The Chinese Economy in the 21st Century

Enterprise and Business Behaviour

Edited by

Barbara Krug

Professor for Economics of Governance at Rotterdam School of Management (RSM) at Erasmus University of Rotterdam

Hans Hendrischke

Associate Professor in Chinese Studies at the University of New South Wales, Sydney

Edward Elgar
Cheltenham, UK • Northampton, MA, USA

Published by
Edward Elgar Publishing Limited
Glensanda House
Montpellier Parade
Cheltenham
Glos GL50 1UA
UK

Edward Elgar Publishing, Inc.
William Pratt House
9 Dewey Court
Northampton
Massachusetts 01060
USA

A catalogue record for this book
is available from the British Library

ISBN 978 1 84542 750 4

Printed and bound in Great Britain by MPG Books Ltd, Bodmin, Cornwall

Contents

List of Figures

List of Tables

List of Contributors

David G. S. Goodman, University of Technology Sydney

Mark Joannes Greeven, Erasmus Research Institute of Management, Erasmus University Rotterdam

Hans Hendrischke, University of New South Wales Sydney

Barbara Krug, Rotterdam School of Management, Erasmus University of Rotterdam

Jeroen Kuilman, Erasmus Research Institute of Management, Erasmus University Rotterdam

Sonja Opper, School of Economics and Management, Lund University

Patrick Reinmoeller, Rotterdam School of Management, Erasmus University of Rotterdam

Xueyuan Zhang, Rotterdam School of Management, Erasmus University of Rotterdam

Ze Zhu, Rotterdam School of Management, Erasmus University of Rotterdam

Preface

This book is about new firms, new sectors, new institutions and ultimately a new business system in China. The novelty of firms, sectors or institutions cannot be judged by comparing them solely with the socialist era or even with highly abstract models of firms, sectors, or institutions that constitute a market economy. Instead novelty needs to include a 'surprise', an outcome that has not been anticipated by theories on economic development, comparative business systems, or economic transformation or indeed the experience gathered by international firms elsewhere. And surprises there are a-plenty in China.

The reader will learn that a stock-listed company in China has not much in common with a company listed at the NYSE. A closer look reveals that the corporatisation of firms did not automatically lead to a corporate governance structure such as one finds in the Anglo-Saxon type of arm's length financial system or the bank-oriented system prevailing in Japan (Opper, Chapter 1). That stock-listed companies 'with Chinese characteristics' should not be too quickly dismissed as part of a unique case is brought to the attention of the reader by the analysis of the foreign bank sectors in which the author emphasises the diversity of organisational forms. Leaving aside the question of whether new firms or sectors in China are more or less market-conforming, there is an argument that the Reforms, i.e. the competitive release, unleashes a variety of organisational forms not easily fitting textbook models (Kuilman, Chapter 2) where politics is (still) a major force in shaping corporate governance, diversity of organisational forms and the (spatial) concentration of industries. Location, diversity and new organisational forms are features that appear in all the following chapters. Both Zhang and Reinmoeller (Chapter 3) analysing the Foreign Direct Investment sector and Greeven (Chapter 4) analysing the IT sector point to the concentration of firms in certain regions, the increasing diversity of different ownership arrangements, and different strategies that link foreign and domestic resources, as well as human capital and financial assets. The challenge therefore is to identify the factors and underlying rationale which made foreign firms change their strategy, or allowed young IT firms to circumvent state intervention but flourish and quickly change from start-up firms to major producers and reliable partners in international supply chains.

As all four chapters describe, China is no longer a socialist party-state where the coordination of resources follows a central plan, nor is China an 'interventionist' state where a technocratic bureaucracy ensures the dominance of political considerations in certain sectors and for certain transactions. By delineating the influence of the state, they point to the missing link, namely that with the decentralisation of decision making power to non-state and lower administrative levels, transformation and economic development can no longer be explained by the doings and non-doings of a party-state alone. The following three chapters of the book take the analysis one step further.

Krug (Chapter 5) strongly argues that an analysis of Chinese development needs to focus on the economic and business behaviour of economic and political actors. With firms being the recipient of institutional change rather than corporate actors *sui generis*, the behaviour of entrepreneurs becomes crucial. Based on fieldwork in three provinces and extensive interviews, the set of institutions which the entrepreneurs regard as binding is identified. The analysis shows that indeed organisational and institutional innovation occurs, but not only as a response to external factors at the macro-level, such as the Reform policy as such, or economic variables. Instead organisational innovation reflects transaction cost considerations, including informal institutions, and is the outcome of the interaction between economic and political actors. It is argued that the transfer of decision making power to non-Party and non-state actors mobilised new economic and political actors whose behaviour and interaction form the basis for institutional change in China and diversity of local business systems across China. One such actor is local government.

Zhu and Krug (Chapter 6) describe a process which, starting with the decentralisation policy at the beginning of the reform period, did not lead to one form of fiscal governance. Instead provincial and even more so sub-provincial agencies use the transfer of decision-making power and tax authority to formulate different local tax regimes. The underlying rationale reads as follows: while entrepreneurs whose need to cope with the high level of uncertainty and asymmetric information makes them search for ways to align the interest of stake-holders, shareholders and local government agencies, sub-provinical agencies find themselves in the situation where both tax authority and tax revenues are negotiated within the state administration and between firms and local tax bureaus. The analysis of the interaction between the non-state private and local state sectors draws attention to the institution of local autonomy, which is strengthened by the fact that private entrepreneurs invest in locally embedded firms for transaction cost reasons, as well as by the central state's offers of local government 'independent' revenue sources via tax farming and landownership. In short, both the diversity of firms (and institutions) and the concentration of certain industries in certain regions can be explained by looking at the processes at the local level and by analysing the behaviour of (micro-level) actors. The local perspective suggests that concentrating on transaction cost considerations when analysing institutional change in China might miss the variety of business cultures within China. After forcefully arguing against the reification (and simplification) of Chinese culture, let alone one represented by Confucianist values, Goodman (Chapter 7) gives three examples of how local culture and local economic development interact, once more stressing the need to take a local and agent-based perspective to explain the emerging, highly diverse economic system in China.

Entrepreneurs and local government agencies respond not simply or solely to political constraints and incentives but carefully weigh uncertainty, asymmetric information, monitoring and enforcement problems in the new private sector. Both came to the same conclusion; namely that a co-operation strategy between private investors, managers, local tax officials and local governments in general promises the highest returns. Thus, new institutions such as corporate governance around incorporated firms (as described by Opper in Chapter 1), or local autonomy, such as tax farming compacts centre around aligning the interests of political and economic actors (as described by Zhu and Krug in Chapter 6).

Networks seem to be different: while one major motivation behind the new governance structures is the need to get access to scarce resources, market information, or political licences, networks seem to be invincible. Regardless of whether they are modelled as a group, and therefore as an actor, or as a social co-ordination mechanism, networking seems to be the answer for all economic and political problems. They are seen as an effective means for overcoming shortages of material as well as the means to skilfully escape official rules and regulations. The thoughtful analysis presented by Hendrischke (Chapter 8) shows that networks are indeed effective mechanisms for aligning the interests of economic and political actors, and re-combining resources for establishing new firms. Yet they are also powerful economic actors if and so long as their social base is employed to serve economic purposes. The analysis of networks (their emergence, functioning and impact on the new institutional architecture of China's economy) has to be seen in contrast to the way networking is introduced as a resource-mobilising and co-ordinating factor in the mainstream literature. Stressing the functional value of networks, the analysis shows how they secure a broad resource base within the new institutional set up as they smoothly 'exit' from one locality, set incentives for co-operation, generate new knowledge and allow for flexibly recombining resources according to expected returns.

This leaves the question of spatial and institutional diversity. On the one hand, Goodman (Chapter 7) provides some powerful evidence that cultural differences in China should be taken seriously to the extent that localities can be modelled as business or innovative systems *sui generis* (Chapter 8). On the other hand, Krug (Chapter 5) and Hendrischke (Chapter 8) identify transactions cost considerations and economic factors (see also Zhang and Reinmoeller in Chapter 3 and Greeven in Chapter 4) as the driving forces behind jurisdictional differences which must disappear in market and jurisdictional competition. The final chapter (Krug and Kuilman Chapter 9), focussing on organisational ecology, speculates about the processes that will cause firms or local government agencies to imitate or dismiss specific organisational forms of firms. The analysis suggests that competition for resources; more precisely the switching from 'political' to market competition is still the single most crucial factor, and one that reminds the reader that organisational and institutional innovation at the local level still cannot completely off-set central and Party- policy guidelines.

The analysis provided by different authors and focusing on different aspects of institutional innovation and change can help to explain specific features of firms and industries and points to a new research agenda. It is shown that agent-based approaches offer useful insights: that the local perspective matters, and that the process unleashed by the reform commitment needs to be analysed in order to understand the diversity that can be observed within the Chinese economy. It also solves some of the puzzles that have evaded textbook explanation so far. For example the puzzle as to why entrepreneurship and investment increased so rapidly despite the absence of private property rights can be explained when one takes the local perspective. Property rights at this level are not missing, and more importantly are enforced whenever local government agencies are in need of a stable tax base, value creation in their jurisdiction, and expect higher returns from private entrepreneurship.

To sum up: the research shows that a theory of endogenous institutional change is needed to supplement approaches in which economic actors respond to changes in relative prices and exogenously given institutions. Aside from conceptual idiosyncrasies, one reason why such a research agenda is conspicuously absent when it comes to explaining economic transformation and development is the limitations of current research methods. The local perspective implies more than acknowledging the problems with the representativeness of data. The perspective rather insists that there is not one integrated market, not one (and uniform) set of institutions, and not one Chinese value-conforming set of behavioural patterns. For this reason the local perspective needs to construct local institutions and set them apart from 'national' legislation and structures, when comparing one locality with another.

For practical purposes, administrative units are taken as a proxy when a specific province or county is accepted as the architect of the effective set of institutions to which economic and political actors respond. As Goodman shows, this procedure can still lead to a too rough picture, yet when statistics are needed there is not much alternative as data collection in China follows administrative units. Likewise, institutional change as negotiated within the political sector mostly follows the administrative state or Party hierarchy. The difference in the institutional architecture of a certain location is a conglomerate of central and local directives and authority structures. Whether local institutions supplement, mitigate or offset national bureaucracies and legislation is often enough an empirical question. In short, the local perspective asks for an extensive study of central and local conditions which next to a thorough knowledge of the general economic situation requires time-consuming research of the local institutions as revealed in local documents, field work and interviews.

The institutional perspective also asks for major modification to the conventional concepts of Institutional Economics. On the one hand, institutions need to describe more than the set of (new) incentives and governance structures defined at the beginning of the reform era at the Central level. As described in the different chapters, the interaction between the new and old economic and political actors is a major force for generating new procedures that govern private exchange, investment, innovation and appropriation of profit. Therefore, the governance of the interaction, its emergence and consequences needs to be analysed. The use of contracts in private business deals, tax farming, sharecropping or networking, and the participation of foreign firms in local administrative units are examples of new institutions that might or might not reflect the revival or modification of institutions known from the pre-socialist past. Which institutions evolved as the dominant form in which kind of transaction and selected by which group of economic and political actors seems (still) to be an empirical question. Fieldwork by other social scientists and interviews provide the most reliable data source.

Interviews are crucial when informal institutions are included in an analysis. It is not only the fact that many informal institutions are means to escape national or formal legislation; it is rather the fact that many informal institutions are regarded as 'the normal way of doing things'. Therefore they are neither questioned, nor are alternative ways examined. Thus, for example, only very few managers or firms would turn to the courts in case of contract enforcement problems, not because they have reason to mistrust the courts and legal system (as they most probably do), but rather because to turn to trusted third parties, i.e. networks or local administration is seen as the normal way.

Economic and political actors matter in their double role as both the object, and initiator of institutional change. Without the Reforms, which started with a broad transfer of resources and the decentralisation of decision making powers, one would not find such diversity in institutions and behaviour as one does today. Aside from questions about the origins of so many risk-taking and innovative actors (never an easy question in the literature of entrepreneurship) the major conceptual problem is how to model their behaviour and more urgently their interaction. Analytical narratives known from economic history come closest to the techniques used in the book. With the help of life histories of firms or career patterns of entrepreneurs the institutional frame, the form of interaction and the subjectively evaluated trade-offs between (notably) a co-operative and competitive strategy can be constructed. Using game theory would be the next step to add more rigour to the descriptive analysis provided in this book. The contributions here provide a more descriptive version, i.e. one that does not include tests. The general idea behind the research design is to first, construct the institutional landscape at the micro-level; second offer an explanation that relies on the findings of transaction costs or institutional economics (or sometimes economic sociology); and third to compare the results that one could expect from the economic analysis with the actual observations.

Such an analysis relies heavily on the fieldwork of other social scientists who have worked in the same location, local statistics and documentation of rules and regulation and on interviews that allow the (re-)construction of the life history of firms and the courses of actions chosen by the economic and political actors. It is worth stressing that the interviews do not attempt to give a representative overview that can be generalised to the whole of China. They rather delineate the spatial or sectoral boundaries of the explanatory value.

The different contributions, all of which have more or less subscribed to the research agenda described above, have been generated by a central research project financed by the Dutch Organisation for Scientific Research (NWO 450-02-460). The NWO grant and the generous support by the Research School of the Rotterdam School of Management (ERIM) and the Trustfonds of Erasmus University allowed us to embark on international co-operation with the University of Technology, Sydney (UTS) and University of New South Wales (UNSW) both in Sydney; Zhejiang University in Hangzhou, China; and Suzhou University in Jiangsu, China. The core group (Goodman, Greeven, Hendrischke, Krug, Kuilman, Reinmoeller, Zhang and Zhu) of the research project profited immensely from support provided by our Chinese colleagues Wan Jieqiu (Suzhou) and Yao Xianguo (Hangzhou) without whose help, expertise, and friendliness we could not have met enough entrepreneurs and managers willing to spend so much time talking to us. Many thanks also to the group of experts who have critically and patiently accompanied the different stages of the drafts and empirical developments: Richard Whitley, Gordon Redding, George Hendriksc and Bart Nooteboom. The conference in Hangzhou in 2006 provided the infrastructure for discussing the methodological and conceptual issues involved. Whether called an attempt to contribute to co-evolutionary theory or a theory of endogenous institutional change, there was a consensus that the research agenda offers fruitful insights. The conference showed also how stimulating and effective discussion between academics from different backgrounds can be, provided they accept the necessity to explain China as a very special case of economic transformation and not merely as a data base for testing already well-established models. Therefore many thanks to Max Boisot, John Child, Steve Casper, Bruno S. Frey, Lars Feld, Andrew Tylecote, and Stephan Rothlin.

Intellectual input is often enough constrained by the lack of logistic and technical knowledge and so it would have been in this case if Wilfred Mijnhardt, Maaike Siegerist, Mark Oskam, Niall Coen, Marije Veldheer, Dicea Jansen and Johannes Meuer had not offered good advice and practical solutions.

1. Going Public without the Public: Between Political Governance and Corporate Governance

Sonja Opper

1.1 INTRODUCTION

The corporatisation and partial privatisation of China's state-owned enterprises and the establishment of China's stock exchanges were originally motivated by the government's goal of recapitalising the ailing, debt-ridden state-owned industrial sector. A transfer of control power to the new shareholders and an encompassing shift of decision-making rights were not intended. Against this background, a distinct type of corporate governance emerged, which neither resembles the Anglo-American model of arm's length finance, nor the bank-oriented system of corporate governance.

Early on, China's corporatisation strategy appeared as an unexpected success-story. Within only eight years, more than 1,000 mostly state-owned firms were listed on the two national stock-exchanges in Shenzhen and Shanghai, market capitalisation rose to almost 54 per cent of GDP and China's stock market outperformed many of the established East Asian markets. Since 2000 however, the situation has changed dramatically. Stock performance has fallen despite persistently high economic growth. A comparison of stock listings and market capitalisation/GDP reveals the reversal of a previously positive trend. While the development of market capitalisation and stock listings were closely correlated until 2000, these trends decoupled in the following years. Chart 1.1 illustrates that market-breadth declined by almost 50 per cent and fell back to a market capitalisation rate of 27 per cent while stock-listings further increased by 289 firms between 2000 and 2004.

Critics identified continuing political interference in firm-decision-making as one of the crucial weaknesses of China's newly listed corporations. Corporate governance (CG) mechanisms seemed deficient and both external interference as well as insider malfeasance remained widespread. While overall this criticism seems justified, the underlying institutional mechanisms that undermine the emergence of sound CG in China's corporations have rarely been discussed.

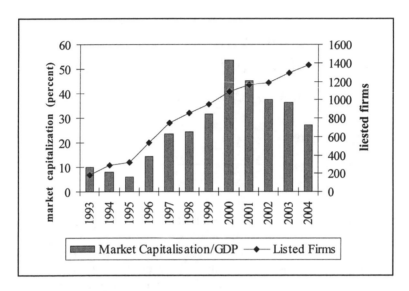

Source: *China Securities and Futures Statistical Yearbook,* 2005

Figure 1.1   Stock listings and market capitalisation, 1992–2004

This study provides a comprehensive assessment of China's newly emerging CG system. Arguing from a political economic perspective, I will introduce the hypothesis that the functionality of imported CG mechanisms as formulated in *China's Company Law* (1994) automatically erodes within the framework of the current political and socio-economic environment. A new, hybrid type of CG evolves, combining certain features of Western-style CG and specific organisational traits of established political governance structures. In order to identify the specific hybrid control mechanisms, the following analysis applies a comprehensive definition of CG. Following Williamson (1996: 11) 'governance structure is... usefully thought of as an institutional framework in which the integrity of a transaction is decided'. Blaire's (1995: 3) definition is even broader, referring to

'a whole set of legal cultural and institutional arrangements that determine what publicly traded corporations can do, who controls them, how that control is exercised and how the risks and returns from the activities they undertake are allocated'.

Similarly, the World Bank (2002: 55) suggests that corporate governance is 'largely a matter of allocation and exercise of control over resources within firms'. Briefly, for the purpose of this analysis, CG includes all aspects that affect control of corporations and may provide mechanisms to contain principal-agent problems arising from ownership separation (Berle and Means, 1968).

The degree of China's transition from political governance to an economic CG system will be assessed within the framework of a three-level analysis. After an introduction to the framework of the political economy of CG (section 1.2), section 1.3 assesses ownership control as determined by the distribution of property rights and the distinct types of shareholders. The following section explores organisational features of CG internal to the firm and examines the quality of state–firm relations (section 1.4). It will be shown that politics and business have not been effectively separated. In contrast, a significant overlap of political and economic control rights resulting from blurred boundaries between the state and the firm constitute a central feature of China's newly emerging CG system. Politicians and bureaucrats still have a variety of options, either formal control rights or informal ties, to remain directly involved in a company's decision making processes. Section 1.5 explores whether the financial system has the capacity to mitigate institutional deficits arising from weak control structures. The final section provides an assessment of China's CG system and future development perspectives.

1.2 BUILDING CORPORATE GOVERNANCE: A POLITICAL ECONOMY PERSPECTIVE

A large number of studies provide evidence that politics is usually a major force shaping the structure of national CG systems (Fligstein, 1990; Fligstein and Freeland, 1995; Roe, 1994). Politics may even be a more powerful tool in transition economies. While the development of joint-stock companies and corresponding CG systems in the Western industrialised nations relied on evolutionary processes based on free exchange of property rights and profit making objectives (Fama and Jensen, 1983), transformative economies face the challenge to ad hoc create national CG systems. However, the problem with CG reforms is that new CG systems are not filling empty institutional spaces or 'control vacuums'. On the contrary, the challenge of introducing market-based CG systems involves the replacement of established political governance structures reaching into the firm.

Generally, the shift of control rights is often retarded by mutually reinforcing interests, which perpetuate a close relationship between the state and the firm. On the one hand, state actors are rarely willing to institute a new economic system that completely deprives them of direct control rights and rent-seeking opportunities at the firm level (Rona-Tas, 1994; Walder, 1995; Bian and Logan, 1996; Parish and Michelson, 1996; Zhou, 2000). On the other hand, managers and workers often prefer the continuation of direct state-firm linkages to gain access to resources in a highly insecure and rapidly changing institutional environment. In addition, weak and often contradictory rules governing markets allow openings for persistent discretionary intervention by bureaucrats and politicians (Vickers and Yarrow, 1988: 114). As a result, 'there is still a much different atmosphere of interaction between government and individual economic agents in ex-socialist countries than in countries with a long tradition of free markets' (Murrell, 1996: 32).

Nee and Opper (2005) call this type of economic order *politicised capitalism*, where state actors set the regulatory framework *and* remain directly involved in guiding transactions at the firm level. In transition from state socialism, politicised capitalism is a hybrid institutional order comprised of recombinant elements of the old economic institutions and new organisational practices and rules oriented to establishing a market economy. It is a mixed economy where market liberalisation and ownership reform are unfinished, preserving partial control rights by the state as both a redistributive allocator and owner of productive assets (Kornai, 1990). Although the new rules of a market economy impose formal limits on state interventions in the firm, the defining feature of politicised capitalism is the absence of clearly defined state–firm boundaries and the overlap of economic and political sphere in the firm's decision-making (Nee, 1992).

To understand political and ideological tensions connected with the creation of CG systems in post-socialist transition economies, it is important to note that socialist-style *political governance* over companies relied essentially on the same control-channels as the various types of market-based CG systems: 1. ownership control, 2. organisational structures internal to the firm connecting principal (state as de facto owner) and agent (for example, factory director), 3. resource allocation, and particularly the allocation of finance. Hence establishing Western-style corporate governance involves the redistribution of control rights from the political to the economic sphere along three dimensions: 1. from state to private ownership; 2. from ideological to purely meritocratic and incentive based command structures and 3. from state allocation to market allocation of finance.

While a reform consensus may be easier to achieve in one field than in others, it has to be noted, that a central though overlooked problem with the creation or reform of CG systems lies in the complementarity of its distinct elements. For instance, changes in the system of management compensation may have efficiency increasing effects in the presence of efficient securities markets, but may have just the reverse effects if complementary institutions are missing. Positive performance effects of executive stock options rest on the efficiency of stock markets. In the presence of illiquid and easy to manipulate markets, stock options do not necessarily lead to improved firm performance, but may simply invite price-manipulation and management self-dealings. In other words, the functioning of distinct governance mechanisms depends on the existence of certain complimentary institutions (Heinrich, 1999).

Problems arising from selective and incomplete reforms, neglecting the systemic character of CG, arise from conflicting stakeholder interests. Politicians in particular often fiercely oppose shifts in governance. As holders of monopoly control rights, they were among the main beneficiaries of the old command structure. A privatisation of control rights and depoliticisation of CG would deprive them of both, a convenient tool to steer economic development (e.g. local employment, welfare, structural change etc) and a source of individual income as political control rights invite rent-seeking behavior and other types of opportunistic practices (Shleifer and Vishny, 1994: 1019). Selective replacement of distinct elements therefore seems more likely than a far-reaching move to complete depoliticisation.

1.3 DEPOLITICISING THE PROPERTY CHANNEL

The CG literature assumes that the effectiveness of corporate control and management performance critically depends on the distribution of shares to different shareholder types characterised by differing individual incentives and monitoring devices. China's privatisation of large-scale SOEs starting in the early 1990s is characterised by two main features shaping the property structure of listed firms. First, in contrast to most Central and Eastern European transition economies, China's government rejected the complete privatisation of its large-scale SOEs, which were instead corporatised and only partly privatised through stock-listings. The official notion was that the participation of non-state-shareholders alongside the state would provide sufficient economic incentives to limit political interference and to turn corporations into profit-making entities. Secondly, the government established a segmented market consisting of different share-types, which impeded free share trading and changes of the overall ownership distribution between the state, legal persons (i.e. state or non-state firms and organisations registered as a legal person) and individual shareholders. Both features jointly reveal one of the initial premises of China's stock market reforms: the government was neither ready nor willing to lose direct ownership control over the production sector; instead stock market listings were regarded in the first place as convenient tools to raise fresh capital. Plans for continuing utilisation of firms as policy tools are, for instance, specified in policy documents, such as the 'Preliminary Method of State Share Administration in Share Companies' (Article 3). A guarantee of a controlling position of state shares to perform industrial policy goals and to influence the overall investment structure is explicitly stipulated.

Transferability. Overall four major share-types were created: state shares, legal person shares, A-shares and B-shares. Among these, A-shares and B-shares are publicly traded at the national Stock Exchanges, while state shares and legal person shares are not publicly traded and only transferable upon state approval. On average the first three types usually amount to about 30 per cent each of the total company shares (see figure 1.2). Shares which are directly valued by the market (A and B shares) average only about 40 per cent of total outstanding shares. Figure 1.2 illustrates that there has been very little variation between share-types until 2004 supporting the strong political preference for a stable, state-dominated securities market.

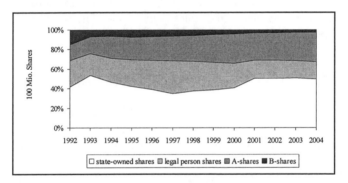

Source: *China Securities and Futures Statistical Yearbook 2005,* p. 179

Figure 1.2   Capital structure, 1992–2004

Monitoring. In addition to relatively weak market incentives, ownership-control suffers from the limited monitoring capacity of shareholders. The group of potentially active shareholders is extremely small among holders of tradable shares. A-shares are predominantly held by domestic individual investors, though recently an increasing amount is held by institutional investors. It is estimated that 'official' funds, whose operations have been approved by the government, hold only around 2.3 per cent of the A-shares (OECD, 2002: 439). More than 20 per cent of the A-shares are actually held by 'grey funds' whose operations are in fact illegal (OECD, 2002: 442).

Within the group of A-shareholders, individuals are unlikely to have incentives to perform monitoring activities, as they are imposed with a legal limit of 0.5 per cent of total shares. Obviously, they are likely to take a free-rider position and leave active controls to holders of larger shares. Only institutional investors of A-shares may accumulate a sufficient amount of shares to be in the position to actually monitor and influence management behavior.

B-shares are tradable for foreign individuals, institutional investors and Chinese nationals able to trade in foreign currency. However, only a minority of 110 firms currently list B-shares; the remaining firms exclusively list A-shares. As a consequence, the portfolio choice remained rather limited and market liquidity was low. Particularly international institutional investors showed little interest in the narrow B-share market. In addition, foreign investors' monitoring capacity suffers from higher information costs owing to their unfamiliarity with China's rapidly changing market conditions and institutional environment.

Entry condition. In order to broaden investment opportunities for international strategic investors, China's Securities Regulatory Commission (CSRC) eventually decided to open the A-share market for institutional investors. Since mid-2003 overseas fund management institutions, insurance companies, securities companies and other asset management institutions approved by the CSRC may, within the Qualified Foreign Institutional Investors-Scheme (QFII), invest in China's ailing A-share market. Since 2006, strategic investors are also able to buy A-shares from existing shareholders and to purchase new shares issued by listed companies. The initial purchase must be for at least 10 per cent of a company, and the investor must hold the stake for at least three years. Free accumulation of shares is still not possible, as foreign investors remain prohibited from buying A-shares on the open market. Also, the current scope of the QFII-Scheme does not keep up with earlier announcements. Investment quotas now total US$ 5.65 billion, while ten billion was previously announced as a target quota (Areddy, 2006). With currently 34 foreign strategic investors participating in the program, the average quota is around US$ 166 million. It is obvious that chances for strong holdings by foreign investors within the A and B-share market are therefore rather limited.

Neither private nor public: hybrid ownership forms. While large shareholders still play a minor role within the A and B-share market, they are primarily found among the groups of holders of state-shares and legal person-shares. State shares are obtained by an institution, as a representative of the central government. These so-called state-asset management companies usually have weak incentives to perform monitoring-activities. Firstly, this is because officials of state asset management agencies usually do not receive any personal benefits from effective monitoring. Secondly, state shareholders do not operate under hard budget constraints; even if budgets are admittedly hardened, state shareholders can almost be sure to be bailed out by the state treasury if companies suffer financial distress. Several empirical studies confirm that state shareholding is linked to a lower share-price, signalling the detrimental effect of continuing state ownership. Xu and Wang (1999) and Qi et al. (2000) found that corporate performance is negatively related to the proportion of a company's state shares. Wong et al. (2004) provided complementary evidence on negative performance effects resulting from state intervention at the firm level. Recent experiments launched in mid 2005 making state shares tradable may mark a turning point for China's split share structure and may gradually lead to a reduction of state shares. China's securities market regulators have emphasised that tradability of state shares does not entail a 'selling out' of state property. The question whether state shares will actually come into circulation will depend on the shareholders' (that is the responsible government level) strategic choice on the size of state-holdings. Furthermore, there is little doubt that the state – in spite of reductions in shareholdings – will not relinquish control.

The incentives and monitoring capacities of legal person shareholders are slightly better than those for state. Legal person-shares are owned by domestic institutions or enterprises of various ownership forms. In contrast to state agencies, legal persons are legal entities, which operate commercially with independent accounting systems and are formally separated from the state bureaucracy and government departments. They therefore have stronger profit-motives than the state asset management companies in charge of the administration of state shares. Furthermore, holders of legal person shares are unlikely to be plagued by the free-riding problem because their shareholding is relatively large (Xu and Wang, 1999; Qi et al., 2000). Wong et al. (2004) calculate that the average shareholding of the top ten shareholders (holding legal person shares) is 20.26 per cent. Such shareholders usually possess seats on the board of directors (BoD) and can thereby directly monitor enterprise policy (Xu and Wang, 1999). However, it is important to note that the majority of legal person shareholders represent state-owned firms which still operate under softer budget constraints than the non-state sector. Also, representatives are typically deeply enmeshed in close network-ties with party and government representatives. Therefore, they may not always be able to exert independent monitoring.

Overall, shareholder distribution and incentives limit chances for a *depoliticisation* of corporatised firms and the creation of purely profit-based monitoring by company shareholders. Table 1.1 presents a stylised overview, summarising material incentives, technical capacity and the average size of shareholdings as major determinants of monitoring effectiveness. Potentially strong and motivated strategic investors capable of effective monitoring activities are only to be found in the groups of institutional investors within the A-share segment and the legal-person segment. Due to China's specific market segmentation, however, these shareholders are rarely in the position of accumulating sizable holdings. Continuing interference by the state is therefore hard to avoid or mitigate.

Table 1.1 Monitoring incentives and capacity of shareholders

Shareholder type	Profit incentive	Technical capacity	Size of holding	Expected monitoring effect
State	Weak	Middle	Large	Weak
Legal person				
State institution	weak/middle	middle	large	weak/middle
Non-state legal person	strong	strong	middle	middle/strong
A-share				
Individual	strong	weak	small	weak
Institutional	strong	strong	middle	middle/strong
B-share				
Individual	strong	weak	small	weak
Institutional	strong	middle	middle	middle

Shareholder protection. Problems due to China's specific property distribution are further aggravated as by weak shareholder protection. A convenient tool to proxy the extent of shareholder protection is the Anti-Director Index (ADI) developed by La Porta et al. (1998), which proxy the extent of shareholder protection along seven dimensions:

1. equal voting rights for shareholders (one share = one vote);
2. the right of shareholders to mail their proxy vote to the firm;
3. the requirement that firms may not ask their shareholders to deposit shares prior to a shareholder meeting;
4. the right that shareholders may cast all their votes for one candidate standing for election to the board (cumulative voting) or the requirement that there should be a proportional representation in the BoD;
5. the availability of legal mechanisms against perceived oppression by directors;

6.   the existence of preemptive rights of shareholders to buy new issues of stocks;
7.   the percentage of share capital needed to call an extraordinary shareholders meeting, with values of up to 33 per cent being regarded as an acceptable level of shareholder protection.

Table 1.2   Anti director rights in China

Types of Shareholder Rights	Granted Rights
One share-one vote	No
Proxy by mail allowed	No
Shares not blocked before meeting	No
Cumulative voting/Proportional Representation	No
Oppressed Minority	Yes
Preemptive Right to New Issues	No
Percentage of Share Capital to Call an extraordinary shareholder meeting less than 15%	Yes

Source: Gensler and Yang, 1994

According to Table 1.2, China grants only two out of seven crucial shareholder rights. Exploitation by major shareholders is therefore hard to prevent or mitigate due to the weak legal position of minority shareholders.

1.4   DEPOLITICISING ORGANISATIONAL SUPERVISION

Effective vertical command structures, making agents responsible to shareholders, are a critical step in establishing market-based CG mechanisms. The dissolution of overriding vertical political command structures reaching into the firm is therefore a central task in establishing effective CG systems. The official policy line was indeed to encourage a separation of government and business (*zhengqi fenkai*) to support a rationalisation of the economic sphere. In retrospect, however, reforms revealed a high degree of ambivalence and inconsistency. Not only did the willingness to fully depoliticise the economic sector seem limited; the vested interests of members of the governmental and party apparatus undermined the credibility of reforms. Under the current political regime, any form of de-politicisation is essentially a form of self-constraint which – due to weak incentives of individual government and party representatives and the lack of truly politically independent checks and balances– seems hard to enforce. The overall picture of firm-level organisational reforms is therefore mixed.

Official propaganda called for a rigorous separation of government and business functions; and *zhengqi fenkai* emerged as one of the new government slogans in China. The state's role was supposed to be comparable to that of a normal shareholder, without any priority rights to interfere in the firm's organisation and governance. In this spirit, the tenth five-year Plan aims

'to complete the establishment of a modern enterprise system under which there will be clearly established ownership, well defined power and responsibility, a separation of enterprise management from government administration, and scientific management' (Xinhua,17 March 2001).

In spite of such statements, China's lawmaking revealed a more ambivalent position towards firm depoliticisation. Article 14 of the Company Law calls for the supervision of enterprises by the government and social masses, so implicitly undermining the concept of independent enterprise. Even more serious deficits result from the continuing influence of the 'three old political committees', i.e. party committee, labour committee and trade union, placed within the firm. Despite the creation of new organisational and governance structures, such as shareholders meetings, Boards of Directors and supervisory committees alongside the position of the CEO, the old political organs were not abolished. Instead, the Company Law guarantees and regulates their future involvement and responsibilities. Although, the 'old three' lost a large amount of their inherited coordination and control rights, their survival invites a continuation of political involvement within firm-decisions. Particularly their long tradition as central political bodies within the firm provides fertile grounds for continuing informal involvement (Wu and Du, 1998: 68).

The Company Law gives the state broad and ill-defined rights of intervention. As to the role of Party committees, the Company Law (Article 17) merely provides that 'the activities of the local Party offices of the CCP must be carried out in accordance with the constitution of the CCP'. The constitution of the CCP, however, contributes very little to limiting the content of Party activities. Article 31 broadly delegates the implementation of Party decisions to the local Party committees, where further specifications of tasks are not to be found. The missing legal specifications on Party coordination rights seem to reflect the dilemma of the leadership, which must respect economic necessities and stabilise the political system at the same time. This requires efficiency-increasing reforms in the former state sector, without a complete loss of political control at the enterprise level. Wu Bangguo (1997), member of the CPC Central Committee and a member of the Politburo of the CPC Central Committee since 1992, for instance, warned that the 'Party must absolutely not lose its political leadership powers with regard to the enterprises', and claimed that the 'Party should take part in the decision-making in the enterprise with regard to major issues.' This is in line with the position of the former General Secretary Jiang Zemin, who drew a detailed sketch of future Party activities at the enterprise level. In conflict with the overall goals of a separation of administration and firm, he suggested that the Party should take on at least four preliminary functions (FBIS-CHI-1999-0817, 9):

1.   implementation of the Party line;
2.   fulfilling tasks with special attention to production and management;
3.   participation in the most important business decisions;
4.   support for the board of directors, the supervisory committee and management.

Interestingly, these goals are consistent with specifications codified in China's constitution (Article 32) with respect to the Party's role in state enterprises. It is worthwhile to note, that this type of personal statement by leading politicians can have norm-setting character in a society such as China's. Fewsmith (2001: 25) argues that objective legal standards are actually not decisive; norms are rather subjective moral judgments on *right* and *wrong* which give the government arbitrary and therefore decisive power. Jiang's accentuation of the role of local Party committees can thus critically influence the subsequent process of adaptation. The preservation of the Party monopoly further supports the strong role of the party within the firm. In spite of the reduction in formal control rights within the firm the government and Party network still enjoy unchallenged authority outside of enterprises. This tension between the formal distribution of power at the micro and macro level can thus trigger a 'voluntary' acceptance or even the request for political involvement at the firm level as long as the enterprise decision-making elite believes that cooperation will actually yield positive economic returns either for the insiders and/or for the firm.

Like the Party committee, the workers congress and the trade union retain limited coordination rights within the firm. The workers congress, for example, has the legal right to representation on the supervisory committee and the board of directors. In addition, the worker congress has the right to make suggestions and to participate in discussions that affect the protection of employee rights according to Article 121 of the Company Law. Thus decisions on wage policy, distribution of bonuses and the use of welfare funds cannot be implemented without worker participation (in theory). The labour union formally operates as the working committee of the workers congress. The union directors have the right to participate in board meetings, in order to protect workers' interests (Article 56). More specifically, the activities of the union directors include monitoring the CEO, calling employee meetings and taking responsibility for collective agreements between unions and enterprises (Yang and Zhou, 1998: 44).

In summary, the three old political committees complement the new organisational bodies in important areas. While formal control rights have been significantly reduced compared to the pre-reform era, they still enjoy the right to attend major decision-making processes and can thereby actively influence enterprise management through procedural and personal relationships. As a result, the coexistence of old and new organisational structures within a firm may cause frictions arising from institutional incompatibilities (Dorn, 1998: 137).

The risk of insufficient separation of political and business functions is further enhanced by the high representation of party members in leading firm positions. A recent study conducted by the World Bank in 2003 revealed that the CEO is at least an ordinary party member in 67 per cent of all 2,351 surveyed firms. In 42 per cent of the surveyed firms, the CEO takes up an active political role as party secretary, deputy party secretary or party committee member. The respective distribution for listed firms is even higher. Overall, 84 per cent of the surveyed listed firms indicate that the CEO is a party member; 55 per cent indicate that the CEO also holds a position within the party. Compared with the relatively low proportion of party members in China's overall population (5 per cent), the specific role of party networks for firm-careers becomes quite obvious. 17 per cent of firms, a strikingly high number, even report that their CEO was appointed by the government and not – as legally required – by the Board of Directors. Effective and unbiased supervision of the CEO is further weakened by the fact that membership allocation on the Board of Directors, is usually not in line with the firm's ownership distribution. Finally, 57 per cent of firms report a mismatch between ownership distribution and board composition.

Overall, the new control structures, though formally modeled on Western-style corporate governance, are still characterised by a severe concentration of power in the hands of a few, politically well connected insiders, as well as Party and government elites.

1.5 DEPOLITICISING FINANCIAL CONTROL

'The ways in which the suppliers of finance to corporations assure themselves of getting a return on their investment' is one of the major control mechanisms of public corporations in Western CG systems (Shleifer and Vishny, 1997). The market for takeovers, as a major sanctioning mechanism in the Anglo-American system, and banking controls as a central pillar of corporate governance in the German and Japanese CG system, represent the two role-models of financial control. It is evident that public corporations can only successfully attract investors and creditors, if providers of finance believe that their investments are sufficiently protected. Effective financial market supervision therefore emerges as a *conditio sine qua non*, for any type of CG system. For transition economies, this involves the need for far-reaching reforms, particularly in the financial sector. Empirical evidence shows that nearly all transition economies implement control-oriented financial systems. The dominance of control-oriented systems is partially attributable to a certain affinity of officials towards interventionist procedures and their deep-rooted skepticism towards the free flow of market forces.

China displays the typical feature of control-oriented financial systems: bank loans are the main source of finance for Chinese companies. There are currently four state commercial banks and three political banks that have been joined by 12 joint-equity banks and around 90 regionally limited city banks. In 1996, the first completely private bank, the Minsheng Bank, entered the market. Growing competition has only slightly modified the oligopolistic structure of the Chinese banking sector. At the end of the 1990s, over 80 per cent of credit balance and 75 per cent of credit was still concentrated in the four state commercial banks. Therefore, the state commercial banks remain the central providers of financial control.

In retrospect, the Chinese government implemented only moderate reforms in the commercial banking sector, particularly when it came to the depoliticisation of state banks. While, for instance, the Commercial Bank Law (effective in 1995) guaranteed the formal-legal independence of commercial banks it still emphasises that loan decisions should be taken under the 'guidance of state economic policies' (Article 34). Conflicts of interest between economic and political interests are therefore inevitable. Abundant evidence confirms that China's commercial banks are not truly independent in their loan decisions (Zhu, 1999; Leung and Mok 2000; Lin 2001). Loan decisions are still subject to political intervention, which the state-owned banks cannot oppose. In addition, state credit plans remained institutionalised until 1998. These specified not only the volume of credits, but also the guidelines for sector distribution and means of credit. Park and Sehrt (2001) confirm that the importance of political credit in the course of reform has by no means been reduced and that credit issuance was not determined by fundamental economic data until the late 1990s. At the local level, governments can easily intervene in credit decisions, as bank directors used to be recruited by the local government authorities (Park and Sehrt, 2001: 618). Even the newly founded joint-equity banks are not completely immune to political interventions (Wong 2000). The aforementioned World Bank-survey reveals a surprisingly high proportion of 39 per cent of listed firms, which indicates that they still rely on government assistance when acquiring bank loans. Particularly noteworthy is the fact, that government involvement in loan decisions of listed firms is far higher than in cases involving other legal forms. Only 16 per cent of state owned enterprises reported government assistance to acquire bank loans. These findings suggest that bank-control is still seriously undermined by discretionary government involvement. The geographical distribution of government-assistance in loan decisions confirms this perspective. Particularly less marketised municipalities such as Wuhan and Chongqing display strong government involvement, while government support is much harder to secure in liberalised municipalities such as Shenzhen.

More recently, stricter lending criteria based on economic considerations have been put in place. The China Construction Bank, for example, strengthened its loan criteria in March 1999 and delegated credit decisions to an allocations committee. Not much seems to speak in favor of a total withdrawal of politics from the financial sector at the moment. The banks were reminded of their political responsibility to provide loss-making enterprises with the necessary capital at the National People's Congress in March 1999 (Wong, 2000). In practice, the state banking system is under the protection of the Ministry of Finance and still works under soft-budget constraints (Steinfeld, 1999). Therefore banks have little incentive to optimise their lending decisions; the accumulation of non-performing loans simply does not affect a bank's survival chances and probability of insolvency.

The plan to trade shares of all four state commercial banks on China's stock exchanges by 2007 – often interpreted as a turning point in China's financial sector reforms – signals an increasing need for modern management skills and money for capital expansion, but does not imply major ownership changes. The current ceiling of 25 per cent for foreign involvement in a single domestic bank and a ceiling of 20 per cent ownership for a single foreign investor signals the government's reluctance to relinquish state control over the financial sector. The question is whether foreign investors, such as Goldman Sachs' who hold a 7 per cent ownership stake in the Industrial and Commercial Bank of China (ICBC), will be influential enough to change the corporate culture and develop modern governance-techniques (Linebaugh, 2006). The suspicion arises that the real motivation for China's stock listings is to generate capital.

Not only soft budget constraints arising from strong government involvement and political loans hamper effective control-based supervision of public corporations, the banks' supervisory function is also weakened by the poor quality of company information. While China invested tremendous efforts in the internationalisation of its accounting standards, effective enforcement mechanisms are not yet in place (Opper, 2003). Sound reforms would have to center on a rigorous upgrading and restructuring of the responsible bodies supervising auditing quality and financial disclosure.

In addition, weak complementary institutions dampen incentives for control-based creditor monitoring. Particularly politicised insolvency and bankruptcy procedures limit the credibility of firm liquidation as the ultimate sanctioning mechanism. China's bankruptcy procedure leaves ample room for negotiations and political interventions. Although China's Bankruptcy Law (Article 8) clearly specifies that insolvent firms are to file for bankruptcy, the Supreme Court advised responsible local courts to apply rather mixed standards for their decision-making:

> Peoples Courts shall be accommodating to the advancement of the adjustment of industrial structure, the creation of a modern enterprise system. They shall prevent evasion of the law and the loss of state-owned capital. They shall eliminate narrow minded regional protectionism and lawfully safeguard the legal rights and interests of creditors and debtors, maintain social stability and help establish and perfect the socialist market economic system.

The mix of structural issues, stability concerns and social policy goals clearly provides grounds for frequent discretionary political intervention. The independence of court rulings is therefore highly doubtful (Kamarul and Tomasic, 1999). The informal provision of 'bankruptcy quotas' further weakens the effectiveness of company liquidations as control instrument (OECD, 2002). Fear of social instability and local unrest provide strong motives for local governments to prefer reorganisation strategies over company liquidation. Large-scale firms typically have good chances to avoid liquidation. For listed firms, the risk of bankruptcy and liquidation seems even weaker. It was only in 2001 that the first public corporation filed for bankruptcy. Local governments can rely on both their ownership rights and their close administrative ties with commercial banks (Gao and Schaffer, 1998: 18) to acquire new loans and reschedule (or cancel) old debts. Since legal creditor protection is relatively low in China, banks usually have little incentives to insist on firm liquidation. Ultimately, bankruptcy and liquidation are political decisions, not economic mechanisms.

1.6   CONCLUSION AND OUTLOOK

Analysis of corporate control mechanisms reveals that China's corporatisation strategy has not been accompanied by a far-reaching depoliticisation of traditional governance mechanisms in terms of ownership, vertical governance structures, and financial system. None of the governance mechanisms exhibits a deep depoliticisation in favor of the establishment of market-conforming corporate control. Instead, channels for political intervention and control remain intact, in spite of a clear reduction of formal political control rights. Particularly, the state's triple function as company shareholder, dominant owner of the commercial banking sector, and norm-setting agent of institutional change almost rules out the emergence of purely economic governance mechanisms. Subsequently, a hybrid system is emerging, which selectively incorporates organisational features of Western corporations, without embedding the firm into a system of full-fledged economic control mechanisms. Due to the high level of state involvement, the system resembles a patronage or network-oriented CG system as it was practiced, for instance, in Italy's post-war economy (Barca and Trento, 1997). Building on structural features of the bank-controlled CG type, network-oriented CG is also characterised by high levels of state ownership and state involvement; markets play a secondary role and bank-controls remain rather ineffective. In this sense, the emerging system of corporate governance perfectly reflects the government's original goal to use the stock market as a tool for capital generation, but not as a mechanism to redistribute control rights of the ailing industrial sector.

From a broader perspective, China's recent corporate development process underlines the fact that corporatisation and the creation of corresponding CG systems are distinct endeavors. Neither does the introduction of public corporations automatically trigger the emergence of corresponding governance mechanisms, nor do political decision-makers necessarily opt for the implementation of matching institutions. The risk of mismatches is high, often because of political or ideological constraints and, all too often, individual motives. Due to the specific motivational basis of China's political decision makers, China's newly corporatised firms remained enmeshed in close-knit networks involving political and economic actors. Subsequently, political involvement is sustained, partly by building on formal control rights assigned to the state's representatives (for instance as company shareholders) and partly by relying on informal ties with managers, board members and bank representatives.

In light of Italy's successful post-war development, close government-firm relations do not necessarily undermine economic performance. However, there is a high risk that the incorporation of multiple social and political goals will eventually weaken company profits. Similarly critical is the risk of insider-malfeasance due to ineffective monitoring mechanisms. Market performance over the recent years seems to support a rather pessimistic view of China's ability to reform its hybrid system of politicised corporate governance.

REFERENCES

Areddy, J.T. (2006), 'China Shares Pile on Gains', *Wall Street Journal Asia*, **13** (January), 20–22.

Barca, F. and S. Trento (1997), 'State Ownership and the Evolution of Italian Corporate Governance', *Industrial and Corporate Change*, **6** (3), 533–559.

Berle, Adolf A. and Gardiner C. Means [1968] (2005), *The Modern Corporation & Private Property*, News Brunswick and London: Transaction Press.

Bian, Y. and J.R. Logan (1996), 'Market Transition and the Persistence of Power: The Changing Stratification System in Urban China', *American Sociological Review*, **61** (5), 739–58.

Blaire, Margaret M. (1995), *Ownership and Control. Rethinking Corporate Governance for the Twenty-First Century*, Washington, D.C.: The Brookings Institution.

Dorn, J. (1998), 'China's Future: Market Socialism or Market Taoism?', *Cato Journal*, **18** (1), 131–146.

Fama, E.F. and M.C. Jensen (1983), 'Separation of Ownership and Control', *The Journal of Law and Economics*, **26** (2), 301–326.

Fewsmith, Joseph (2001), *Elite Politics in Contemporary China*, New York, NY: Armonk.

Fligstein, Neil (1990), *The Transformation of Corporate Control*, Cambridge, MA: Harvard University Press.

Fligstein, N. and R. Freeland (1995), 'Theoretical and Comparative Perspectives on Corporate Organisation', *Annual Review of Sociology*, **21** (1), 21–43.

Foreign Broadcast Information Service (FBIS), various volumes.

Gao, S. and M.E. Schaffer (1998), 'Financial Discipline in the Enterprise Sector in Transition Countries: How Does China Compare?', Centre for Economic Reform and Transformation.

Gensler, Howard and Jiliang Yang. 1995. *A Guide to China's Tax & Business Laws.* Hong Kong: FT Law & Tax Asia Pacific.

Heinrich, Ralph P. (1999), 'Corporate Governance: A Systemic Approach with an Application to Eastern Europe', in Eckhard F. Rosenbaum, Frank Bönker and Hans-Jürgen Wagener (eds), *Privatization, Corporate Governance and the Emergence of Markets*, New York, NY: St. Martin's Press, pp. 83–97.

Kamarul, Bahrin and Roman Tomasic (1999), 'The Rule of Law and Corporate Insolvency in Six Asian Legal Systems', in K. Jayasuriya (ed.), *Law, Capitalism and Power in Asia*, London: Routledge, pp. 151–172.

Kornai, Janos (1990), *The Road to a Free Economy: Shifting from a Socialist System*, New York, NY: Norton.

La Porta, R.F. Lopez-de-Silanes, A. Shleifer, and R.W. Vishny (1998), 'Law and Finance', *Journal of Political Economy*, **106** (6), 1113–1155.

Leung, M. and V. Wai-Kwong Mok (2000), 'Commercialization of Banks in China:

Institutional Changes and Effects on Listed Enterprises', *Journal of Contemporary China*, **9** (23), 41–52.

Lin, J.Y. (2001), 'WTO Accession and Financial Reform in China.' *Cato Journal*, **21** (1), 13–18.

Linebaugh, K. (2006), 'Next China Bank Deal: ICBC', *The Wall Street Journal Asia*, **13** (January), 27–29.

Murrell, P. (1996), 'How Far has the Transition Progressed?', *The Journal of Economic Perspectives*, **10** (2), 25–44.

Nee, V. (1992), 'Organisational Dynamics of Market Transition', *Administrative Science Quarterly*, **37** (1), 1–27.

Nee, V. and S. Opper (2005), 'Economic Transformation in Post-Communist Societies', in Jens Beckert and Milan Zafirovski (eds), *International Encyclopedia of Economic Sociology*, London: Routledge, pp. 200–204.

OECD (2002), *China in the World Economy. The Domestic Policy Challenges*, Paris: OECD.

Olson, M. (1993), 'Dictatorship, Democracy, and Development', *American Political Science Review*, **87** (3), 567–576.

Opper, S. (2003), 'Enforcement of China's Accounting Standards: Reflections on Systemic Problems', *Business and Politics*, **5** (2), 151–173.

Parish, W.L. and E. Michelson (1996), 'Politics and Markets: Dual Transformations', *American Journal of Sociology*, **101** (4), 1042–1059.

Park, A. and K. Sehrt (2001), 'Tests of Financial Intermediation and Banking Reform in China', *Journal of Comparative Economics*, **29** (4), 608–644.

Qi D., W. Woody, and Z. Hua (2000), 'Shareholding Structure and Corporate Performance of Partially Privatized Firms: Evidence from Listed Chinese Companies', *Pacific–Basin Finance Journal*, **8** (5), 587–610.

Roe, Mark J. (1994), *Strong Managers, Weak Owners: The Political Roots of American Corporate Finance*, Princeton, N.J.: Princeton University Press.

Rona-Tas, A. (1994), 'The First Shall Be the Last? Entrepreneurship and the Communist Cadres in the Transition form Socialism', *American Journal of Sociology*, **100** (1), 40–69.

Shleifer, A. and R.W. Vishny (1994), 'Politicians and Firms', *The Quarterly Journal of Economics*, **109** (4), 995–1025.

Shleifer, A. and R.W. Vishny (1997), 'A Survey of Corporate Governance', *Journal of Finance*, **52** (2), 737–783.

Steinfeld, Edward S. (1999), *Forging Reform in China: The Fate of State-Owned Industry*, 2nd ed., Cambridge: Cambridge University Press.

Vickers, John and George Yarrow (1988), *Privatization: An Economic Analysis*, Cambridge, MA.: MIT Press.

Walder, A.G. (1995), 'Local Governments as Industrial Firms: An Organizational Analysis of China's Transitional Economy', *American Journal of Sociology*, **101** (2), 263–301.

Williamson, Oliver E. (1996), *The Mechanisms of Governance*, Oxford: Oxford University Press.

Wong, R. (2000), 'Competition in China's Domestic Banking Industry', Part II, *China Online*, 3 October.

Wong, S.M.L., S. Opper and R. Hu (2004), 'Shareholding Structure, De-politicization and Enterprise Performance: Lessons from China's Listed Companies', *Economics of Transition*, **12** (1), 29–66.

World Bank (2002), *Building Institutions for Markets, World Development Report 2002*, Washington, DC: World Bank.

Wu, B. (1997), 'Several Questions Concerning the Reform and Development of State-Owned Enterprises', *The Chinese Economy*, **30** (2), 6–47.

Wu, S. and Y. Du (1998), 'Jiyu jiankong zhuti de gongsi zhili moshi tantao', *Zhongguo Gongye Jingji*, **9**, 64–68.

Xu, X. and Y. Wang (1999), 'Ownership Structure and Corporate Governance in Chinese Stock Companies', *China Economic Review*, **10**, 75–98.

Yang, D. and Y. Zhou (1998), 'Lun liyi xiangguanzhe hezuo luoji xia de qiye gongtong zhili jizhi', *Zhongguo Gongye Jingji*, **1**, 38–45.

Zhu, T. (1999), 'China's Corporatization Drive: An Evaluation and Policy Implications', *Contemporary Economic Policy*, **17** (4).

Zhou, X. (2000), 'Economic Transition and Income Inequality in Urban China: Evidence from a Panel Data', *American Journal of Sociology* **105**, 1135–74.

2. Institutional Change, Diversity and Competition: Foreign Banks in Shanghai, 1847–2004

Jeroen Kuilman

2.1 INTRODUCTION

In the last 25 years, Shanghai has experienced a rapid increase in the number of foreign banks. While only four 'quasi-foreign' banks were present in Shanghai in the early 1980s the Hong Kong and Shanghai Banking Corporation (HSBC) most notably, this number grew to over 100 foreign banks after 1997. To many casual observers, this may not seem surprising given the fact that this city receives the lion's share of foreign direct investment (FDI) in China and accounts for a large proportion of foreign trade, both of which increased substantially after China embarked on its Open Door Policy in the early 1980s. In 2004 for instance, Shanghai, with a population of only 1.3 per cent of China's total and a land area of only 0.1 per cent, accounted for more than 10 per cent of the total level of FDI in China and a similar share of China's total foreign trade, more than any other city. Foreign enterprises have also come to play an important role in Shanghai's local economy: foreign invested enterprises accounted for more than 60 per cent of Shanghai's gross industrial output in 2004.

However, many are surprised to learn that foreign direct investment and the inflow of foreign banks into Shanghai are not new phenomena. The history of foreign banking in Shanghai dates back to 1847, when the first international bank established itself in this city. Much later, in the 1920s and early 1930s (before China slipped into a phase of economic isolationism), Shanghai functioned as one of Asia's main financial centres; out competing other financial centres such as Hong Kong, Singapore and Yokohama. Shanghai's development as a financial centre was stimulated by the founding of many modern local banks, along with industry associations and a stock exchange. At the time, Shanghai's riverfront boulevard, 'The Bund', housed a relatively large number of foreign financial institutions and was widely referred to as the 'Wall Street of the Orient'.

The protracted and volatile history of foreign banks in Shanghai provides a useful window on long-term industry evolution. We are centrally interested in observing how organisational diversity evolves over time, along with more intensively studied aspects such as density (defined as the number of organisations) and the role of institutional change. Diversity in corporate demography has not been adequately addressed by models of density-dependent market entry and exit (Hannan and Carroll, 1992). For the purpose of this discussion, diversity can be quantified in terms of the variety of countries-of-origin of the international banks in Shanghai. This is in line with the approach used by Xu (2006) who studied diversity among newspapers in terms of their ethnicity. In the case of Shanghai banking, diversity here may be expected to reflect diversity as well in governance structures, corporate culture, size and strategies.

The main objective of this chapter is to illustrate how diversity in Shanghai banking evolved over time, to correlate this with density and institutional change, and in this way to counterbalance the thrust of many other conceptual studies in organisation theory and strategic management (e.g. Carroll and Hannan, 2000: 439–451). This review should thus be seen as a companion text to the theoretical work in this area. A focus on abstract concepts such as diversity and density will facilitate comparative analysis, and this may generate insights that go beyond the single-industry focus. Second, it provides institutional and historical knowledge about an important element of China's financial sector. This sector deserves attention because it plays a pivotal role in China's ongoing reform efforts today (Keister, 2002). Although the industry has changed markedly over the past 150 years, there are also some parallels between historical developments and today's situation which may shed some light on current and future developments. These continuities include for instance the competitive interactions between foreign and domestic banks, as well as the location choices of foreign banks in China.

The following historical account distinguishes four distinct phases of foreign banking in Shanghai:

1. the British hegemony in financing foreign trade with China, 1847-1889;
2. the rise of international banking, 1890-1933;
3. decline and virtual disappearance of foreign banks from the Shanghai scene, 1934-1981;
4. the re-emergence of foreign banks in Shanghai, 1982-2004.

Although the boundaries between these time periods are often not sharp and alternative ways of identifying the industry's phases are possible, these time periods do reflect substantial differences in the industry's competitive and institutional structure.

2.2   BRITISH MONOPOLY: 1847–1889

The first emergence of foreign banks in Shanghai is generally seen to be a direct consequence of the Opium War (1839–1842) between China and Great Britain. This war started when China demanded an end to British imports of opium, which were having devastating effects on the Chinese population. Growing addiction, smuggling and official corruption led the Chinese to take active steps to cut off the opium trade in June 1839. The British, who imported the goods mostly from their territories in India, retaliated against these attempts. British imperial forces started a series of attacks on the Chinese mainland and finally defeated China. The war officially ended with the Treaty of Nanking signed on August 29, 1842, which required the Chinese government to pay war indemnities and exempted Westerners in China from the operation of Chinese law. It also opened five coastal cities to foreign residence and trade. These 'treaty ports' were Canton (Guangzhou), Amoy (Xiamen), Fuzhou, Ningbo and Shanghai. In addition, Hong Kong was ceded to Britain.

Shanghai opened for foreign trade in November 1843 and, like the other treaty ports, it experienced rapid economic growth. Shanghai was particularly successful since it had a favorable geographic position: it offered easy access to large silk producing areas and major tea plantations close to the city (McElderry, 1976). In addition, Shanghai is situated at the mouth of the Yangtze River, so it was positioned to benefit from the ensuing increase in shipping between the upstream provinces and the delta region (Bergère, 1996). Later, the city's position as a trading hub was further enhanced due to the internal disruptions that China experienced between 1850 and 1865, most notably the Taiping Rebellion[1]. These disruptions closed off many of the other treaty ports from the resources in their hinterland, but the hostilities did not spread to the city of Shanghai. As a result, treaty ports such as Canton saw their trade in silk and tea largely diverted to Shanghai, leading to substantial growth in the exports of these commodities through Shanghai's port (McElderry, 1976).

In the midst of this increase in trade, foreign banks were needed to mediate between Chinese and foreign merchants, to finance the imports and exports of foreign firms and to provide foreign currency exchange (Tamagna, 1942). The first foreign bank to set up in Shanghai was the Oriental Bank

Corporation in early 1847[2], a British bank which established itself on The Bund. This boulevard, part of the so-called 'International Settlement' in which foreign firms enjoyed extraterritorial rights, later housed many other local and foreign banks financial institutions. Then, in 1854, the Chartered Mercantile Bank of India, London and China established its own branch office in Shanghai. Later, on April 3, 1865, what would become one of the most important foreign banks in Shanghai's financial history, the Hong Kong and Shanghai Banking Corporation (HSBC), started operations after opening for business in Hong Kong a month earlier. By the end of 1865, the number of foreign banks in Shanghai totalled eleven (see Figure 2.1), of which ten had British origins.

In 1866, these banks were hit hard by an international financial crisis caused by excessive speculation in shares of limited liability companies. The so-called 'Overend-Gurney Crisis' (named after the company that took a leading role in this speculation boom) led to widespread failure within world banking circles and beyond. Compared to their domestic banks, British banks with offices overseas were particularly vulnerable, since the panics caused by the Overend-Gurney Crisis led to runs on the branches of these banks worldwide (Baster, 1929). In Shanghai, the offices of such banks as Agra and Masterman's Bank, the Bank of India and the Commercial Bank of India were closed down as a result of heavy losses. Of these banks, only Agra and Masterman's Bank was able to re-establish itself after the crisis. In May 1870, it re-opened in Shanghai under the name Agra Bank.

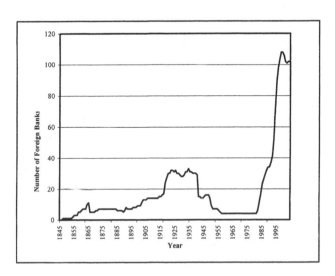

Figure 2.1   Number of foreign banks in Shanghai, 1847–2004

During the following years, British banks nevertheless maintained their dominant position. With London being the centre of the world's silver market and of international finance, British banks controlled the foreign exchange business in China. Firms and governments from other nations wishing to engage in trade with China had to do so through these British banks. British banks also de facto created their own institutional environment in Shanghai following the Treaty of Nanking. Not only did they enjoy the benefits of extraterritoriality throughout China, but Shanghai's International Settlement had its own police force, a Municipal Council and a (liberal) legal system. The local banking system then was dominated by a relatively small and homogeneous set of British banks that faced little competition from other foreign banks, and as a consequence mainly competed with each other. This lack of diversity apparently did not induce non-British banks to establish a presence in Shanghai and the situation persisted for much of the nineteenth century. As Hannan and Freeman (1989: 142) have noted

'When diversity is low, a few organisations or a few organisational forms can more easily dominate a sphere of activity. If these few organisations have high market power, they may be able to prevent other organisations from getting started'.

There is some evidence that this might have happened in Shanghai in this period. In the early decades of foreign banks in Shanghai, banks from rival nations did not fare well there. Deutsche Bank opened its first office in Shanghai in 1872, however this venture does not appear to have been very successful. Silver prices declined sharply in the mid 1870s and its Shanghai office was closed down in 1875 as a result. Furthermore, from 1875 to 1884, not a single new branch of a foreign bank was opened. In this period, incumbent British banks consolidated their positions by seeking further expansion throughout China[3] (Tamagna, 1942).

2.3   EXPANSION OF INTERNATIONAL BANKING: 1890–1933

In the last decade of the nineteenth century, the hegemony of British foreign banks slowly started to erode for two major reasons: first, China's trade with other nations had increased substantially (Table 2.1); and second, foreign banks had also increasingly moved into financing government projects, the number of which had increased substantially by the end of the nineteenth century. Such projects included investment in railway and telecommunications infrastructure and were part of an effort by the Chinese government to modernise and strengthen the national economy. Since China at the time lacked a well developed internal capital market, foreign banks were well positioned to play a pivotal role in lending to the Chinese government[4]. A particular expansion in the number of loans to the Chinese government by the foreign banks came after the Sino-Japanese War. Following her defeat in 1894, China was obliged to pay heavy war indemnities, and to finance this they turned to foreign banks (Cheng, 2003).

As a consequence of these factors, financiers in countries other than Britain increasingly recognised the disadvantages of not having a direct presence in Shanghai, such as a lack of local information (Jones, 1993). Countries that traded with China had been doing so through British merchant banks, but there was an increasing desire to reduce the transaction costs here. This pushed banks from other nations towards setting up their own branch offices in China and building up direct ties. On 2 January 1890, a consortium bank opened an office in Shanghai representing German interests (among them was the aforementioned Deutsche Bank). Later, in 1893, the first Japanese bank (the Yokohama Specie Bank) established a branch office in Shanghai[5], and with the creation of the Russo-Chinese Bank in 1896, the first foreign-Chinese jointly owned bank was founded. The International Banking Corporation (a predecessor of Citibank) opened an office in Shanghai on 15 May 1902. A Dutch bank, the Nederlandsche Handel-Maatschappij, opened its Shanghai office on 11 February 1903[6]. In short, from only five foreign banks in 1889, the number grew to 13 by 1903.

Table 2.1   Trade of various countries with China, 1880–1910

	United States	Japan	Great Britain	Germany	France
1880	71,000	103,000	1,539,000	88,000	69,000
1885	80,000	144,000	1,640,000	226,000	39,000
1890	22,000	267,000	2,032,000	262,000	114,000
1895	36,000	49,000	3,052,000	478,000	170,000
1900	131,000	751,000	3,240,000	638,000	281,000
1905	587,000	308,000	4,812,000	1,322,000	662,000
1910	289,000	2,655,000	4,943,000	1,326,000	553,000

Note: Measured in tonnage of vessels.

Source: Hsiao (1974).

Figure 2.2 shows the historical trajectory of the diversity of foreign banks in terms of their nationality. Diversity is quantified as one minus the Herfindahl index[7], which can be interpreted as a measure of the likelihood that two random foreign banks in Shanghai have different countries-of-origin.

This diversity of foreign banks in Shanghai in terms of their nationality reflected the diversity in trade and financing relations that China maintained with various countries. Institutional theory predicts that dependence on one single source of support for vital resources will give rise to homogeneity (DiMaggio and Powell, 1983), however if multiple sources for resources become available, then the diversity among organisations is likely to increase as well. Similarly, organisational ecology predicts that as the number of dimensions that characterise a resource environment increases, the opportunities for new types of organisations will increase as well (Péli and Nooteboom, 1999). Diversity in the resource environment provides a possibility for new entrants to position their organisations further away from incumbents in the competitive space, reducing the negative effects associated with a proximate positioning (e.g. Baum and Mezias, 1992). Here, the increase in diversity in China's trade and financing relations (the relevant resource environment for foreign banks) provided an opportunity for banks with other nationalities to operate under reduced competitive pressure.

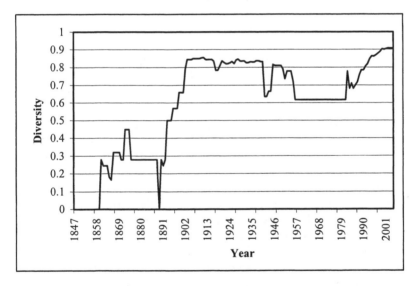

Figure 2.2   Diversity in country-of-origin among Shanghai foreign banks, 1847–2004

Although the rise in organisational diversity in the early twentieth century was exceptional, Figure 2.2 also reveals a more general pattern in which diversity had an overall tendency to increase as the industry aged in Shanghai, a tendency that can also be observed in earlier work studying diversity in other contexts (Boone et al., 2005; Solari and Rossi, 2000).

Obviously, these empirical patterns are in sharp contrast to the predictions of institutional theory (Dacin, 1997; DiMaggio and Powell, 1983; Kraatz and Zajac, 1996), but they are in line with the recent observations of Hambrick et al. (2005).

While the competitive boundaries of the industry changed dramatically in the early twentieth century, the business of foreign banks appeared to be immune to some of the institutional changes that took place at that time. For instance, foreign bank failures did not increase substantially as a result of the revolution of 1911 and the subsequent change of regime, i.e. the founding of the Republic of China. Also, during the First World War the number of foreign banks in Shanghai remained relatively stable (although the assets of the Deutsch-Asiatische Bank were frozen in 1917 when China joined the war). After the First World War, however, some European banks had to take a step back. Preoccupied with post-war reconstruction, these banks retrenched or reduced their financial interests in China by channelling funds to their home country. Nevertheless, the total number of foreign banks increased steadily in the post-war period. This growth was largely due to the arrival of banks representing new foreign financial powers, most notably new American and Japanese banks. These banks basically moved into the void left by the European banks. In 1918 alone, seven banks established a presence in Shanghai, two of which were from the United States (the American Express Company and the American Oriental Banking Corporation) and three from Japan (the Bank of Chosen, the Exchange Bank of China and the Shanghai Bank).

In the following years, Shanghai experienced a period that is sometimes referred to as its 'golden age' (Ji, 2003). In this period, Shanghai gained a reputation as a centre of international finance, not only through the prosperity of the foreign banks present in the city, but also through the rapid development of modern local banks and other financial institutions, such as the stock exchange. It was in this period that Shanghai's Bund, which housed many of the foreign banks, became known as the 'Wall Street of the Orient'. At the end of 1934, the number of foreign banks peaked at 33. For comparison, alternative financial centres such as Singapore (21 'full-license' banks in 1934, many of which were foreign banks, see Carroll and Hannan [2000: 23]) and Hong Kong (17 foreign banks, excluding banks from mainland China) hosted a much lower number of foreign banks. Jones (1992: 407) states that Hong Kong 'was essentially a smaller version of Shanghai throughout the interwar years'.

Such a rise in the density of organisations is typically associated with a growth in their perceived legitimacy. Growth in numbers gives force to claims of institutional standing and facilitates the social recognition of an organisational population. Tests of a theory of density dependent industry evolution proposed by Hannan and Carroll (1992) suggest that, especially in the period following World War I, Shanghai gained widespread legitimacy as a centre for international finance (Kuilman, 2005). However, despite this legitimation, in the mid-1930s Shanghai's position as a major finance and trading hub quickly started to crumble.

2.4 DEMISE OF FOREIGN BANKS: 1934–1981

Numerous factors contributed to the decline of Shanghai's role in international finance. Starting in 1934, there was a currency crisis that resulted from the adoption of the Silver Purchase Act by the United States. This change in U.S. monetary policy caused silver to flow out of China and world silver prices to climb sharply. Responding to this crisis, the silver standard was abandoned and issuing bank notes became the sole right of three government banks (the Central Bank of China, the Bank of China and the Bank of Communications). This was a shift in financial authority from the foreign banks, many of which had previously issued their own notes, to the Chinese government. In addition, in connection with abandoning the silver standard, banks had to hand over their silver supplies to the government. Foreign banks which previously had operated almost autonomously in the Chinese financial market, now found themselves in a position of 'subordinate dependence' (Tamagna, 1942: 119). The role of foreign banks then diminished further as they increasingly faced competition from the growing number of local banks. Cheng (2003) notes that domestic banks, which had matured substantially in the 1920s and 1930s, made successful efforts to attract depositors away from foreign banks. In addition, many of the more modern domestic banks were able to break into the financing of government debts, an area which the foreign banks had previously controlled. The balance of power in the financial market thus shifted from foreign to domestic banks.

The onset of another Sino-Japanese War in 1937 (and the subsequent occupation of substantial parts of China by the Japanese), did not have immediate consequences for the presence of foreign banks in Shanghai, although their financing activities were hampered by a decrease in trade flows. Protected by the extraterritorial rights of the International Settlement, they continued their banking activities in, for example, currency exchange. The Japanese, however, attempting to gain more control over China's financial system, expanded their financial interests in the occupied territories. In May 1939, the Japanese-supported Hua Hsing Bank was established. Later, in January 1941, the Central Reserve Bank of China was founded. Both the Hua Hsing Bank and the Central Reserve Bank of China issued their own banknotes and were instrumental in financing the expenditures in China of Japan's armed forces.

The immunity of foreign banks in the International Settlement lasted until December 1941 when, immediately after the Japanese attack on Pearl Harbor, Japanese military forces entered the settlement. The Japanese took control of the American, Belgian, British and Dutch banks in Shanghai and turned them over to Japanese banks, such as the Yokohama Specie Bank, for liquidation. Banks of friendly or neutral nationalities (French, German and Italian banks) continued to operate, together with the Japanese banks, albeit on a more limited scale (Tamagna, 1942).

The end of the Second World War led to the closing down of all Japanese and Japanese-supported banks and the confiscation of their assets (Ji, 2003). In total, ten foreign banks had to close their banking facilities in Shanghai in 1945. On the other hand, banks from other countries whose branches had been liquidated at the end of 1941 started to re-establish themselves in Shanghai. Initially, these returning foreign banks hoped they could rapidly restore their banking business, including the elaborate networks of branches they had previously maintained in various parts of China. However, civil war between communist and nationalist factions spread across the country, and when the communists prevailed, these hopes were soon disappointed. The civil war was accompanied by economic and financial chaos: heavy inflationary pressures troubled the banking business in particular. For instance, the wholesale price index for Shanghai in September 1947 was 4,635,700, based on an index of 100 for the first half of 1937. As a result, the foreign banks were never able to fully recover from the turbulence generated by the Second World War even though they were able to restore their presence.

The Communist Party formally seized power on October 1, 1949, and this event presaged the end of the foreign banks' China operations. An adverse economic environment combined with a socio-political environment in which foreign banks were seen as agents of Western imperialism created resource scarcity and led to the temporary demise of international banking activities in the city. In the years that followed 1949, foreign banks disbanded their China operations one by one. American banks, such as Chase Bank and the National City Bank of New York, were among the first to shut down their operations at the end of 1950 because of the tensions generated by the Korean War. A United Nations trade embargo imposed on China in May 1951 worsened the economic climate for the remaining foreign banks in Shanghai. Banks such as the Nederlandsche Handel-Maatschappij, the Banque Belge pour l'Etranger and the Banque de l'Indo-Chine all closed their branches.

By the late-1950s, only four 'quasi-foreign' banks were left in Shanghai: HSBC; the Bank of East Asia; the Chartered Bank of India, Australia and

China (later to become the Standard Chartered Bank); and the Overseas Chinese Banking Corporation (incorporated in Singapore)[8]. These four banks were granted a special legal status and were only permitted to provide such financial services as the government deemed necessary for China's national economic development (MacCormac, 1993). In practice, this resulted in a small, continuing business in inward remittances and export bills, while China moved into a period of economic isolation.

Ruef's (2004) generic model of the demise of organisational forms fits well with this stage of the historical development of the Shanghai banking industry. He points out that exogenous factors such as regulatory actions and material resource conditions can lead to the disappearance of organisational forms. In the context of Shanghai banking, regulatory actions such as the abandonment of the silver standard and the requirement that foreign banks hand over their silver reserves, both serve as a partial explanation for the decline of foreign banking in Shanghai. In addition, wars disrupted the industry and led to resource scarcity and inflation. Ruef offers competition from related, alternative populations as another possible explanation. In the 1950s, Shanghai became an industrial city under heavy state control and Hong Kong was able to position itself as one of the main international trade and financial centre in the Far East at this time (Tian, 1996; Schenk, 2001). Kuilman (2005) discusses how the more favourable institutional environment of Hong Kong provided an alternative for the foreign banks in Shanghai. As a consequence of the adverse conditions in mainland China, the foreign banking population in Hong Kong started to grow rapidly in the 1960s and 1970s.

2.5 RE-EMERGENCE OF FOREIGN BANKS: 1982–2004

Starting in 1978, a series of steps were introduced in the form of a new reform program[9] which ended China's economic isolation. The reforms aimed to stimulate economic growth and to improve living standards, and included the opening of the national economy to foreign trade and investment. The part of the reform program regarding foreign trade and investment became known as China's Open Door Policy. Within this policy, foreign financial institutions were not only encouraged to invest in the country, but also to promote reform of the financial system and to foster China's economic and financial relationships with other countries (Lees and Liaw, 1996).

In 1980, the first foreign banks started to open representative offices in Beijing, since the relevant ministries and headquarters (notably that of the Bank of China) were based there. Establishing a representative office in

Beijing facilitated liaison activities, which were, in effect, the only activities that were permitted for these early representative offices. However, the most important locations for foreign banks later proved to be the four Special Economic Zones (SEZs) in Southern China: three in Guangdong Province and one in Fujian. These SEZs were granted a degree of autonomy, greater infrastructural investment and tax incentives. Foreign investment projects in these areas proliferated rapidly.

With the SEZs designated by the central government as the main recipients of foreign investment in the 1980s, Shanghai was put at a relative disadvantage. Tian (1996) suggests that one of main reasons for not including Shanghai in the initial implementation of the open-door policy was a fear of political instability: in the 1950s and 1960s Shanghai had become a heavy contributor to the central government's tax revenues (85 per cent of its local revenue was remitted to the central government in the period 1958–1982), so a failure of the reform policy in Shanghai would have greatly upset the national budget.

Nevertheless, Shanghai did see some considerable growth in the 1980s, most notably in the development of its financial functions. Shanghai experienced the entry of new foreign banks for the first time since 1949. In December 1982, the Industrial Bank of Japan and the Bank of Tokyo established representative offices in the city. In April 1984, Shanghai and 14 other coastal cities were 'opened' for foreign investment, and this led to additional bank entries. Shanghai also started to strengthen its financial system in other areas. In 1986, an interbank lending market was established, and in 1988, a forex swap market was introduced. By 1989, the number of foreign banks in Shanghai had reached 34, exceeding the highest number of foreign banks before 1949. This reflects at least a partial revitalisation of Shanghai's identity as a financial centre, and a continuation of its historical role (Lees and Liaw, 1996).

However, new limitations on entry to China's financial markets were introduced after the Tian'anmen Incident in June 1989 (MacCormac, 1993). Foreign banks adopted a cautious wait-and-see attitude towards the Chinese market. The earlier boom in the entry of new foreign banks (in the form of new representative offices) came to a halt. Moreover, the austerity program (1989–1991)[10] put in place after Tian'anmen led to loan defaults, and foreign banks which had already opened branches elsewhere in China found that collecting debts or enforcing guarantees was difficult (MacCormac, 1993).

In the aftermath of Tian'anmen, the central government wanted to show the outside world that China was still open for investment and was continuing its reforms (Gold, 1991). This could be seen, for example, in the acceleration of the development of a previously planned zone for trade and finance in Pudong, formerly a rural hinterland east of Shanghai. This new financial zone was announced in 1990 and foreign banks were encouraged to open branch offices there[11]. In addition to this initiative, other ways to further Shanghai's economic development were explored. Investments were made in physical infrastructure, such as a ring road bypassing the city centre, public transportation, and gas and water works. In December 1990, the Shanghai Stock Exchange re-opened for business, stimulating the growth of China's financial market. The events of 1990 heralded a period of rapid economic growth.

Since 1991, Shanghai's annual growth in gross domestic product has generally exceeded the national average: reaching 14–15 per cent between the years 1992 and 1995. Foreign direct investment figures have also improved substantially. In 1995, Shanghai attracted China's second largest amount of FDI after the province of Guangdong (Tian, 1996). This improved economic climate, together with a thriving real estate market and a more attractive capital market, led to a further increase in the number of foreign banks in the 1990s. From the 34 foreign banks present in Shanghai in 1990, this number increased to a total of 108 foreign banks by the end of 1999[12]. Despite the increase in the number of foreign banks, their share of the Chinese financial market remained small; and in fact decreased in the late 1990s, from 2.5 per cent in 1996 to 2 per cent in 2000 and 1.2 per cent by the end of 2002[13]. To a large extent, this is a result of the restrictions that foreign banks have faced in the Chinese market. Foreign banks have throughout China's reform era mainly been permitted to provide foreign currency services to non-Chinese individuals and enterprises, i.e. foreign corporations and joint-ventures in China. Despite the fact that this potential customer base has been growing rapidly, this has not resulted in a larger market share for the foreign banks. Foreign banks have thus appeared to be merely peripheral players in a market dominated by large, state-owned domestic banks.

However, further deregulation of the banking system (see Table 2.2) agreed upon as a condition of China's accession to the World Trade Organisation (WTO) in December 2001 is generally expected to enlarge the market for foreign banks. Among others stipulations, China was to allow foreign banks to provide local currency services to all types of local enterprises by the end of 2003, and to Chinese citizens by the end of 2006 (i.e. five years after WTO accession).

During the second half of the 1990s, it became evident that deregulation had generated what Barnett and Carroll term 'competitive release' (Barnett and Carroll, 1993, p. 116). This has manifested itself in several ways, most notably in the fact that competition between domestic and foreign banks has been intensifying.

In this connection, Kuilman (2005) has shown that a gradual increase in the number of domestic banks has slowed down the time-to-profitability for foreign banks with branch offices. Another manifestation of the increased competition is the increasing number of equity stakes in domestic banks purchased by foreign financial institutions (see Table 2.3).

Table 2.2   Deregulation of Shanghai's foreign banks, 1980–2006

Date	Event	Business Scope Implications
30 Oct. 1980	Representative offices permitted	Foreign banks are allowed to: - liaise with the Bank of China - give advice to foreign firms in China - develop business with Chinese commercial and trade organisations
Dec. 1990	Upgrading to branch possible*	Foreign banks are allowed to engage in profit-making operations but prohibited from accepting deposits from or making loans to private domestic enterprises and Chinese individuals. All restricted to foreign currency transactions.
31 Dec. 1996	Local currency licenses*	Foreign banks can obtain a local currency license provided that they have been profitable for two consecutive years.
17 Dec. 2001	China's WTO entry	Selected foreign banks are allowed to expand their foreign currency business to all institutions and individuals in China.
17 Dec. 2003	Two years after WTO entry	Foreign banks with a local currency license will be allowed to lend to and accept deposits from private domestic enterprises.
17 Dec. 2006	Five years after WTO entry	Foreign banks with a local currency license are allowed to lend to and accept deposits from Chinese citizens. Private banking will also be permitted.

Note: *Local regulations (only in Shanghai), other regulatory changes are on the national level.

Table 2.3   Foreign investments in Chinese banks, 1996–2004

Date	Chinese Bank	Foreign Investor	Percentage
1996	China Everbright Bank	Asian Development Bank	1.9
Sep. 1999-Mar. 2002	Bank of Shanghai	HSBC/ International Finance Corporation/ Shanghai Commercial Bank (HK)	8 7 3
Nov. 2001	Nanjing City Commercial Bank	International Finance Corporation	15
Jan. 2003	Shanghai Pudong Development Bank	Citigroup	5
Oct. 2003	China Minsheng Banking Corporation	International Finance Corporation/ Temasek	1.6 4.55
Dec. 2003	Fujian Industrial Bank	HSBC (Hang Seng Bank)/ International Finance Corporation/ Government of Singapore Investment Corporation	15.98 4 5
Dec. 2003	Dalian City Commercial Bank	SHK Financial Group	10
Jun. 2004	Shenzhen Development Bank	Newbridge Capital	17.89
Sep. 2004	Xi'an City Commercial Bank	Bank of Nova Scotia/ International Finance Corporation	2.5 2.5
Aug. 2004	Bank of Communications	HSBC	19.9
Sep. 2004	Jinan City Commercial Bank	Commonwealth Bank of Australia	11
Nov. 2004	Tianjin Bohai Bank	Standard Chartered Bank	19.99

These phenomena suggest that the boundaries between the two organisational populations are slowly blurring. The growing competitive overlap between domestic and foreign banks also signals a resurrection of the competitive relationship between foreign and domestic banks that existed in the 1920s and 1930s. Although the market has so far remained fragmented due to the legacy of socialist attitudes, recent years have seen renewed direct competition between the two organisational populations.

2.6   CONCLUSION

Institutional change can have dramatic effects on the number and diversity of organisations in an industry, and those effects are best seen across a long historical time frame. The history of foreign banking in Shanghai shows that the role of the state has been crucial in determining the level of diversity. At the end of the nineteenth century, for example, the Chinese government increasingly sought loans in the international capital markets, and an increased number of nations became involved in financing government projects. Banks from these nations increasingly felt the need to establish a direct presence in China rather than depending on the then-dominant British banks. American, Dutch, French, German and Japanese banks all established a presence in Shanghai. These changes fundamentally altered the industry's competitive structure. The increase in organisational diversity thus appears to have been a direct effect of institutional change.

However, some important institutional changes in mainland China, such as the revolution of 1911, affected neither the diversity nor the density of foreign banks in Shanghai. There are two reasons why this might have been the case. First, foreign banks may have been protected from failure by their parent banks and by home-country authorities. As affiliates of larger organisations, they may have had easy access to funds in times of adversity. In addition, these banks often also represented the financial interests of their home-country government. As such these banks were political agents as they facilitated inter-governmental finance. Second, prior to the Second World War, foreign banks in Shanghai had operated in their own institutional environment in the form of the International Settlement. This prevented some of the hostilities elsewhere in China spilling over to Shanghai.

Currently, however, given the volatile progress of contemporary reforms in China, institutionally i.e. state generated change is likely to continue to dominate the dynamics of foreign banking in Shanghai. The de-regulation process that started in the 1980s will continue to unfold. So far it seems to have generated a 'competitive release' (Barnett and Carroll, 1993) with an increase in density surpassing any level that the local industry has ever seen, and a restoration of nationality diversity to pre-1949 levels. Expectations are that, at least in the short-term, the trends towards higher density and diversity will continue and that Shanghai will increasingly compete with alternative financial centres such as Hong Kong and Singapore. Diversity will increase not only in terms of nationalities, but also in terms of the financial services being offered. As deregulation continues and the scope of operations for foreign banks expands, they will increasingly compete with domestic banks, which in the long term could cause downward pressure on the density and diversity of foreign banks.

NOTES

1. The Taiping Rebellion was one of the largest peasant upheavals in Chinese history, directed at the educated Confucian elite. 20 million Chinese died as a result of this rebellion. See also Feuerwerker (1975), Kuhn (1978), and Nee and Peck (1975).

2. Among historians there seems to be little consensus regarding the founding year of this bank in Shanghai. Authors such as Cheng (2003), McElderry (1976), and Tamagna (1942) claim its branch office was opened in 1848. Others, such as Hong et al. (2003) and Ji (2003) point to 1847 as the starting year. I find Ji's (2003) source and argumentation the most convincing. Moreover, 1847 is mentioned by two museums in Shanghai (the Bank History Museum and the Bund History Museum) as the year of establishment.

3. For instance, the Hong Kong and Shanghai Banking Corporation also opened offices in Xiamen (1873), in Fuzhou (1877), and in Tianjin (1881).

4. This is in contrast to, for instance, the modernisation of Japan, which was largely financed by a domestic government debt market, modeled after successful Western models (Han 1998).

5. Earlier however, on 9 April 1878, the First National Bank of Japan installed an agent at the Shanghai branch of Mitsui & Co. for the purpose of assisting in exchange transactions. This agent was recalled on 4 February 1881.

6. Earlier, from 1825 to 1827, the Nederlandsche Handel-Maatschappij (NHM) maintained a trading post in Shanghai, but the NHM at the time was not yet active in the banking business.

7. This measure has earlier been used by Carroll, Xu and Koçak (2005), Koçak and Carroll (2005), and Xu (2006).

8. But even if these quasi-foreign banks wanted to leave they ran into severe difficulties. This is shown most clearly by the experiences of the Hong Kong and Shanghai Banking Corporation. The bank tried to sell its local assets and withdraw its funds from the Chinese mainland, but was not allowed to do so. After years of negotiation, the Chinese authorities eventually confiscated HSBC's prominent building on the Bund, but insisted that the branch itself remained active in Shanghai. Its staff

therefore moved into rented premises where it continued its (limited) business activities (Collis 1965).
9.   For a detailed account of various aspects of the reform program, see Qian (1999).
10. This austerity program was introduced to prevent the economy from overheating. In this period, the Chinese government also attempted to re-centralise investment and financial powers (Weingast, Qian, and Montinola 1995).
11. Branch offices, in contrast to representative offices, are allowed to engage in profit-making operations, such as the granting of loans. By allowing foreign banks to open branch offices in the city, the local government created a source of working capital and funds for the development of Pudong.
12. A wave of mergers and acquisitions in the global banking industry, most notable among Japanese financial institutions, was among the main factors that caused the number of foreign banks to decline after 1999.
13. People's Bank of China 2005.

REFERENCES

Barnett, W.P. and G.R. Carroll (1993), 'How institutional constraints affected the organization of early U.S. telephony', *Journal of Law, Economics and Organization*, **9**, 98–126.

Baster, Albert S.J. (1929), *The Imperial Banks*, London: P.S. King and Son.

Baum, J.A.C., and S.J. Mezias (1992), 'Localized competition and organizational failure in the Manhattan hotel industry, 1898–1990', *Administrative Science Quarterly*, **37**, 580–604.

Bergère, Marie-Claire (1996), 'The Geography of Finance in a Semi-colonial Metropolis: The Shanghai Bund (1842–1943)', in Herman Diederiks and David Reeder (eds), *Cities of Finance*, Amsterdam: North-Holland.

Boone, Christophe, F.C. Wezel, and A. Witteloostuijn (2005), 'An Ecological Theory of Population-level Diversity Dependence', presented at the annual Organizational Ecology Conference at the University of Durham.

Carroll, Glenn R. and Michael T. Hannan (2000), *The Demography of Corporations and Industries*, Princeton, NJ: Princeton University Press.

Carroll, Glenn R., H. Xu and O. Koçak (2005), 'Diverse organizational identities of newspapers: An empirical study of election turnout in American local communities 1870–1972', presented at the Academy of Management Meeting, Honolulu.

Chang, Kia-Ngau (1958), *The Inflationary Spiral: The Experience in China, 1939–*

1950, Cambridge, MA: The Technology Press of the Massachusetts Institute of Technology.

Cheng, Linsun (2003), *Banking in Modern China: Entrepreneurs, Professional Managers, and the Development of Chinese Banks, 1897–1937*, Cambridge: Cambridge University Press.

Collis, Maurice (1965), *Wayfoong: The Hong Kong and Shanghai Banking Corporation*, London: Faber and Faber.

Dacin, M.T. (1997), 'Isomorphism in context: the power and prescription of institutional norms', *Academy of Management Journal*, **40** (1), 46–81.

DiMaggio, P.J. and W.W. Powell (1983), 'The iron cage revisited: Institutional isomorphism and collective rationality in organizational fields', *American Sociological Review*, **48**, 147–60.

Feuerwerker, Albert (1975), *Rebellion in Nineteenth-Century China*, Ann Arbor, MI: Center for Chinese Studies, University of Michigan.

Gold, T.B. (1991), 'Can Pudong Deliver?', *The China Business Review*, **18** (6), 22–29.

Hambrick, D.C., S. Finkelstein, T. S. Cho, and E. M. Jackson (2005), 'Isomorphism in reverse: Institutional theory as an explanation for recent increases in intraindustry heterogeneity and managerial discretion', *Research in Organizational Behavior*, **26**, 307–50.

Han, Joon (1998), *The Evolution of the Japanese Banking Industry: An Ecological Analysis*, Ph.D. dissertation, Stanford, CA: Stanford University.

Hannan, Michael T. and Glenn R. Carroll (1992), *Dynamics of Organizational Populations: Density, Legitimation, and Competition*, Oxford: Oxford University Press.

Hannan, Michael T. and John H. Freeman (1989), *Organizational Ecology*, Cambridge, MA: Harvard University Press.

Hong, Xiaguan, Xinxin Wang, and Anding Li (2003), *The History of Shanghai Finance*, Shanghai: Shanghai Academy of Social Sciences Press.

Hsiao, Liang-Lin (1974), *China's Foreign Trade Statistics, 1864–1949*, Cambridge, MA: Harvard University Press.

Ji, Zhaojin (2003), *A History of Modern Shanghai Banking: The Rise and Decline of China's Finance Capitalism*, Armonk, NY: M.E. Sharpe.

Jones, Geoffrey (1992), 'International financial centres in Asia, the Middle East, and Australia: A historical perspective', in Youssef Cassis (ed.), *Finance and Financiers in European History*, 1880–1960, Cambridge: Cambridge University Press, pp. 405–28.

Jones, Geoffrey (1993), *British Multinational Banking, 1830–1990*, Oxford: Clarendon Press.

Keister, L.A. (2002), 'Financial markets, money, and banking', *Annual Review of Sociology*, **28**, 39–61.

Koçak, O. and G.R. Carroll (2005), 'Growing Church Organizations in Diverse U.S. Communities 1890–1906', Research Paper no. 1920, Stanford, CA: Stanford University.

Kraatz, M.S. and E.J. Zajac (1996), 'Exploring the limits of the new institutionalism: The causes and consequences of illegitimate organizational change', *American Sociological Review*, **61** (5), 812–36.

Kuhn, Philip A. (1978), 'The Taiping rebellion', in Denis Twitchett and John K. Fairbank (eds), The Cambridge History of China, **10**, Cambridge: Cambridge University Press, pp. 264–316.

Kuilman, Jeroen G. (2005), *The Re-emergence of Foreign Banks in Shanghai: An Ecological Analysis*, Ph.D. dissertation, Rotterdam: Erasmus University Rotterdam.

Lees, Francis A. and K. Thomas Liaw (1996), *Foreign Participation in China's Banking and Securities Markets*, Westport, CT: Quorum Books.

MacCormac, S.H. (1993) 'Foreign banking in China: Opportunities for U.S. investors in the 1990s', *Journal of Chinese Law*, **7** (2), 225–75.

McElderry, Andrea L. (1976), *Shanghai Old-style Banks* [Ch'ien Chuang], 1800–1935, Ann Arbor, MC: Center for Chinese Studies, University of Michigan.

Nee, Victor and J. Peck (1975), 'Introduction: Why uninterrupted revolution?' in Victor Nee and James Peck (eds), *China's Uninterrupted Revolution: From 1840 to the Present*, New York, NY: Pantheon Books, pp. 3–56.

People's Bank of China (2005), *Quarterly Statistical Bulletin*, Beijing: People's Bank of China.

Péli, G.L. and B. Nooteboom (1999), 'Market partitioning and the geometry of the resource space', *American Journal of Sociology*, **104**, 1132–53.

Qian, Y. (2000), 'The process of China's market transition (1978–1998): The evolutionary, historical, and comparative perspective', *Journal of Institutional and Theoretical Economics*, **156** (1), 151–71.

Ruef, M. (2004), 'The demise of an organizational form: Emancipation and plantation agriculture in the American South, 1860–1880', *American Journal of Sociology*, **109**, 1365–410.

Schenk, Catherine R. (2001), *Hong Kong as an International Financial Centre: Emergence and Development 1945–65*, London: Routledge.

Solari, Luca, and Ruggero Rossi (1999), 'The Lost Twin Strikes Back: Rejoining Heterogeneity and Density Dependence within Organization Ecology', unpublished manuscript.

Tamagna, Frank M. (1942), *Banking and Finance in China*, New York, NY: Institute of Pacific Relations.

Tian, Gang (1996), *Shanghai's Role in the Economic Development of China: Reform of Foreign Trade and Investment*, Westport, CT: Praeger.

Weingast, B., Y. Qian and G. Montinola (1995), 'Federalism, Chinese style: The political basis for economic success in China', *World Politics*, **48** (1), 50–81.

Xu, H. (2006), 'Organizational Diversity and Museum Formation: A study of American Local Communities, 1872–1976', presented at the Hong Kong University of Science and Technology, Hong Kong.

3. Foreign Firms in China: Success by Strategic Choices

Xueyuan Zhang and Patrick Reinmoeller

3.1 INTRODUCTION

Ever since the beginning of economic reform in 1978, China has attracted the attention of Western academics and the business world (e.g. Organisation for Economic Cooperation and Development, 2005; Prasad, 2004; Shenkar, 2006). With an average annual GDP of 9.4 per cent between 1979 and 2004 this cannot come as a surprise. Rather unexpected, however, was the fact that China outperformed the European transition economies. One reason given for this development is the contribution made by foreign direct investment (FDI), more precisely the establishment of subsidiaries (i.e. foreign firms hereafter) in China (see Economist Intelligence Unit, 2003; and Lardy, 1995). China was the largest FDI recipient among developing countries in 2004, attracting FDI inflows of US$60.63bn, and surpassed only by the United States and the UK. This development raises some questions. First, to which extent does China's overall development depend on past and ongoing FDI? Second, what actually explains the trend? In what follows, an attempt is made to analyse the processes and activities of foreign firms investing and producing in China. After all, if China was not regarded as an attractive location for investment and production, the observed FDI inflow would not have occurred. If enough foreign firms succeeded in China to induce more firms and/or more capital to follow then we assume that one or more of the following factors must have played a role:

1. *A selection effect.* By carefully choosing the best suited entry strategy only firms with a high probability of success invested in China.

2. *An integration effect.* By acknowledging the specificity of the local business environment and developing complementary capacities foreign firms can exploit the business opportunities offered in China. It is worth mentioning that once production has started and increasingly more since the middle of the 1990s firms are confronted with locally rather than nationally

designed constraints and opportunities (e.g. Clissord, 2004; Segal and Thun, 2001).

3. *A learning effect.* By flexibly reacting to an unfamiliar business environment characterised by frequent and sometimes drastic changes, firms need to employ structures and routines that allow for smooth adaptation to new chances and constraints. These three factors are not independent from each other. In what follows they will however be treated separately for analytical reasons.

The chapter is organised as follows: after a general overview of the FDI landscape since 1978 (Section 3.2), our analysis describes the factors which lead firms to invest in China (Section 3.3); identifies factors that inform firms of their entry choices (Section 3.4); and examines the ideas of local embeddedness and adaptation (Section 3.5). This analysis is offered in the context of a generally dynamic situation (Section 3.6).

3.2 OVERVIEW

The Open Door Policy of 1978 parted the Bamboo Curtain between China and the Western world. At the beginning (realised) FDI increased gradually, yet remained small. Nevertheless, by 1990 annual realised FDI was about four times that of 1983. This picture changed dramatically again in the 1990s. In 1992 alone, realised FDI amounted to US$11bn, almost three times the amount of 1991. In 2004, it reached more than US$60bn, which is almost five times the amount of 1992 and 17 times that of 1990. To put these figures into perspective it is worth having a look at the cases of Russia (another transition economy) and India (another large economy at a similar level of income).

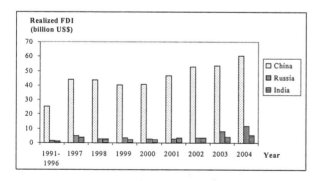

Source: United Nations Conference on Trade and Development 2003, 2005[1].

Figure 3.1 FDI inflows: China, Russia and India

As Figure 3.1 shows, FDI inflows in all three economies increased during the 1990s, yet those in Russia and India remained far behind China. In 2004 for example, China received about 9 per cent of the total FDI globally, as compared to Russia's 1.8 per cent and India's 0.82 per cent.

FDI means more than the transfer of capital and technology. It changes the ecology of the Chinese economy when more and more foreign firms operate in China (see column 2 in Table 3.1), after decades in which China had remained outside the international division of labour. By the end of 2004 more than 242,000 foreign firms were operating in China. However, it should be noted that more than 90 per cent of these entered the market after 1990. The contribution of these firms became considerable. They became a major source for tax revenue (see Table 3.1, column 3). In 2004 for example, foreign firms generated more than one-fifth of the total tax revenue indicating their crucial role in the economy and the state's finances.

Table 3.1   The performance of FDI in China: 1980–2004

Year	FDI realised amount (billion US$)	No. of foreign firms in operation	Share of tax revenue (per cent) p.a.
1980	-	7	-
1982	1.8^2	330	-
1985	2.0	4912	-
1990	3.5	25389	-
1991	4.4	37215	-
1992	11.0	84371	4.25
1993	27.5	167507	5.71
1994	33.8	206096	8.51
1995	37.5	233564	10.96
1996	41.7	240447	11.87
1997	45.3	235681	13.16
1998	45.5	227807	14.38
1999	40.3	212436	15.99
2000	40.7	203208	17.50
2001	46.9	202306	19.01
2002	52.7	208056	20.52
2003	53.5	226373	20.90
2004	60.63	242284	20.80

Source: China Ministry of Commerce 2004, 2005; China National Bureau of Statistics 2004, 2005; United Nations Conference on Trade and Development 2005

Moreover, foreign firms are also the driving force behind China's integration into the international market as can be seen in the foreign trade statistics (see Figure 3.2). Since the beginning of reform, China's imports and exports have rapidly increased, well above global increases. By the end of 2004, the imports and exports reached US$561.38bn and US$593.36bn respectively, with an average annual growth rate of 17.5 per cent and 17.7 per cent respectively. As a consequence, China's contribution to world exports increased from 1 per cent (in 1980) to more than 6 per cent (in 2004). The export success of China's economy is to a great extent the export success of foreign firms in China (Figure 3.2). While in 1986, foreign firms' share of total exports was only 1.9 per cent, this share had increased to 57.1 per cent in 2004.

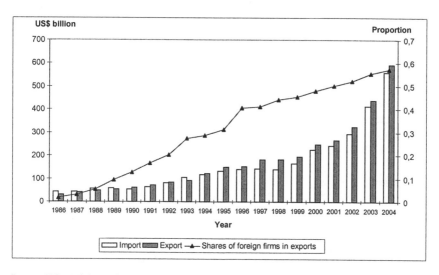

Source: China Ministry of Commerce 2004, 2005; Liang, 2004

Figure 3.2   Imports and exports of China, 1986–2004

Even more striking is the extent to which the composition of exports changed. China's exports have shifted from natural resource-based products (e.g. grain and oil) to labour-intensive products (e.g. garment and textile products), and lately to technology-related products (e.g. machinery and computer products). In 2004, machinery and electronic products amounted to 54.5 per cent of the total export values, of which more than 70 per cent were produced by foreign firms (China National Bureau of Statistics, 2005). Another example is the emergence of a Chinese IT sector in the 1990s, which proved to be so internationally competitive that China is one of the top three exporters in the world today (Amighini, 2005). In this case too, foreign firms dominate China's exports: 87.3 per cent of exports of high-tech and new technological products were produced by foreign firms in 2004 (China Ministry of Commerce, 2005).

All in all, the picture summarised above demonstrates the remarkable performance of FDI and foreign firms in China at the macro level, and invites a more detailed analysis of the underlying processes. The first question is why foreign firms would go to China?

3.3   WHY INVEST IN CHINA?

Economic analysis of foreign trade and foreign direct investment in China often cites determinants such as market size, economic development, labour market conditions and infrastructure (Cheng and Kwan, 2000; Wei, 1995; Wei and Liu, 2001; and Zhao, 2003). Market size (measured by GDP or GDP per capita) and economic growth translate into business opportunities for foreign investors. Likewise, a huge, low cost labour force with remarkably well trained technical personnel adds to the attractiveness of China as a factor market (Kearney, 2004; Lu and Liu, 2004). China's infrastructure (especially in transportation and communications) is also beginning to contribute to its attractiveness as a location for FDI (China National Bureau of Statistics, 2005).

Another group of studies stress institutional factors, i.e. institutional incentives for FDI. The reforms were accompanied by liberalisation in the foreign trade sectors, which included the establishment of Special Economic Zones (SEZs), and special tariffs and tax rates. These were designed to attract FDI (Fu, 2000; Ng and Tuan, 2002; Organisation for Economic Cooperation and Development, 2000; Wei and Liu, 2001) by keeping the operating costs within China low (Kim and Lau, 1994; Krug, 2004; Krugman, 1994). Corruption and regulatory complications though ubiquitous have so far only started to deter investors from North America and Europe (Khan, 2001). Investors closer to China or her culture do not seem to be worried (Wei and Liu, 2001), as exemplified by the fact that Asian investors from Hong Kong, Taiwan, Macao, Singapore, South Korea and Japan, still dominate FDI inflow in China (Chen and Chen, 1998; Lu and Zhu, 1995; Li et al., 2001; Wei, 1995; Yang, 1997; Zhang, 2000, 2005).

All in all, these studies suggest that both economic advantages and institutional incentives attract FDI to China. However, studies at the macro level dismiss two crucial aspects. First, China cannot be modelled as a unified economy, let alone one integrated market. Thus foreign firms need to respond to local rather than national boundaries of markets and institutions

(Demurger, 2001; Dollar et al., 2003). Second, the success of FDI in China depends crucially on the strategic decisions of foreign firms: what and where they produce, in particular; how they manage their business relationships; and how they deal with local jurisdictions.

Thus it is assumed in what follows that a firm-level analysis is needed to identify (systematic) factors by which the performance of the FDI sector can be explained in relation to its specificity. Studies in international business and strategy addressing this issue point to the importance of choosing the 'right' entry strategy, responding flexibly to the local environment while developing the capacity to adapt to changing circumstances (Buckley and Casson, 1976; Caves, 1996; Dunning, 1977; Ghemawat, 2003; Peng, 2003). In the following, we discuss entry choices and local embeddedness of foreign firms in China respectively, attempting to sort out the major underlying considerations and their dynamic features in order to understand the behaviour of foreign firms in China.

3.4 INVESTING BY STRATEGIC ENTRY CHOICES

3.4.1 Perspectives from International Business and Management

One promising starting point for explaining why China has been chosen by foreign companies or multinational corporations (MNCs) is Dunning's widely accepted 'eclectic approach' (1977, 1988, 2003). At the core of the eclectic approach lies the question of why foreign companies establish subsidiaries instead of exporting their products. *Internalising production* refers to the decision to invest in subsidiaries and is assumed to depend on two further considerations. The first consideration is *location advantage,* which according to this approach is not limited to different resource endowments or labour costs, but also accounts for transaction costs in cross-border trade, which can be circumvented when production is localised. The second consideration is *ownership advantage* when companies that need to keep control over their firm-specific assets, such as intellectual property rights, brand names, or research and development will forego contracts with Chinese partners but insist on subsidiaries.

In other words, the approach suggests that firms will sooner establish subsidiaries when the value they attach to their firms-specific assets is higher; that firms will sooner establish subsidiaries when the locational advantages offered by a host country are higher; and that firms will sooner establish subsidiaries when transaction costs in conventional foreign trade are higher. In the case of China, as described earlier, the decision where to locate needs to take into account the costs and benefits of various locations within the

Chinese economy. Therefore, firms will establish subsidiaries in that part of China which offers the best comparative advantage with respect to location. *Risk diversification* arguments, while not part of the original Dunning model, are useful in this case. They suggest that investors or MNCs benefit from locational diversification when doing so offers scale and scope economies, more flexibility, and learning opportunities (Hall and Lee, 1999; Rugman, 1979). Thus, it can be assumed that firms will diversify risks by investing in different locations selected according to their respective advantages.

What is, however, not explicitly addressed by the Dunning model is the question of how exactly production in China (or any other place) gets organised. *Entry mode studies* offer further insights by drawing attention to different forms of ownership and collaboration with local partners. These studies show that the three dominant foreign ownership modes, i.e. contractual joint venture (CJV), equity joint venture (EJV) and wholly foreign owned subsidiary (WFOE) can be explained by three considerations: transaction costs, exploitation/exploration capability and institutional constraints.

Transaction cost considerations will cause foreign investors to seek more shares and control when confronted with asset specificity and/or opportunism; and conversely, to seek less when facing uncertainty such as political or economic risks (Anderson and Gatignon, 1986; Delios and Beamish, 1999; Hennart, 1988; Meyer, 2001). Exploitation/exploration capability considerations will cause foreign investors to opt for an EJV when they expect additional returns from broadening their resources and knowledge base (exploration) via a Chinese partner's distributional networks or local knowledge (Gomes-Casseres, 1990; Madhok, 1997). On the other hand, firms will insist on a WFOE when they expect higher returns from exploiting their firm-specific resources and capabilities (Agarwal and Ramaswami, 1992; Delios and Beamish, 1999; Luo, 2001). Institutional considerations remind firms that often enough the envisaged ownership form depends not only on (Chinese) regulations, but also on perceived political risk (Contractor, 1990; Gomes-Casseres, 1990; Xu et al., 2004; Yiu and Makino, 2002).

In what follows it is assumed that both streams of literature, the eclectic approach and entry mode studies, together provide a fruitful guideline for investigating the behaviour of foreign firms in China.

3.4.2   Choosing the Right Location in China

We next look for the reasons behind locational choice within China. The statistics show that foreign firms are unevenly spread within the country. As can be seen from Table 3.2, when listed according to province the ten most favoured locations are all to be found in the Eastern region[3]. The Eastern region hosted 82.43 per cent of the total foreign firms that had been established by the end of 2004. This has to be seen in contrast to the twelve provinces called the Western region, seven of which are found at the end of the list. The Western region altogether hosted 6.53 per cent of the total foreign firms up to 2004. That leaves the eight provinces that are called the Central region hosting 11.04 per cent of the total foreign firms up to 2004 (China Ministry of Commerce, 2005). This pattern has not changed much since the 1980s (Organisation for Economic Cooperation and Development, 2002).

Empirical studies analyzing the reasons for patterns of locational choice in China point to factors such as openness to trade, different economic growth rates, manpower, infrastructure and preferential investment policies at the sub-national level (Broadman and Sun, 1997; Chadee et al., 2003; Gao, 2005; Wei et al., 1999; Zhou et al., 2002). However, these patterns also reflect the varying investment climate, which are often generated locally (Dollar et al., 2003; Demurger, 2001; Li et al., 2000).

Thus, for example, many consulting reports and empirical studies attribute the high concentration of FDI in the *Eastern region*, i.e. the *Pearl Delta and Yangtze areas*, to the general investment climate, based on higher GDP per capita, higher concentrations of modern small and medium enterprises, higher educational levels, advanced transportation infrastructure, good shipping connections, and proximity to major international ports such as Shanghai and Hong Kong (Chadee et al., 2003; KPMG, 2003, 2005; PricewaterhouseCoopers, 2004; Wei et al., 1999).

A closer look however, points to another determinant, namely the institutional advantages offered by SEZs, 'open' coastal cities and development zones. Since the early eighties, China has opened certain jurisdictions (mostly found in the Eastern region) to foreign investors. These jurisdictions are often endowed with better infrastructure, less state intervention and a more developed legal system. Empirical studies confirm that foreign firms positively respond to these institutional advantages by deliberately locating their investment in these locations (Li and Park, 2006; Ng and Tuan, 2002; Zhou et al., 2002).

In a second step, sub-national administrative levels were allowed to establish their own *development zones*. This did not lead to a wider geographical spread however, instead the new development zones closely followed the locational choices of FDI (see Table 3.2).

Within these jurisdictions, industrial sites are parcelled out, roads and public utilities are provided. Most crucial however is the fact that foreign firms in the special zones enjoy tax privileges.

Table 3.2   Geographic distribution of foreign firms by province (to 2004)

Rank	Province (Region)	Proportion of foreign firms in total	Number of development zones[4]
1	Guangdong (E)	21.95%	31
2	Jiangsu (E)	12.64%	30
3	Shandong (E)	9.29%	29
4	Shanghai (E)	7.14%	22
5	Fujian (E)	7.04%	17
6	Zhejiang (E)	6.35%	22
7	Liaoning (E)	5.84%	15
8	Beijing (E)	4.27%	5
9	Tianjin (E)	3.37%	6
10	Hebei (E)	2.32%	10
11	Hubei (C)	1.98%	10
12	Hainan (E)	1.89%	4
13	Guangxi (W)	1.62%	7
14	Jiangxi (C)	1.54%	6
15	Hunan (C)	1.50%	5
16	Henan (C)	1.50%	5
17	Jilin (C)	1.43%	9
18	Heilongjiang (C)	1.41%	5
19	Sichuan (W)	1.34%	15
20	Anhui (C)	1.21%	8
21	Shaanxi (W)	0.81%	6
22	Chongqing (W)	0.72%	4
23	Yunnan (W)	0.51%	6
24	Shanxi (C)	0.48%	5
25	Inner Mongolia (W)	0.39%	4
26	Guizhou (W)	0.33%	9
27	Gansu (W)	0.32%	4
28	Xinjiang (W)	0.25%	5
29	Ningxia (W)	0.14%	1
30	Qinghai (W)	0.08%	1
31	Xizang (W)	0.02%	1

Notes: E in the bracket indicates that the province is found in the Eastern region; C in the bracket indicates that the province is found in the central region; and W in the bracket indicates that the province is found in the Western region in China.

Source: China Ministry of Commerce, 2005; China Association of Development Zones, 2005.

Technologically advanced firms and export-oriented firms can expect even further tax reductions after these five years. Harder to assess is the effect of regulation and state intervention in these zones. As empirical studies have shown, the zones have enough leeway to design their own 'industrial policy', often enough in consultation with the foreign companies already operating in the zone. As a consequence the special zones together offer a comparative advantage when compared with the 'rest of the country'. As different special zones offer different sets of rules and regulations, foreign firms will decide on location not only according to (short term) cost advantages, or infrastructure, but also according to the best 'fitting' regulatory regime.

To sum up, investment patterns point to the influence institutional factors have on the investment decisions of foreign firms. By diversifying their total investment across different localities (regulatory arbitrage) they mitigate 'confiscation risk' and the risks associated with weak contractual enforcement (Clissord, 2004; Organisation for Economic Cooperation and Development, 2005; Stuttard, 2000). This explains why most MNCs who have a presence in China have invested in two or more locations, with Mitsubishi as the extreme having established 131 subsidiaries in 31 locations (Wang, 2004). A detailed case study of Coca-Cola (Mok et al., 2002) finds that Coca-Cola, facing regulation and contractual risks in different locations, have bottling plants in 21 locations to diversify the risk and exploit regulatory arbitrage.

3.4.3. Ownership Choice

So far it has been shown that firms reduce their investment risk or improve their expected returns by carefully selecting their location or spreading total investment across different locations. The next question is to which extent firms attempt to mitigate risk or ensure best use of their capabilities by choosing an appropriate ownership mode.

That there has been a striking change in the relationship between foreign firms and domestic economic actors is underlined by the fact that by 1982, 86 per cent of foreign investors had set up a contractual arrangement or contractual joint venture (CJV) with Chinese companies, yet this dropped to only 3 per cent by 2004 (see Figure 3.3). Since then most foreign firms have opted for equity joint ventures (EJV), or wholly foreign owned enterprises (WFOE). The percentage of EJVs in the total foreign firms reached its peak (72.5 per cent) in 1992 and dropped to 26.5 per cent in 2004. While up to 1982 only 3.6 per cent of foreign investors established WFOEs, the percentage jumped to 70 per cent in 2004, when a change in law (1986) allowed the establishment of completely foreign affiliates. The question is therefore, why do foreign companies prefer to establish subsidiaries instead of opting for joint ventures with Chinese partners who could be expected to provide valuable (market) information and business related knowledge.

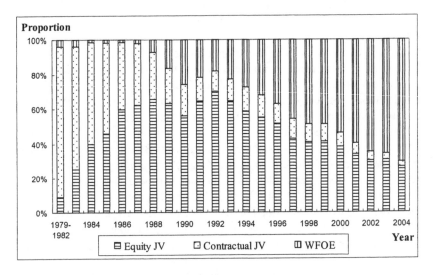

Source: *China Ministry of Commerce 2004, 2005.*

Figure 3.3   Ownership choices of foreign firms in China by year

On a more general level, what considerations determine the ownership choices of foreign firms in China? Once more, *transaction cost, capabilities and institutional considerations* play a role. Empirical studies reveal that both asset specificity (plus risk), firm-specific capabilities and government regulations have been crucial for foreign firms in choosing between contractual arrangements and EJVs (Pan and Tse, 2000; Tse et al., 1997) as well as between EJVs and WFOEs (Guillén, 2003; Luo, 2001; Pan, 1996). When firms possess specific assets such as R&D, proprietary product information and marketing expertise, an EJV is preferred to a contractual arrangement, and a WFOE to an EJV. When foreign investors seek local knowledge or capabilities (such as distribution networks and local technologies), they prefer EJVs over WFOEs. Once again, government regulations interfere with economic considerations. Not only does the perceived risk and opportunism of domestic partners matter, but also the degree of liberalisation for choosing the best organisational form.

The further question is whether all three considerations determine the decision equally. An analysis of the *dynamics of interaction* with government regulation and agencies provides further insights. Empirical studies point out that ownership choices are based on rational calculations, and institutional constraints (at the national and local level). Under strict, but weakly enforced government regulations, foreign firms are less able to implement their rational choices but need to compromise instead (Contractor, 1990; Gomes-Casseres, 1990). Thus, for example, in the early 1980s, foreign firms continued to opt for CJVs although the EJV Law was promulgated in 1979. The ambiguity of the new law made contractual arrangements more attractive by offering more flexibility in changing the terms of the business relation with the Chinese partner. The amendments to the EJV Law in 1983 which clarified specific rules and signalled the seriousness of the policy changed the picture: an increasing number of foreign firms opted for EJVs, as this organisational form offered more effective ways to protect their China investment and promised a higher co-operation rent. After the WFOE Law was promulgated in 1986, the institutional environment changed again allowing investment that left firms 'exclusively' in the hands of foreigner. The shift to WFOEs promised better control over the operation of a company and its assets to foreign investors, in particular patents and product-specific know-how. For example, Johnson & Johnson, although running some successful pharmaceutical EJVs, shifted to WFOEs in 1992 claiming better monitoring capabilities and less government restrictions (Vanhonacker, 1997). Gradual movement in response to institutional changes reveals that foreign firms' ownership choices are responsive to the institutional situation, selecting that alternative that promises the best protection for their investment and greater freedom for their strategic operation.

In addition, the decentralised structure of the Chinese economy and the differences between economic zones allowed some foreign firms to be proactive in their choices. Thus, a total of 120 WFOEs had been established in several locations before the WFOE Law was enforced in 1986 (Fu, 2000). The reason given was that only by granting investors the right to establish a WFOE would they introduce their advanced technologies; as was the case with 3M in Shanghai, for example (Brown, 1986).

As the examples demonstrate, the *protection of property rights*, especially intellectual property rights, remains one of the major concerns of foreign investors (Pearson, 1991; Roehrig, 1994). The Chinese government responsed to these concerns with laws such as the Trademark Law, Patent Law, Contract Law and Copyright Law. In addition, China has subscribed to the Berne Convention for the Protection of Literary and Artistic Works and the Universal Copyright Convention. Nevertheless the general feature of weak protection of property rights and weak enforcement of contracts cannot be argued away (Krug, 2004; Michael and Rivette, 2004). This explains why foreign firms prefer WFOEs, though they forego the comparative advantage of having a Chinese partner in particular in industries where intellectual property rights are at stake (Michael and Rivette, 2004).

On the other hand foreign firms prefer EJVs when they use standardised technology, and when they depend on local complementary resources including local networks. One such an example is Phillips' EJV with Neusoft, one of China's leading software companies, to jointly develop medical information systems. Another example is 3COM's EJV with Huawei to utilise Huawei's advantages in data communications.

All in all, foreign firms are involved in an interactive process where they respond to changes in Chinese law, while trying to negotiate further changes. It is this interaction which once more points to the significance of locational choice. On one side 'endowments' such as good infrastructure, a cheap labour force or a transparent regulatory regime are linked to different locations, thus offering incentives for foreign firms to search for the best fitting place. On the other hand, as was shown above, these features are not stable but change over time due to market development and policy change. Moreover, foreign firms do not need to remain 'institution takers' (to use the analogy with 'price taking' firms). Instead they can actively search for ways to directly (via negotiation) or indirectly (via 'exit' and investment in other locations) influence further institutional change. As will be seen in what follows this situation is not China-unique but reflects strategic choice by foreign firms.

3.5   FOREIGN INVESTMENT AND LOCAL EMBEDDEDNESS

The institutional business context of firms has long been recognised as crucial to firm's performance (Galbraith, 1973) and gained new prominence with globalisation and the emergence of transition economies (Child and Tse, 2001; Henisz, 2000; Peng, 2003). Thus, it is argued that the more 'foreign' a potential host country the more important it is for a foreign firm to gain legitimacy (Kostova and Zaheer, 1999; Xu and Shenkar, 2002) particularly in China's case (Khanna et al., 2005). One way to do so is to closely cooperate with local business communities and local governments, by jointly searching for an organisational 'fit' with the overall, i.e. national institutional environment. The 'fitting' strategy helps foreign firms to gain access to and better understand local business routines and government regulations. By doing so, foreign firms build up resources and abilities to better cope with institutional idiosyncrasies, which in turn increases the value of their business relations in China (Frynas et al., 2006; Henisz, 2003).

In short, *local embeddedness* (Granovetter, 1985) becomes a business strategy which offers high returns in particular in a country such as China where the business context differs widely across the country. In what follows, we describe the specific features of the heterogeneous business context and provide evidence that foreign firms do indeed take the advantage of local embeddedness into account when they invest and when they operate in China.

3.5.1 Local Governments and Transaction Costs

To understand the local embeddedness feature of foreign firms in China, it is important to understand the decentralised character of the Chinese government which facilitated the emergence of different business environments (see also Chapter 6).

Previous studies, especially in international business and management do not acknowledge the wide ranging effects of the reforms in the 1980s which led to decentralisation. Decentralisation in China does not refer to the legislative or regulatory power of provinces. Instead it refers to shifting resources (such as land) and regulatory power to the local (i.e. sub-provincial) administrative level (Economist Intelligence Unit, 2003; Lau et al., 2000; Nee, 1992; Qian and Weingast, 1997; Walder, 1995). While, on the one hand, local governments are expected to implement and/or interpret central policy, on the other hand, they enjoy considerable leeway to design their own policies. Local sources of income (tax revenues, profits from commercial activities and/or land deals) severely limit the central government's ability to control the localities via budget constraint. In short, the Chinese economy is characterised by a weak central state, with local government agencies as the primary economic actor. This form of local autonomy (see Chapter 6) explains why foreign firms have a variety of commercial experiences depending on the locality they operate in, or more precisely, the local government they are confronted with. *Local governments are the key actors, the main institutions foreign firms have to reckon with* when they intend to build up local knowledge.

Lacking local knowledge or local protection generates transaction costs for firms (Wei, 1996; Zhao and Zhu, 2000, Clissord, 2004) such as economic and policy uncertainty, arbitrary interpretation of policies, weak enforcement of regulations and corruption (World Bank, 2005).

Yet, these transaction costs can be lowered by actively searching for ways which turn local governments into co-operating economic actors (Krug and Hendrischke, 2005; Segal and Thun, 2001). As the example of the TVEs and other private companies in China shows, formal or informal co-operation with local government agencies offers an effective way for not only lowering transaction costs, but also for getting access to more business opportunities (Che and Qian, 1998; Li, 1996; Wong et al., 2004).

Table 3.3   Comparatively perceived obstacles to doing business in China

Indicator	China	Russia	Indonesia	Philippines
Economic and regulatory policy uncertainty (%)	31.54	32.85	48.25	28.35
Macroeconomic instability (%)	28.06	28.74	50.07	39.66
Business licensing and permits (%)	18.81	14.53	20.48	12.45
Consistency of officials' interpretations of regulations	68.43	25.18	44.04	49.90
Senior management time spent dealing with requirements of regulations (%)	20.24	10.04	5.47	8.24
Unofficial payments for firms to get things done (% of sales)	1.99	1.50	1.76	1.73
Gifts requested by government officials	100.00	..	5.61	0.00
Time firms spent in meetings with tax officials (days)	14.55	..	1.97	3.75
Firms expected to give gifts in meetings with tax inspectors (%)	45.93	53.62	11.22	28.15
Value of gift expected to secure government contract (% of contract)	2.31	1.62	0.75	1.92
Confidence in the judiciary system (%)	82.87	34.89	59.19	64.80

Source: World Bank (2005).

3.5.2   Alliances and Networks as Governance

As discussed above, it is assumed that foreign firms will invest in relation building at the local level in China. Indeed, empirical studies on foreign firms' success in China emphasise cooperation with local institutions and the ability to manage cultural distance or understand local knowledge, while pointing also to traditional firm-specific advantages such as quality input of technology, management skills, control rights over operations, and support from parent corporations (Child and Yan, 2003; Isobe et al., 2000; Luo, 2002; Luo and Park, 2004; Peng and Luo, 2000; Shenkar, 1990; Yan and Gray, 2001). Such cooperation with local institutions allows the firm to be embedded into the local institutional environment.

Cooperation provides advantages such as reducing the complexity of the institutional environment, characterised by ambiguous property rights, incomplete transmission of information, uncertainty, and inconsistent government policies (Boisot and Child, 1999; Krug and Pólos, 2004; Shenkar, 1990). At the local level, additional factors such as regulatory and policy inconsistency (in interpretation), corruption, bureaucratic inefficiency, capital controls, local protectionist policies (entry and exit barriers), and cultural adaptation (Hallward-Driemeier, 2003; International Finance Corporation, 2005), add to the problems firms need to learn to cope with. *Investing in good relations with local governments is as necessary a strategy as investing in business networking* for reducing transaction costs and acquiring market (and political) information in China (Lau et al., 2000; Luo, 1997; Peng, 2000b; Qian, 2002).

First, foreign firms deliberately embark on an *alliance or coalition with local governments* to safeguard their operation. Local governments in China are actively involved in shaping the local institutional environment and the business activities that take place in this environment (Nee, 1992; Oi, 1995; Walder, 1995). In the interaction with foreign firms, local governments play a double role. On the one hand, local governments collaborate with foreign firms in bargaining with the central government to change regulations (locational competition effects); and on the other hand, local governments implement and reinforce national and local policies and regulations that affect foreign firms. Therefore, cooperation (or alliance) with local governments becomes the best choice, providing foreign firms with both the political leverage and strategic resources to their operation (Krug and Hendrischke, 2005; Peng, 2000a; Yeung, 2000). In an information poor environment like China, it provides advantages in both information costs and transaction costs. Peng (2000a) notes that Beijing Jeep, Shanghai Volkswagen and Guangzhou Peugeot all benefited from the coalition with local authorities which helped them to bargain with the central government to get preferential treatments.

In practice, secondly, foreign investors do not have to directly interact with local authorities, but can *rely on partners* who have knowledge of local culture, language and institutions (Henisz, 2000). A cross-sectional analysis demonstrates the significance of choosing the right local business partners (Luo, 1997). The right local partners can help foreign firms to boost market expansion, obtain insightful information, mitigate operational risks and obtain context-specific knowledge. In this sense, overseas Chinese enjoy an advantage over western investors, who know more about doing business in China. In addition, overseas Chinese have also an advantage over local agents who lack international experience. Therefore, besides local partners, Hong Kong firms are often sought by western investors for partnerships (Pan and Tse, 1996). These studies show that such cooperation provides leverage in an uncertain environment and hence has a positive effect on firm performance.

Developing a formal business alliance certainly is not the whole story. In the context of China, business is often done through *interpersonal networks* (*guanxi* in Chinese)[5]. *Guanxi* networks are regarded as an information and resource pool (Park and Luo, 2001; Tsang, 1998). In an environment where formal economic institutions are ill-functioning, *guanxi* networks, as informal institutions, are often decisive for foreign investors in capturing local knowledge, enforcing business deals and increasing the efficiency of private exchanges (Krug and Hendrischke, 2005). Local partners (or personnel), including overseas Chinese partners, often act as agents of foreign investors to access local *guanxi* networks which are cultivated through a trust-building process (Yang, 1994). This aspect of *guanxi* building demonstrates that successful foreign firms are often locally embedded while capturing social capital. One revealing fact is that foreign firms gradually tend to hire local managers to replace expatriates. Partly this is due to lower costs and the improved quality of local managers, but more importantly, it is due to the advantage of managers with local knowledge and local (business) networks (Kamis, 1996). Yeung and Li (2000) confirm this, pointing to Shanghai where the managerial structure has been highly localised with most foreign firms having local chairpeople and management staff. Even in the more conservative Japanese subsidiaries, a high degree of control has been ceded to local managers (Taylor, 1999).

To conclude, foreign firms in China adopt both formal alliances and informal *guanxi* networks (Peng and Luo, 2000). These interrelated mechanisms allow foreign firms to obtain access to local authorities, gain tacit information on policies, explain their policy concerns and negotiate on regulations, mitigate official arbitration, and avoid government intervention (Child, 1994; Luo and Park, 2001; Peng and Luo, 2000; Shenkar, 1990). In other words, local embeddedness helps a firm to get an understanding of, and subsequently leverage of, the local institutional environment in order to mitigate transaction costs.

3.6   CONCLUSION

The chapter describes the strategic choices of foreign firms on entry and in operation, in order to provide an interpretation of the success of FDI in China. The description reveals that institutional factors play a significant role in the choices of foreign firms, which require 'fit' and adaptability. In a dynamic view, these choices change over time in response to institutional changes (for an overview, see Appendix).

First, location choices reflect institutional differences across the country. Foreign MNCs deliberately choose coastal regions to establish subsidiaries, where the overall investment climate is better than other regions. It is highly consistent with theoretical prediction and other similar observations of international investment (Dunning, 1986; Henisz, 2000; Organisation for Economic Cooperation and Development, 2002). With the expansion of open regions inland, more foreign firms gradually invested or re-invested in the central or western regions of China to exploit the low-cost production factors (labour, land and resources), but the institutional momentum is not strong enough to alter the geographical imbalances of uneven distribution. In addition, the first-mover institutional advantage of the eastern region can not be played away by overall openness.

Second, ownership choices demonstrate dynamism over time, with preferences changing in response to the process of institutional liberalisation. While the contractual arrangement was mostly opted for by subsidiaries in the early 1980s, WFOEs have become the preferred option since ownership restrictions were lifted and the protection of property rights has become more assured. In the current landscape, EJVs and CJVs still exist along with WFOEs. In other words, ownership choice was highly constrained by the regulation, but now mainly reflects foreign MNCs' consideration regarding capability/market exploitation and exploration.

Third, local embeddedness has always been crucial to the success of an operation, which helps them to deal with the complexity and uncertainty of the local institutional environment in China. Foreign firms learnt to form alliances with local governments and build up *guanxi* networks (through local managers or other personnel) at the local level. It makes them closely linked to local institutions, the advantage of which is economising on transaction costs and information costs involved (Wei, 1995; Zhao, 2003). The choice of blending formal alliance with informal *guanxi* networks has been widely acknowledged by foreign firms in China, which provides them with the capability to manage institutional deficits in the context.

As was shown, the behaviour of foreign firms is a response to institutional conditions and changes in China. To better absorb the above findings, it is worthwhile to review the process of institutional liberalisation and its effects on firms, as shown in the Appendix. The process takes place in both time and spatial dimensions. Over time, the changes liberalise foreign firms' ownership choices in China and access to locations (from SEZs to open coastal cities then to inland cities), reduce tariffs, and provide improving legal supports for contractual issues and protection of (intellectual) property rights. It has been an interactive process through which local governments also learn, by monitoring the behaviour of foreign investors, to improve the legal systems and clarify policy ambiguity (Pearson, 1991).

By interacting, foreign firms learn to understand the context and develop 'fit' strategies for success. This chapter shows that, perhaps the most striking feature of the experience of foreign firms in China is that an entry strategy is much less important than was assumed 20 years ago. Once operations start, no concern is more pressing than the question of negotiating the local business environment. In this sense, localising seems to be the most promising strategy. It is worth stressing that unlike 25 years ago, when foreign firms negotiated with representatives of the ministries in Beijing, localisation today refers not only to attempts to cope with the 'Chineseness' of the environment, but also the attempt at virtually 'going local'. Firms meet representatives of local governments which also are the major agents for establishing and running SEZs or any other lower-level jurisdiction. Investing in the accumulation of local 'knowledge' promises high returns, especially in cases where local governments invite the business community in the jurisdiction to participate in the operation of the zone. By doing so, foreign firms can influence the tax and regulatory framework to the effect that the environment looks more familiar and allows more familiar business practices. The high concentration of foreign firms in specific places points in the same direction: proximity between foreign firms allows knowledge-sharing and joint 'lobbying' for favourable local policies.

All in all, the behaviour of foreign firms seems to confirm what other chapters in the book have already mentioned: firms react more strongly to transaction costs generated in the external environment than to contract-specific transaction costs that characterise their interaction with other foreign or Chinese firms. Localisation proves to be the most suitable choice for their success.

NOTES

1. The amount indicated to 1991–1996 is the average annual FDI inflows in this period.
2. This amount is the sum of the period 1980–1982.
3. Three regions are separated in China. The eastern region includes: Beijing, Tianjin, Hebei, Liaoning, Shanghai, Jiangsu, Zhejiang, Fujian, Shandong, Guangdong, and Hainan. The central region includes Shanxi, Jilin, Heilongjiang, Anhui, Jiangxi, Henan, Hubei and Hunan. The western region includes Guangxi, Inner Mongolia, Sichuan, Chongqing, Guizhou, Yunnan, Shaanxi, Gansu, Qinghai, Ningxia, Xinjiang and Xizang.
4. The data are as of September 2005 when the website was searched. The number is counted for development zones at the provincial level and above.

5. Though some studies show that larger firms with greater level of internationalisation are more likely to have capabilities to leverage on the uncertain environment (Gaba et al., 2002), the preponderance of overseas Chinese firms proves that *guanxi* networks do play a greater role in China in reducing information costs and transaction costs, which facilitate the entry and operation of smaller firms but with higher level of local knowledge (Gao, 2003; Li et al., 2001; Wang and Ellis, 2002). In addition, the diversity in local cultures implies that *guanxi* networking is eminent and crucial in business (Tse et al., 1997).

REFERENCES

Agarwal, S. and S.N. Ramaswami (1992), 'Choice of foreign market entry mode: impact of ownership, location, and internalization factors', *Journal of International Business Studies*, **26**, 1–27.

Amighini, A. (2005), 'China in the international fragmentation of production: evidence from the ICT industry', *European Journal of Comparative Economics*, **2**, 203–219.

Anderson, E. and H. Gatignon (1986), 'Modes of foreign entry: a transaction cost analysis and proposition', *Journal of International Business Studies*, **17**, 1–26.

Boisot, M.H. and J. Child (1999), 'Organizations as adaptive systems in complex environments: the case of China', *Organization Science*, **10** (3), 237–252.

Broadman, H. and X. Sun (1997), 'The Distribution of Foreign Direct Investment in China', The World Bank Policy Research Working Paper 1720, World Bank.

Brown, David G. (1986), *Partnership with China: Sino-foreign Joint Ventures in Historical Perspective*, Boulder and London: Westview Press.

Buckley, Peter J. and Mark Casson (1976), *The Future of Multinational Enterprises*, Macmillan.

Caves, Richard E. (1996), *Multinational Enterprises and Economic Analysis*, Cambridge: Cambridge University Press.

Chadee, D.D., F. Qiu and E.L. Rose (2003), 'FDI location at the subnational level: a study of EJVs in China', *Journal of Business Research*, **56**, 835–845.

Che, J. and Y. Qian (1998), 'Institutional environment, community government and corporate governance: Understanding China's Township-Village Enterprises', *Journal of Law, Economics and Organization*, **14**, 1–23.

Chen, H. and T. Chen (1998), 'Network linkages and location choice in foreign direct investment', *Journal of International Business Studies*, **29**, 445–467.

Cheng, L.K and Y.K. Kwan (2000), 'What are the determinants of the location of foreign direct investment? The Chinese experience', *Journal of International Economics*, **51**, 379–400.

Child, John (1994), *Management in China During the Age of Reform*, Cambridge, UK: Cambridge University Press.

Child, J. and D.K. Tse (2001), 'China's transition and its implications for international business', *Journal of International Business Studies*, **32**, 5–17.

Child, J. and Y. Yan (2003), 'Predicting the performance of international joint ventures: an investigation in China', *Journal of Management Studies*, **40** (2), 287–320.

China Association of Development Zones (2005), www.cadz.org.cn, Beijing, 1 September.

China Ministry of Commerce (2004), *2003 Report of Foreign Investment in China*, www.mofcom.gov.cn, Beijing: Ministry of Commerce of the People's Republic of China.

China Ministry of Commerce (2005), *2004 Report of Foreign Investment in China*, www.mofcom.gov.cn, Beijing: Ministry of Commerce of the People's Republic of China.

China National Bureau of Statistics (2004), *China External Economic Statistical Yearbook*, Beijing: China Statistical Press.

China National Bureau of Statistics (2005), *Statistics Yearbook 2005 of China*, Beijing: China Statistical Press.

Clissord, Tim (2004), *Mr. China*, New York: HarPerBusiness.

Contractor, F.J. (1990), 'Ownership patterns of US Joint Ventures Abroad and the Liberalization of Foreign Government Regulations in the 1980s: Evidence from the Benchmark Surveys', *Journal of International Business Studies*, **21**, 55–73.

Cui, L., J. Liu and Y. Yao (2005), 'No close-up of foreign firms with 10-year lose-making, protection of local governments for their tax evasion', (in Chinese) *Economic Reference* (Chinese newspaper), **1 November**.

Delios, A. and P.W. Beamish (1999), 'Ownership strategy of Japanese firms: transactional, institutional and experience influences', *Strategic Management Journal*, **20**, 915–933.

Demurger, S. (2001), 'Infrastructure development and economic growth: an explanation for regional disparities in China?', *Journal of Comparative Economics*, **29**, 95–117.

Dollar, D., A. Shi, S. Wang and L. Colin Wu (2003), 'Improving City Competitiveness through the Investment Climate: Ranking 23 Chinese Cities', The World Bank Working Paper 3323, World Bank.

Dunning, John H. (1977), 'Trade, Location of Economic Activity and the MNE: a Search for Eclectic Approach', in Bertil Ohlin, Per-Ove Hesselborn and Per Magnus Wijkman (eds), *The International Allocation of Economic Activity*, New York: Holmes & Meier Publishers, Inc., pp. 395–418.

Dunning, J.H. (1986), 'China's open door policy and the prospects for FDI', *Multinational Business*, **4**, 28–31.

Dunning, J.H. (1988), 'The Eclectic Paradigm of International Production: A Re-statement and Some Possible Extensions', *Journal of International Business Studies*, **19**, 1–31.

Dunning, J.H. (2003), 'Some antecedents of internalization theory', *Journal of International Business Studies*, **34**, 108–115.

Economist Intelligence Unit (2003), *Country Profile 2003: China*, London: The Economist Intelligence Unit.

Frynas, J.G., K. Mellahi and G.A. Pigman (2006), 'First mover advantages in international business and firm specific political resources', *Strategic Management Journal*, **27**, 321–345.

Fu, Jun (2000), *Institutions and Investments: Foreign Direct Investment in China during an Era of Reforms*, Ann Arbor: The University of Michigan Press.

Gaba, V., Y. Pan and G.R. Ungson (2002), 'Timing of entry in international market: an empirical study of U.S. fortune 500 firms in China', *Journal of International Business Studies*, **33**, 39–55.

Galbraith, Jay R. (1973), *Designing Complex Oorganizations*, Reading, MA: Addison-Wesley.

Gao, T. (2003), 'Ethnic Chinese networks and international investment: evidence from inward FDI in China', *Journal of Asian Economics*, **14**, 611–629.

Gao, T. (2005), 'Labor quality and the location of foreign direct investment: evidence from China', *China Economic Review*, **16**, 274–292.

Ghemawat, P. (2003), 'Semiglobalization and international business strategy', *Journal of International Business Studies*, **34**, 138–152.

Gomes-Casseres, B. (1990), 'Firm ownership preferences and host government restrictions: an integrated approach', *Journal of International Business Studies*, **21**, 1–22.

Granovetter, M.S. (1985), 'Economic action and social structure: the problem of embeddedness', *American Journal of Sociology*, **91**, 481–510.

Guillén, M.F. (2003), 'Experience, imitation, and the sequence of foreign entry: wholly owned and joint-venture manufacturing by South Korean firms and business groups in China, 1987–1995', *Journal of International Business Studies*, **34** (March), 185–198.

Hall, E.H. Jr. and J. Lee (1999), 'Broadening the view of corporate diversification: an international perspective', *International Journal of Organizational Analysis*, **7**, 25–53.

Hallward-Driemeier, M., S. Wallsten and L.C. Xu (2003), 'The Investment Climate and the Firm: Firm-level Evidence from China', World Bank Working Paper 3003, World Bank.

Henisz, W.J. (2000), 'The institutional environment for multinational investment', *Journal of Law, Economics and Organization*, **16**, 334–364.

Henisz, W.J. (2003), 'The power of the Buckley and Casson thesis: the ability to manage institutional idiosyncrasies', *Journal of International Business Studies*, **34**, 173–184.

Hennart, J-F. (1988), 'A transaction cost theory of equity joint ventures', *Strategic Management Journal*, **9**, 361–374.

Huang, Yasheng (2001), *Selling China: Foreign Direct Investment during the Reform Era*, New York: The Cambridge University Press.

International Finance Corporation (2005), *Survey on the Business Environment in China*, www.ifc.org, International Finance Corporation (IFC), 1 September.

Isobe, T., S. Makino and D.B. Montgomery (2000), 'Resource commitment, entry timing, and market performance of foreign direct investments in emerging economies: the case of Japanese international joint ventures in China', *Academy of Management Journal*, **43**, 468–484.

Kamis, T.L. (1996), 'Education for the PRC executive', *China Business Review*, **23**, 36–39.

Kearney, A.T. (2004), *Making Offshore Decisions*, www.atkearney.com, Chicago: A.T. Kearney.

Khan, Z.S. (2001), 'Patterns of Direct Foreign Investment in China', World Bank Discussion papers 130, World Bank.

Khanna, T., K.G. Palepu and J. Sinha (2005), 'Strategies that fit emerging markets', *Harvard Business Review*, **2005** (June), 63–76.

Kim, J.I. and L. Lau (1994), 'The Source of Economic Growth of the East Asian Newly Industrialized Countries', *Journal of the Japanese and International Economies*, **8**, 235–271.

Kostova, T. and S. Zaheer (1999), 'Organizational Legitimacy under Conditions of Complexity: the case of the multinational enterprise', *Academy of Management Review*, **24**, 64–81.

KPMG (2003), 'Ningbo Investment Environment Study', www.KPMG.com.cn, KPMG.

KPMG (2005), 'Changsha Investment Environment Study 2005', www.KPMG.com.cn, KPMG.

Krug, Barbara (2004), *China's Rational Entrepreneurs: The Development of the New Private Business Sector*, London: Routledge.

Krug, B. and H. Hendrischke (2005), 'From Initial Commitment to Economic Regimes to Business Systems: Institutional Change in Transition Economies: the Case of China', presented at the annual meeting of EGOS 2005, Berlin.

Krug, Barbara and László Pólos (2004), 'Emerging markets, entrepreneurship and uncertainty: The emergence of private sector in China', in Barbara Krug (ed.), *China's Rational Entrepreneurs: the development of the new private business sector*, London: Routledge, 72–96.

Krugman, P. (1994), 'The Myth of Asia's Miracle', *Foreign Affairs*, **73**(6), 62–78.

Lau, L., Y. Qian and G. Roland (2000), 'Reform without losers: an interpretation of China's dual-track approach to transition', *Journal of Political Economy*, **108**, 120–142.

Lardy, N.R. (1995), 'The Role of Foreign Trade and Investment in China's economic transformation', *The China Quarterly*, **144** (December 1995), 1065–1082.

Li, D.D. (1996), 'A theory of ambiguous property rights in transition economies: the case of the Chinese non-state sector', *Journal of Comparative Economics*, **23**, 1–19.

Li, J., G. Qian, K. Lam and D. Wang (2000), 'Breaking into China: strategic considerations for multinational corporations', *Long Range Planning*, **33**, 673–687.

Li, J., K. Lam, and G. Qian (2001), 'Does culture affect behaviour and performance of firms? The case of joint ventures in China', *Journal of International Business Studies*, **32**, 115–131.

Li, S. and S.H. Park (2006), 'Determinants of locations of foreign direct investment in China', *Management and Organization Review*, **2**, 95–119.

Liang, Guoyong (2004), *New competition: Foreign Direct Investment and Industrial Development in China*, Ph.D. dissertation, Rotterdam: Erasmus University Rotterdam.

Lu, D. and G. Zhu (1995), 'Singapore foreign direct investment in China: features and implications', *ASEAN Economic Bulletin*, **12**, 53–63.

Lu, L.Y.Y. and J.S. Liu (2004), 'R&D in China: an empirical study of Taiwanese IT companies', *R&D Management*, **34**, 453–465.

Luo, Y. (1997), 'Partner selection and venturing sources: the case of joint ventures with firms in the People's Republic of China', *Organization Science*, **8**, 648–662.

Luo, Y. (2001), 'Determinants of entry in an emerging economy: a multilevel approach', *Journal of Management Studies*, **38**, 443–472.

Luo, Y. (2002), 'Contract, cooperation, and performance in international joint ventures', *Strategic Management Journal*, **23**, 903–919.

Luo, Y. and S.H. Park (2001), 'Strategic alignment and performance of market-seeking MNCs in China', *Strategic Management Journal*, **22**, 141–155.

Luo, Y., and S.H. Park (2004), 'Multiparty cooperation and performance in international equity joint ventures', *Journal of International Business Studies*, **35**, 142–160.

Madhok, A. (1997), 'Cost, value and foreign market entry mode: the transaction and the firm', *Strategic Management Journal*, **18**, 39–61.

Meyer, K.E. (2001), 'Institutions, transaction costs, and entry mode choice in Eastern Europe', *Journal of International Business Studies*, **32** (2), 357–367.

Michael, D. and K. Rivette (2004), 'Facing the China Challenge: Using an Intellectual Property Strategy to Capture Global Advantage', www.bcg.com, Boston Consulting Group.

Mok, V., X. Dai and G. Yeung (2002), 'An internationalization approach to joint ventures: Coca-Cola in China', *Asia Pacific Business Review*, **9**, 39–58.

Nee, V. (1992), 'Organizational Dynamics of market transition: Hybrid forms, property rights, and mixed economy in China', *Administrative Science Quarterly*, **37**, 1–27.

Ng, L.F-Y. and C. Tuan (2002), 'Building a favourable investment environment: evidence for the facilitation of FDI in China', *The World Economy*, **25**, 1095–1114.

OECD (2000), 'Main Determinants and Impacts of Foreign Direct Investment on China's Economy', OECD Working Papers on International Investment 2000/4, www.oecd.org,

OECD (2002). *Foreign Direct Investment in China: Challenges and Prospects for Regional Development*

OECD (2005), *Governance in China*, www.oecd.org

Oi, J.C. (1995), 'The role of the local state in China's transitional economy', *The China Quarterly*, **1995**, 1132–1149.

Pan, Y. (1996), 'Influences on foreign equity ownership level in joint ventures in China', *Journal of International Business Studies*, **27**, 1–26.

Pan, Y. and D.K. Tse (1996), 'Cooperative Strategies between foreign firms in an overseas country', *Journal of International Business Studies*, **27**, 929–946.

Pan, Y. and D.K. Tse (2000), 'The hierarchical model of market entry modes', *Journal of International Business Studies*, **31**, 535–554.

Park, S.H. and Y. Luo (2001), 'Guanxi and organizational dynamics: organizational networking in Chinese firms', *Strategic Management Journal*, **22**, 455–477.

Pearson, Margaret M. (1991), *Joint Ventures in People's Republic of China*, Princeton: Princeton University Press.

Peng, M.W. (2000a), 'Controlling the foreign agent: how governments deal with multinationals in a transition economy', *Management International Review*, **40**, 141–165.

Peng, Mike W. (2000b), *Business Strategies in Transition Economies*, Thousand Oaks, CA: Sage.

Peng, M.W. (2003), 'Institutional transition and strategic choices', *Academy of Management Review*, **28**, 275–296.

Peng, M.W. (2005), 'Perspectives – from China Strategy to global strategy', *Asia Pacific Journal of Management*, **22**: 123–141.

Peng, M.W. and Y. Luo (2000), 'Managerial ties and firm performance in a transition economy: the nature of a micro-macro link', *Academy of Management Journal*, **43**, 486–501.

Prasad, E. (2004), 'China's Growth and Integration into the World Economy: Prospects and Challenges'. International Monetary Fund (IMF) Occasional Paper 2004/232, www.imf.org, International Monetary Fund.

PricewaterhouseCoopers (2004), 'The Guangzhou Development District Investment Environment Study'. www.pwccn.com, Beijing: PricewaterhouseCoopers China.

Qian, Yingyi. (2002), 'How Reform Worked in China', Berkeley, CA: University of California, Center for Economic Policy Research.

Qian, Y. and B.R. Weingast (1997), 'Federalism as a commitment to perserving market incentives', *Journal of Economic Perspectives*, **11**, 83–92.

Roehrig, Michael F. (1994), *Foreign Joint Ventures in Contemporary China*, London: Macmillan.

Rugman, Alan M. (1979), *International Diversification and the Multinational Enterprise*, Farnborough: Lexington.

Segal, A. and E. Thun (2001), 'Thinking globally, acting locally: local governments, industrial sectors, and development in China', *Politics and Society*, **29**, 557–588.

Shenkar, O. (1990), 'International joint ventures' problems in China: risks and remedies', *Long Range Planning*, **23**, 82–90.

Shenkar, Oded (2006), *The Chinese Century: The Rising Chinese Economy and its Impact on the Global Economy*, Upper Saddle River, NJ: Wharton School Publishing.

Stuttard, John B. (2000), *The New Silk Road*, New York: John Wiley & Sons, Inc.

Taylor, B. (1999), 'Patterns of control within Japanese manufacturing plants in China: doubts about Japanization in Asia', *Journal of Management Studies*, **36**, 853–873.

Tsang, E.W.K. (1998), 'Can guanxi be a source of sustained competitive advantage for doing business in China?', *Academy of Management Executive*, **12**, 64–73.

Tse, D.K., Y. Pan, and K.Y. Au (1997), 'How MNCs choose entry modes and form alliances: The China experience', *Journal of International Business Studies*, **28**, 779–805.

United Nations Conference on Trade and Development (2003), *World Investment Report 2003: FDI policies for development*, Geneva: United Nations Conference on Trade and Development.

United Nations Conference on Trade and Development (2005), *World Investment Report 2005: Transnational Corporations and the Internationalization of R&D*, Geneva: United Nations Conference on Trade and Development.

Van den Bulcke, Daniel and Haiyan Zhang (2003), *European Union Direct Investment in China*, London: Routledge.

Vanhonacker, W. (1997), 'Entering China: an unconventional approach', *Harvard Business Review*, March-April, 1997:130–140.

Walder, A.G. (1995), 'Local Governments as Industrial as Industrial firms: An Organizational Analysis of China's Transitional Economy', *American Journal of Sociology*, **101**, 263–301

Wang, P.L-K. and P. Ellis (2002), 'Social ties and partner identification in Sino-Hong Kong international joint ventures', *Journal of International Business Studies*, **33**, 267–289.

Wang, Zhile (2004), *2004 Report of Transnational Corporations in China* (in Chinese), Beijing: Economics Press of China.

Wei, S. (1995), 'Attracting foreign direct investment: has China reached its potential?', *China Economic Review*, **6**, 187–199.

Wei, Shangjin (1996), 'Foreign Direct Investment in China: Sources and Consequences', In: Takatoshi Ito and Anne O. Krueger (ed.), *Financial Deregulation and Integration in East Asia,* Chicago and London: The University of Chicago Press, pp. 77–106.

Wei, Yingqi and Xiaming Liu (2001), *Foreign Direct Investment in China: Determinants and Impact*, Cheltenham, UK: Edward Elgar.

Wei, Y., X. Liu, D. Parker and K. Vaidya (1999), 'The regional distribution of foreign direct investment in China'. *Regional Studies*, **33**, 857–867.

Wong, Sonia M.L., S. Opper and R. Hu (2004), 'Shareholding structure, de-politicization and enterprise performance: lesions from China's listed companies', *Economics of Transition*, **12**, 29–66.

World Bank (2005), *Investment Climate Surveys*, www.worldbank.org, World Bank, 1 September.

Xu, D., Y. Pan, and P.W. Beamish (2004), 'The effect of regulative and normative distances on MNE ownership and expatriate strategies', *Management International Review*, **44**, 285–307.

Xu, D. and O. Shenkar (2002). 'Institutional distance and the multinational enterprise', *Academy of Management Review*, **27**, 608–618.

Yan, A. and B. Gray (2001), 'Antecedents and effects of parent control in international joint ventures', *Journal of Management Studies*, **38**, 393–416.

Yang, J. (1997), 'The emerging patterns of Taiwanese investment in mainland China', *Multinational Business Review*, **5**, 92–99.

Yang, Mayfair M. (1994), *Gifts, Favors, And Banquets: The Art of Social Relationships in China*, Ithaca & London: Cornell University Press.

Yeung, H.W-C. (2000), 'Local politics and foreign ventures in China's transitional economy: the political economy of Singaporean investments in China', *Political Geography*, **19**, 809–840.

Yeung, Y. and X. Li (2000), 'Transnational corporations and local embeddedness: company case studies from Shanghai, China', *Professional Geographer*, **52**, 624–635.

Yiu, D. and S. Makino (2002), 'The choice between joint venture and wholly owned subsidiary: an institutional perspective', *Organization Science*, **139**, 667–683.

Zhang, K.H. (2000), 'Why is US direct investment in China so small?', *Contemporary Economic Policy*, **18**, 82–94.

Zhang, K.H. (2005), 'Why does so much FDI from Hong Kong and Taiwan go to mainland China', *China Economic Review*, **16**, 293–307.

Zhao, H. (2003), 'Country factor differentials as determinants of FDI flow to China', *Thunderbird International Business Review*, **45**, 149–169.

Zhao, H. and G. Zhu (2000), 'Location factors and Country of origin difference: an empirical analysis', *Multinational Business Review*, **8**, 60–73.

Zhou, C., A. Delios and J.Y. Yang (2002), 'Locational determinants of Japanese foreign direct investment in China', *Asia Pacific Journal of Management*, **19**, 63–86.

Appendix: Institutional changes in the FDI regime in China[1]

Phases	Year	Law	Year	Spatial 'Opening'
1979–	1979	EJV Law	1980	4 SEZs.
1985:	1980	Income Tax Law of EJVs	1984	14 coastal cities;
Permitt-	1981	Economic Contract Law		Hainan Island
ing FDI	1982	Trademark Law; Income Tax Law of Foreign Enterprises	1985	Yangtze River Delta; Pearl River Delta;
	1983	Exchange control for foreign enterprises		'Golden Triangle'
	1984	Patent Law		
	1985	Accounting Law; Imports and Export Duties		
1986–	1986	WFOE Law; HR liberalisation; Bankruptcy Law;	1988	Liaodong, Shandong .
1991:			1990	Pudong .
Selective	1987	Tariff reduction		
incentive	1988	CJV Law; Procedural rules for		
for FDI		arbitration		
	1989	Administrative Litigation Law		
	1991	Integrated Income Tax Law; Copyright Law		
1992–	1994	Arbitration Rules; Consumer Protection Law; Labour Law; Foreign Trade Law	1992	21 cities (including border cities and most provincial capitals)
1996:				
FDI				
liberalisa	1996	Litigation law		*From 1992, special*
tion				*economic zones could be*
				established by local
				jurisdictions
1997–	1999	Individual Wholly Invested Enterprises Law	1997	Inland regions
on:				
Routinis-	2000	Liberalisation of Labour Market		
ation of	2003	Mergers and Acquisitions by		
FDI		foreign investors; Protection of		
		Intellectual Property Rights		

Source: China Ministry of Commerce, 2005; Huang, 2001; Van Den Bulcke et al., 2003:23–24.

1. What open cities or regions and SEZs have in common is a more positive attitude toward domestic and foreign entrepreneurship. The difference is that SEZs' explicit purpose is to attract FDI and firms.

4. The New Great Leap: The Rise of China's ICT Industry

Mark Joannes Greeven

4.1 INTRODUCTION

A dramatic revolution in information and communications technology at the end of the last century has changed the industrial landscape of China. The information and communication technology industry (ICT industry) is one of the fastest growing industries and has recently been ear-marked as a pillar industry (Meng and Li, 2002), surpassing even some traditional industries such as oil and steel in sales growth (Liang, 2004). The industry ranks first among all national industries in output, gross sales scale, as well as the contribution to national economic growth (United Nations, 2002; China Statistical Press, 2005). The total amount of ICT sales doubled in the past five years and accounts for 18 per cent of the world total. China even surpassed Japan in 2003 and became the second largest producer of ICT products in the world, a surprising feature of an otherwise under-developed economy. Which factors can explain this remarkable development? Did the global ICT revolution boost China's ICT industry? And is China gaining the benefits of being a close follower? Is it directly related to China's economic growth of approximately 10 per cent annually for the past decade? Or is it the strong hand of the government which facilitated the growth of the ICT industry?

What makes the ICT industry rather unique is that it became the recipient of state intervention of a special kind. Usually state intervention refers to regulation, taxation or resource control, all of which serve the purpose to either set hard (budget or regulatory) constraints or formulate negative incentives. In the case of the ICT industry, state intervention refers to the opposite: deregulation of the sector, liberalisation or positive incentives in the form of tax exemptions, if not subsidisations of firms or activities. Some of the so-called state interventions are not sector-specific but refer to general programmes such as reforms in the educational system (indirect state intervention). Some forms of state intervention, however, are sector-specific such as tax rebates (direct state intervention). The overall effect of these policies cannot be assessed by looking at one set of interventions only. The question therefore is: did the state succeed in speeding up the development of the ICT industry via the chosen interventions? Likewise, the competing assumption, namely that foreign direct investment (FDI) is behind China's success in the ICT industry, deserves empirical scrutiny. Here too, one has to distinguish two effects. First, the overall effect of FDI on economic growth, average income, workplace generation and revenues of central and local governments. Second, the direct involvement of foreign companies in the ICT industry, as producers and 'gates' to international value chains.

This chapter will show, using qualitative analyses of policy and statistics, that state intervention has been a major factor in mobilising more and new resources in the ICT industry, using both direct intervening measures – such as providing investment incentives and promoting entrepreneurship – and indirect, non-sector specific measures – such as reforming the educational system, encouraging private investment and attracting foreign investment by deregulation. I will show which factors give rise to what kinds of incentives and constraints that shape the operations of firms in China's ICT industry and illustrate this with a case study of a local software firm in Hangzhou that managed specific incentives and constraints.

The first section starts with an introduction to the *ICT industry* in China, in terms of composition, performance, and players. The second section provides an overview of *previous research* with respect to the factors that have influenced the operation of firms in the ICT industry: state intervention, foreign investment and other factors. Section three deals with China's *dynamic economic environment*: the importance of this relatively straightforward factor is often underestimated. The subsequent sections deal with the general argument: the state attempted to mobilise more and new resources using direct and indirect intervention to provide incentives and pose constraints to firms in the ICT industry. Section four, introduces the argument and goes into detail with respect to direct *state intervention*. In section five, I discuss the deregulation of *foreign investment* and the inflow, source, mode and effects of foreign investment and, in particular, the role of Hong Kong and Taiwan. Section six discusses the upgrading of the *human capital* base in terms of reforming the formal educational system and on the job training programmes. Section seven analyses the accumulation of *private capital* and private investment and how it is still hindered by an uncertain regulatory system. In section eight, a study of a local firm shows how various incentives and constraints affected the operations of the firm. The chapter concludes with a discussion of and directions for further research.

4.2 THE ICT INDUSTRY

In this chapter the ICT industry refers to those firms that produce products or provide services related to the input, process or output of information. The analysis is limited to the following three sectors: telecommunications, computer software and hardware (see for instance Kreamer and Dedrick, 2001; Liang, 2004; Yuntin, 2004; IFC, 2005).

4.2.1 Impact

Of all science and technology intensive industries, the ICT industry is the most telling in terms of impact and rate of development[1]. Over the period 1997–2002, the computer hardware sector had an average annual growth rate in gross industrial output value (current prices) of almost 35 per cent. In the same period, the electronic and telecommunications equipment sector had an average annual growth rate in gross industrial output value (current prices) of almost 20 per cent and the software sector grew with a steady 30 per cent. The High-Technology industries growth of gross industrial output value including the ICT sectors is 20 per cent, excluding these sectors only 12 per cent. Thus, showing the relatively fast growth of the ICT sector, even compared to other fast-growing high-technology sectors. If we compare the growth rates to the overall growth of the manufacturing in China, which is approximately 10 per cent, we can see that the growth of the ICT industry is truly remarkable.

4.2.2 Geographic Concentration

The geographic distribution of firms in the ICT industry over China is unequal: most of the best performing firms in the industry are located in the following regions: the Yangtze River Delta; the Pearl River Delta; the Bohai Sea Rim; and areas along the Shenyang–Dalian expressway. Beijing, Shanghai, Shenzhen and Xian are the country's four best-known high-tech cities. Of them, Beijing has (by far) the largest high-tech area with approximately 8,000 enterprises and 280,000 employees generating 17 per cent of all high-tech enterprises' gross output value and 13 per cent of all high-tech exports in 2002.

4.2.3 Telecommunications: Operators and Equipment Producers

In the early 1950s, China's telecommunications sector was relatively advanced, mainly because of the strong foreign presence in the coastal areas (Harwitt, 2004). For instance, Shanghai had the largest manual exchange station in Asia. In later years, the government wanted to expand its network over the whole of China. During the Great Leap Forward era, network expansion plans failed and led to few low-quality connections. In the Cultural Revolution era, the network did expand modestly, even though the quality of the connections remained poor. As Harwitt (2004) mentioned, the goal of the government was not to get a telephone in every house but to get one in every political station around the country as a new way of political control. Many of the lines were later removed because of their poor quality. It was in the early 1980s, starting with Deng Xiaoping's economic reforms, that the telecommunications system really started to take off. In the late 1980s and 1990s telephone access expanded into the homes of the Chinese and the 1990s are characterised by phenomenal growth and revenues in the telecommunications sector (DeWoskin, 2001), which is still under the control of the Ministry of Information Industries (formerly the Ministry of Post and Telecommunications).

Currently, China has the world's second largest telecom network and the world's largest paging network. The overall market penetration, however, remains very low: 25 per cent for fixed lines and 26 per cent for mobile services (IFC, 2005). In total six telecom operators are in business, i.e. China Telecom, China Netcom (fixed line network operators), China Mobile, China Unicom (mobile carriers), China Railcom, and China Satellite (of minor importance). Most of them are listed in Hong Kong and New York but are still under the control of the state. With respect to the services and network providers, the Chinese enterprises are in control. The six companies provide the basic services and 4,400 companies deliver value added services. Internet access is provided by China Telecom, China Netcom, China Unicom and China Mobile, Ministry of Education and the Chinese Academy of Science operating seven data communication networks: ChinaNet, GBNet/China 169, CERNet, CSTNet, CNCNet, UNINet, CMNet (IFC, 2005).

Market leaders in production of equipment are foreign producers like Nokia, Motorola and Siemens[2]. Moreover, these firms are among the largest foreign investors in China (IFC, 2005). However, domestic manufacturers are closing in. For instance, in mobile handsets they have almost 50 per cent of the market coming from almost nothing several years earlier (IFC, 2005). Some of the major domestic producers are: Huawei, Shenzhen Zhongxin Technology Corporation (ZTE), Datang Telecom Technology (DTT), Great Dragon Information Technology (GDT), TCL, Bird, Keijan, Haier and Shouxin. With the 3G technology being introduced to the market in 2006, the market will become even more competitive. Many domestic firms, like Huawei, have developed 3G equipment and can become very competitive for foreign producers.

Although there is foreign investment in China's telecommunications market, it is only in manufacturing equipment to supply the operating companies. The operations side is exclusively domestic: China Telecom and China Netcom operate the fixed lines; China Mobile and China Unicom operate the mobile carriers (with the 3G technology standards in place, China Telecom will also enter these operations and become a competitor); and China Satcom and China Railcom as minor actors (IFC, 2005). So, the role of foreign investment in this sector is limited to the operations side. The role of the state is substantial in the telecommunications industry as both a 'guard', promoter and owner/investor (Mu and Lee, 2005). Although attempts are made to open up specific sectors within the telecommunication market, many crucial services and operations remain under state supervision.

4.2.4   Computer Hardware

The computer hardware industry in China has its roots in the late 1950s. The first Chinese-made computer was completed in 1958. In the 1970s and early 1980s, policy aimed at developing a self-sufficient industry. In the 1980s, China increased its imports of large and mid-range computers from the US and Japan (IBM, DEC, Unisys, Fujitsu, Hitachi and NEC). The main activity was the assembly of imported kits. In the mid-1980s, the growth of the sector was driven by a strong market demand for consumer electronics in China. In the 1990s, policy shifted to a more pragmatic approach. With the opening-up after 1992, China's computer industry entered a period of growth and intensified competition; the personal computer dominated the market. It is also in this period that the state's promotion of entrepreneurship allowed firms such as Lenovo to develop competences within a supportive institutional environment (Lu, 2000; Gu, 1999).

The late 1990s are characterised by a change in composition of the computer market (Liang, 2004). Whereas the foreign[3] PC makers had 60 per cent of the market in the early 1990s, domestic companies had 80 per cent of the market by the late 1990s (Kreamer and Dedrick, 2001). In recent years, the largest shares belong to Chinese firms and most new players are Chinese. The domestic vendors have two-thirds of the PC market, since the high tariffs on imported PCs and peripherals drive foreign competitors to build production facilities in China (as, for instance, IBM, Dell, HP and Acer did).

Taiwan and Hong Kong firms continue to play a leading role in the industry (Kreamer and Dedrick, 2001). Hong Kong's computer industry is a mixture of SME local firms and foreign multinationals. The major products are PCs, motherboards, printers and more. Most of the companies are small, labour-intensive assembly or subcontractor operations, relying on imports from Japan and the US (Dedrick and Kreamer, 1998). Hong Kong is China's second largest trading partner after Japan, and China provides the Hong Kong electronics industry with abundant supplies of cheap land, subsidised factory leases and low-cost labour. Hong Kong has been a major investor in China in large-scale production and its manufacturing firms provide support services, such as packaging, promotion, design, technical assistance and technology and management transfer. Especially the transfer of skills and knowledge was crucial for mainland Chinese firms, since the development of human capital was insufficient.

Taiwan, on the other hand, is specialised in the production of electronic data processing and components and depends heavily on technologies, components and equipment from the US, Japan and Europe (Kreamer and Dedrick, 2001). In the early 1990s, Taiwanese PC makers entered China with low-end operations to take advantage of low production costs there. Since 1995, competition from US firms has grown and Taiwan has increased its investment, most of which is directed to Jiangsu Province, Shanghai and nearby cities. Between 1999 and 2001, Acer, Twinhead, Inventec, Compal, Quanta, FIC and Arima invested in China. The level of technology is increasing, with notebooks, LCD monitors, scanners and motherboard production. Besides producing for foreign multinationals in China, the Taiwanese firms also manufacture for China's domestic companies (Kreamer and Dedrick, 2001). Half of Taiwan's IT production is now outside Taiwan, mostly in China.

Foreign investment played a significant role in the early years of the computer sector. Foreign firms dominated the sector in the early 1990s, partly driven by strong market demand and the liberalisation of foreign policy. Throughout the 1990s, Taiwan and Hong Kong were responsible for a large part of the investments made in the coastal regions and in the process enhanced the technology level and management skills there. Furthermore, the shift of attention to the promotion of entrepreneurship in high-tech industries facilitated the development of indigenous technology.

4.2.5   Software

As a relatively new industry, the software sector started to develop only in the 1990s. In the 1980s most software products were sold together with computer hardware and were very specific (Zhang and Wang, 1995). There were some software projects scattered around various institutions but hardly any commercial software development existed. The global internet hype and an increasingly strong national economy brought resources to the software industry and the industry started to expand. Especially foreign investors, like Microsoft, IBM and Oracle, and private domestic investors were attracted and still dominate the market. For instance, in Shenzhen 95 per cent of all software firms are either private or foreign. From 1992 to 2000 there was an average annual growth rate of over 30 per cent (Saxenian and Quan, 2005; Tschang and Xue, 2003). However, as Saxenian and Quan (2005) and Brizendine (2002) observe, the software sector remains the 'weakest link' in the ICT industry. For instance, only 1.4 per cent of total ICT industry exports come from software. However, it must be noted that software development in China primarily started with developing Chinese language software and serving the growing domestic market. So, even though the export rates are very low (compared to, for instance, India) that does not necessarily mean that the industry is ill-performing. Still, the state introduced many preferential policies, most notably tax cuts, to increase domestic companies share and software exports.

Currently the focus clearly is on the domestic market, with an increasing focus on software production. In 2003, there were over 8,700 registered software firms, of which 2,000 were newly founded in 2003. In total 51 per cent of the revenues came from software products, 33 per cent came from systems integration and 16 per cent from software services. Even though the preferential treatment of domestic firms over foreign firms has helped the domestic producers to gain momentum, foreign firms still dominate the market (IFC, 2005). Domestic software producers are specialised in financial software and supply chain management software. The market is fragmented with thousands of small enterprises producing niche applications and adapting software to the Chinese language. In addition, many hardware producers, such as the Lenovo Group, developed software arms. The Lenovo Group separated its software arm and renamed it Digital China. Many of the largest software developers are diversified firms, since it is difficult to be a specialised software producer in China (Saxenian and Quan, 2005). The reason for this is that more than half of China's total software output is in software services (primarily systems integration). Due to the weak property rights regime, many companies choose for integrated services, to reduce the risk of piracy. The lack of a supporting institutional environment is clearly a constraint for software firms and strongly influenced the type of operations they perform.

To sum up, the development of the ICT industry in China rests on three components:

1.   a redirection of resources and production to the effect that inherited SOEs become major players in the industry;
2.   the establishment of foreign firms in this industry which produce for the international markets thereby contributing to the county's export earnings. The increasing production for the domestic market whereby they help to satisfy increasing demand for ICT products, and assist to

change the capital stock of China's industrial base, to the effect that more 'modern' technology is employed;

3.   domestic entrepreneurship leading to an increasing number of new firms.

This begs the question of whether the state, through intervening, aims to maintain a segregated market where SOEs play a key role in the telecommunications sector and become major players in the computer hardware market, FDI dominates in computer hardware manufacturing, while new Chinese firms concentrate on software development – and whether this segregation can be kept by state regulation.

4.3   LITERATURE

The growth of China's economy and its industries has received much attention in the economic literature. Most of the studies that deal with aggregate explanations such as productivity gains or capital accumulation (see for instance: Chow, 1993; Borensztein and Ostry, 1996; Hu and Khan, 1997; Wu, 2003) see the similarities with the development of the economies of the 'East Asian Tigers'[4] (Stiglitz, 2003; Krugman, 1994; Young, 1994) but remain too general to be able to explain the development of a specific industry[5], in this case the ICT industry. There is no comprehensive study of the ICT industry as such[6]. On the one hand, one finds studies focused on sub sectors, such as the software industry (for example Yang, Ghauri and Sonmez, 2005). On the other hand, one finds studies that focus on single cases, such as Lu's (2000) in-depth investigation of computer firms. The following tries to fill the gap and provide a more comprehensive study of the ICT industry. The existing literature is organised around two topics: studies that highlight the role of the state in the development of the ICT industry; and studies which concentrate on the role of FDI. This is done in order to review the two most frequently mentioned factors and identify several shortcomings. Subsequently, studies which mention other – missing – factors such as human capital development, private capital accumulation and the proximity to Hong Kong and Taiwan are discussed and summarised in a third paragraph.

4.3.1   State Intervention

The role of the state in the development of the ICT industry is particularly large as other authors suggested (see for instance: Tschang and Xue, 2005; Wang and Wang, 2002; Saxenian and Quan, 2005; Lu, 2000). However, it remains unclear how the state plays a role or, more precisely, which incentives and constraints arise from the state's involvement and how these find their effect on firms in the ICT industry. It is common knowledge that China's economy, but also its political, legal and social systems, is under reform since December 1978. Not going into detail with respect to the general reform program of China's central state, the main consequence of the reforms is that the incentives and constraints to firms continuously change. As Smith (1995) acknowledges in the context of the development of the East Asian Tigers, it is very hard to draw conclusions about the general effect of such state interventions. Garnaut (1990) argues that this depends on the specific type of intervention and the context of the intervention. Since the state – be it the central or the local state – is the driver of reform, the state's policy with respect to the ICT industry is a crucial factor in the industry's development (Kreamer and Dedrick, 2001).

The intervention by China's central state in the ICT industry is highly selective, that is, the intervention is a policy measure to change the allocation of resources, thereby favouring individual or groups of activities (Lall, 1994). The ICT industry has received many forms of preferential treatment and re-allocation and distribution of resources, often in the form of subsidisation rather than mere regulation or taxation measures, in contrast to other industries. For instance, Gu (1996) investigated new technology enterprises. Encouraged and supported by the state, R&D institutes started to commercialise their technology – often ICT related technology – via establishing profit-oriented enterprises or joint ventures with private investors. These enterprises are usually collective or collective-private enterprise subordinated to the specific R&D institute and often referred to as New Technology Enterprises (NTEs). She identified the important role of state support and the availability of resources from existing institutions. Studying the software sector, Saxenian and Quan (2005) stresses the widespread institutional changes and the persistent role of the government and *guanxi* in the development of the software sector. In the same sector, Yang, Ghauri and Sonmez (2005) conducted a competitive analysis – identifying strengths, weaknesses, opportunities and threats – of the software industry in China and paying particular attention to the role of government policies in shaping the competitiveness of the industry[7].

Even though *direct* state intervention is an important factor in the development of the various sectors in the ICT industry, we need a more detailed analysis of the mechanism by which state intervention plays a role. This kind of explanation still stays at a very general level and does not allow the identification of specific incentives and/or constraints that firms are faced with. It is also *indirect* state intervention in, for instance, the development of the educational system or the liberalisation of investment rules and regulations that provides incentives and poses constraints to firms. It is this mechanism of incentives and constraints that helps us to understand how state intervention influenced the growth of Chinese ICT firms. In short, a more detailed account of incentives and constraints that arise from both direct and indirect intervention is necessary to understand the effect of state intervention.

4.3.2   Foreign Investment

Foreign investment is usually viewed as contributing to economic growth by facilitating technology transfer and marginal productivity improvement. This occurs through the externalities technology transfer may engender-technology transfer in this context means the flow of technology from developed to developing countries (Berthelemy and Demurger, 2000). Numerous studies find that increased foreign investment and international trade have positive effects on economic growth (Berthelemy and Demurger, 2000; Chuang and Hsu, 2004; Hobday, 1995) and industrial upgrading (Gereffi, 1999). Gereffi, for instance, argues that better positions in international trade networks allowed East-Asia's apparel manufacturers to upgrade from labour-intensive assembly to skill-intensive full-package supply of new goods and services. However, it remains to be seen whether such upgrading actually takes place in the case of China. As several interesting studies on the role of foreign trade and investment in China suggest, the strong reliance on foreign investment may not be so forthcoming to China's domestic private entrepreneurs (Huang, 2003). Huang argues quite convincingly that FDI came to China because of the opportunities presented by the state's preferential treatment and the large involvement of FDI in state-owned enterprises (SOEs) because of the political capital necessary to invest. Subsequently, China has had rapid export growth rates but this has depended highly on foreign invested firms. This high reliance on FDI for maintaining export rates and aiding the privatisation of SOEs, actually inhibited the growth of the private sector, mainly by missing backward linkages and low domestic content of exports.

These studies, however, are on a national economic level. Many other studies – on an industrial or firm level – suggest the positive effects of foreign investment in the ICT industry, indicating that the preferential treatment of this sector in combination with large foreign investments directed at this industry might actually have had a positive impact. Zhao (1995) finds that the foreign investment boom aided many firms in the ICT industry to accumulate capital, acquire new technology, imitate and learn from foreign firms and develop skills. This finding is supported by a World Bank study (1996) and Liang's (2004) investigation of FDI and industrial development in China's ICT industry (among other industries in his analysis).

In short, a more comprehensive assessment of the specific incentives and constraints arising from foreign investment is necessary to be able to draw more precise conclusions about the effect of foreign investment on firms in the ICT industry.

4.3.3 Other Factors: Economic Growth, Human and Private Capital, Governance and the Proximity to Hong Kong and Taiwan

Several studies direct our attention to a combination of explanations for the success of (firms in) China's ICT industry: overall economic growth, human capital development, private capital accumulation and investment, the role of SOEs and the proximity to Hong Kong and Taiwan. Studying the software industry, Tschang and Xue (2005) identify state intervention as the main factor in software industry growth. However, they also stress that overall economic growth played an important role in the growth of the software industry by providing investment and increasing demand. Furthermore, they identified the low quality and quantity of human resources as inhibiting growth, a conclusion shared by the earlier study of Wang (2003) on the role of human capital in the economic growth of China. Wang and Wang (2002) try to explain the growth of the personal computer industry in China. State intervention and the accumulation of private capital, which spurs demand and investment, are the two main reasons found by them for the growth of the PC industry. The latter explanation finds support by studies of Rodrik (1994), Huang (2003) and Lardy (1995) which point at the important role of state intervention in the promotion of private investment and saving. China witnessed a large increase in private capital and private investments. Two further reasons are suggested: 1. the evolution of many successful firms out of older state enterprises and 2. the interaction with Hong Kong and Taiwan.

The first reason is in line with Lu's (2000) findings in his study on how and why 'indigenous Chinese companies [were] able to catch up in a high-tech industrial sector such as computers' (Lu, 2000: 2). The in-depth study of four Chinese computer companies leads him to stress the importance of innovative learning. Moreover, the specific institutional structure of corporate governance in these companies was conducive to such learning and innovation. Basically, firms evolved out of state-owned organisations with access to science and technology resources and a market. Having a socialist past, the Chinese economy has both the disadvantages and advantages of a socialist legacy. On the one hand, many former state-owned enterprises have the burden of complex bureaucratic structures and the uncertainty of the outcomes of economic reforms. On the other hand, organisations – such as the computer enterprises investigated by Lu (2000) – had the advantages of a secure customer base and access to state developed technology.

The second reason, the proximity of the southern coastal provinces to Hong Kong and Taiwan, is strongly related to the foreign investment thesis, but the influence of Hong Kong and Taiwan is especially significant in the ICT industry. Taiwan started to develop its electronics industry in the 1950s (Hobday, 1995) and has many small firm innovation clusters. Technological development in Hong Kong, on the other hand, is characterised by *laissez-faire*, market-led industrialisation. In the early 1990s, large numbers of firms relocated into China, as wages rose. Hong Kong and Taiwan became the largest investors in China (Sun, Tong and Yu, 2002). Both Hong Kong and Taiwan provided domestic Chinese ICT firms access to the international market, although it is unclear whether this actually led to better positions in international trade that helped upgrading the operations, as Gereffi (1999) would argue. It is clear, however, that the economies in the region – Hong Kong, Taiwan and China – have become more intertwined. Adams and Davis (1994) and Elek (1994) argue that this might reduce the significance of government policies. In short, there is a range of other factors that influence the firms in the ICT industry, beyond direct state intervention and foreign direct investment.

The review highlights the state intervention and foreign investment theses as dominant explanations for the growth of the ICT industry but also identifies several shortcomings in the sense that it remains an incomplete explanation. On the one hand, state intervention is both direct and indirect and an exploration of both types is necessary to understand which incentives and constraints ICT firms have to manage. On the other hand, the effects of foreign investment are inconclusive, meaning that it can lead to both incentives and constraints. In the following, I propose an exploration of direct and indirect state intervention and foreign investment and identify several incentives and constraints arising from both factors. Furthermore, I will include other factors that some of the studies point at to make a more comprehensive assessment of incentives and constraints: human capital development, accumulation of private capital and investment, proximity to Hong Kong and Taiwan. The analysis starts with an assessment of the overall economic environment, a factor often mentioned but underestimated in impact.

4.4 ECONOMIC GROWTH: BETWEEN INCREASING DEMAND AND UNCERTAINTY

The fact that China's economic growth is unsurpassed in the last decades can hardly be doubted. With an average annual growth in GDP of 10 per cent, China is growing faster than any other country in the region (Figure 4.1).

Except for some pessimistic authors (for example Chang, 2001), the overall image is one of growth and opportunity. Viewing it as a window of opportunity, economic growth boosts investment and increases consumption (i.e. GDP per capita increased from RMB 2,000 in 1992 to RMB 4,000 in 2003). Investment in information infrastructure, for instance, is an important factor, considering the relatively underdeveloped state of the art compared to other developing and advanced economies in Asia in terms of internet use, personal computers installed and ICT expenditures (Dahlman and Aubert, 2001; China Statistical Press, 2005). It does not only help firms, institutions and entrepreneurs to reduce costs, increase market coverage and achieve economies of scale, it also increases awareness and understanding of new technologies among (future) customers.

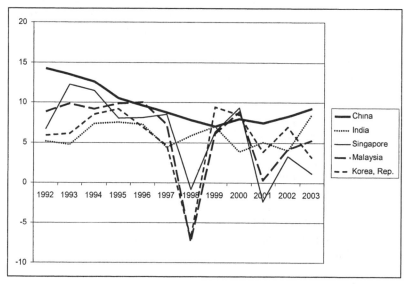

Source: World Bank, 2006.

Figure 4.1   GDP growth rates compared, 1992–2003

The expansion of the market not only creates business opportunities for domestic firms. At the same time it attracts foreign (see the case study at the end of the chapter) producers to the effect that domestic companies need to learn how to compete. The competitive pressures force underperforming firms out of the market, save for those still protected by state preferential treatment. Furthermore, with more competition and a faster pace of development, the rules of the game change. The Chinese economic environment has often been characterised as adverse (for instance

Hendrischke, 2004). This translates into uncertainty that confronts firms with severe resource, management and other challenges. This is especially so for firms in newly emerging industries such as the ICT industry (Aldrich and Fiol, 1994; Feeser and Willard, 1990; Shan, 1990; Zahra and Covin, 1993). They lack managerial and technical skills (amongst other things) and there is no past experience or a template for success or failure.

In fact, the market – the firms – are demanding more market-oriented institutions. As a result of the co-existence of socialist institutions and newly created, market-based institutions (Krug and Polos, 2004), the economic environment has weak economic institutions. The institutions are not weak because they have a socialist hue, which traditionally is unsupportive of private capitalists, but because there are institutions in place coming from both the socialist era and more market-oriented institutions. Both of them are not complete in the sense that they do not provide a stable institutional frame (Qian, 2000), which would reduce the uncertainty emanating from external shocks, value changes or innovation (Krug and Polos, 2004). Thus, even though rapid economic growth creates opportunities, it also poses constraints to the development of firms in the ICT industry.

4.5 ICT INDUSTRY: DIRECT AND INDIRECT STATE INTERVENTION

Both the literature and development patterns in the ICT industry suggest that state intervention has both a direct and indirect influence on firms in the ICT sector. This section will analyse the general regulatory frame, ICT industry–specific incentives and regulations, the promotion of entrepreneurship and the role of SOEs (the direct factors) and introduce several factors related to the reform of China's wider economic environment (the indirect factors).

4.5.1 The General Regulatory Frame

The central state initiated restructuring and reforms to encourage technology development within China since 1978. There are basically four phases of reform. The first phase (1978–1984) was a period of restoration, in which the central government tried to restore the level of technology to the pre-Cultural Revolution level and commercialise results from the state S&T system. The second phase (1985–1986) started with the idea that collaboration between state research and enterprises would facilitate the commercialisation of technologies from the state S&T system (Lu, 2000). However, most of the resources went to state-owned institutes rather than the potentially more innovative non-governmental enterprises (Saxenian and Quan, 2005) and not many new products were brought to market. The third phase (1987–1992) was characterised by the intention to further merge industrial research and development (R&D) institutes into enterprises. The Torch Plan of 1988 aimed at creating a supportive institutional environment for the development of new technology enterprises. Entrepreneurship was promoted and actually led to the creation of several High-Tech Industrial Development Zones and many new technology ventures. The most recent phase started in 1992 with Deng Xiaoping's famous Southern Tour. Government policy offered for the first time significant domestic market access to firms that brought in advanced technology. The policy reforms led to a massive flow of foreign (direct) investment into China. Furthermore, (private) entrepreneurship was promoted by the adoption of the Company Law (December 1993, amended in 1999) and the important constitutional change in 1999, which established the status of private and non-state sector enterprises (Sole Proprietorship Enterprise Law, 1999). Further, WTO membership in 2001 clearly involves many consequences for trade and foreign investment, mainly increasing the foreign presence and influence in the Chinese market.

4.5.2 Incentives in the ICT Industry: Knowledge Sharing and Arm's Length Regulation

The state has been – and still is – very active in promoting and regulating the high-technology industry and the development of science and technology in general. The Ministry of Science and Technology (MOST) is responsible for many promotion programs: the 'Key Technologies R&D Program', the '863 Program' and the 'Torch Program' to name but three. The programs funded S&T projects in institutes of higher education, R&D institutes, enterprises and companies. The Chinese Academy of Sciences (CAS) is China's science and technology (S&T) research organisation and has 123 research institutes, employing over 60,000 scientific and technical personnel. Research focuses on mathematics and physics, chemistry, earth sciences, biology and technology.

The CAS has been very active in commercialising R&D from CAS research. At the end of 2001, 13 CAS institutions had been transformed (CAS, 2006) into enterprises: 12 became limited-liability firms and one merged into a state-run company. The firms reached a total turnover of 81 billion RMB (US$9.7bn) in 2001. The Chinese Academy of Engineering (CAE) and the state Natural Science Foundation Committee (NSFC) are two other important institutions in the technology sector. The CAE was established in 1994 and is a key advisory institution for the engineering community. The NSFC was established in 1986 to promote and finance S&T research. All in all, the central government and associated institutions are very active in the provision of incentives for the development of technology in general and ICT specifically.

Overall, state intervention often takes the form of subsidisation. The rules and regulations for the ICT industry are relatively broad and focused on the promotion of sectors or technologies. The overall ICT development and commercialisation facilitating environment is illustrated by the case of an ERP software firm in Hangzhou, at the end of the chapter. However, there is no clear set of rules and regulations (yet) that regulate the ICT industry. The newness of the industry and the rate of development make it difficult for policy makers to keep up. As DeWoskin (2001) observed, sometimes the changes in technology are one step ahead of policy, eventually forcing policy to fit the technology. In this kind of regulatory environment entrepreneurship can also be promoted by the lack of specific institutional requirements. Entrepreneurs are not burdened by complex sets of rules and regulations that characterise traditional industries. Of course, the lack of a straightforward institutional system is a burden, especially in the case of piracy-sensitive software development, but it also means less rules and regulations that need to be obeyed and thus less interference from the state. So, it is not possible to single out positive or negative effects conclusively, which adds uncertainty to the institutional environment.

4.5.3   Stimulating Entrepreneurship: Carving Out a Hospitable Niche

Many programs promote the establishment of new technology enterprises and entrepreneurship at large. One of the most striking endeavours is the Torch Plan (Gu, 1996; 1999; Wang, Wu and Li, 1998; Sigurdson, 2004; White, Gao and Zhang, 2002) and the subsequent development of technology development zones and the creation of new enterprises with a special legal status (Gu, 1999; Lu, 2000)[8], which led to a strong concentration of ICT firms. The Zones facilitate the operation of the ventures and provide preferential treatments (for example tax cuts), infrastructure and access to capital (from state banks and foreign investors), including venture capital. In return, the government obliges the enterprises to meet certain requirements. Firms have to meet the following criteria (Lu, 2000):

1. operate in the area of new and high technology as indicated by the Ministry of Science and Technology;
2. have appropriate capital and physical resources, market potential and acceptable organisational and managerial abilities; and
3. the chief manager should be a scientific or technical professional.

These Zones are different from the Special Economic Zones that had been established earlier. The technology zones are more geographically distributed over China, there is preferential treatment for both foreign and domestic investors, though less favourable than in the Special Economic Zones.

The promotion of entrepreneurship in the ICT industry has been – and still is – one of the main goals of state intervention in high-technology industries. The reforms in enterprise policy have been substantial and created opportunities for entrepreneurship. The adoption of the Company Law in December 1993 (amended in 1999) and the Sole Proprietorship Enterprise Law in 1999 paved the way and allowed private enterprises as an organisational form and this opened up possibilities for technology entrepreneurs, especially in enterprise development zones[9].

4.5.4 The Emergence of New SOEs

Strongly influenced by state intervention and clearly a result of reform policies and industrial experimentation is the governance mechanism of many (former) state-owned enterprises or organisations (Lu, 2000). Ever since the reforms started, the central government has tried to commercialise state R&D; first by reforming the state R&D system to its pre-Cultural Revolution level, later by trying to create a technology market. Both attempts proved to be harder to realise than expected, as argued by Gu (1999), because there were many uncertainties with respect to technological innovation, inexperience of users in general and underdeveloped market institutions. In the late 1980s and early 1990s, the attempts were more successful. Several decisions and policies supported the integration of R&D assets with commercial production within newly-created enterprises, which were basically spin-offs of state R&D institutions (for example universities). The state as a partner enabled these enterprises to use resources and customers from the state sector. Support was given through financial incentives, preferential stipulations and basic intellectual property rights (Gu, 1996). The institutional environment provided ways to tap into networks of finance: R&D institutions (some venture capital), banks (expansion funds) and Technology Zones (infrastructure). The arrangement combined state ownership with market-oriented, enterprise management enabling a 'collective rationality of building strong organisational capabilities with the strong financial commitment within the institutional framework' (Lu, 2000: 187). Examples of such successfully created enterprises are Lenovo and Founder.

4.5.5   Not only Incentives

State intervention also poses constraints to the population of ICT firms at large. The most straightforward constraint is that preferential treatment of sectors or even individual firms hinders the market process. Only the firms that fall into the categories chosen by the central or local governments are supported but this does not mean that firms that do not fit the categories are not potentially innovative or successful. An example is that in many cases large funds for creating innovative new enterprises actually go to state-owned or controlled firms (Saxenian and Quan, 2005). Intervention also inhibits risky investments with potential higher returns and the development of a venture capital market. Another example is the high-tech zones. In principal these prove to be very beneficial for the enterprises within them, but they are also an institutional device of the government to control resources and influence decisions. The enterprises were obliged to meet certain requirements, such as the number of technical personnel, the allocation of retained earnings and the percentage of sales spent on innovation (Lu, 2000). Such preferential treatment also meant direct control over several sectors – such as the telecom sector – prohibiting foreign investment and any other 'interference'. The main reason of the state was to keep an eye on the internet and telecommunications. This severely limited the possibilities for firms in this sector.

Besides many successful interventions, many plans, such as the technology auction and forced merging of organisations, did not work as well as the central state had hoped. Experimentation – in technology and policy – has lead to the failure of firms and inhibited firms' own initiatives. It was only after initial experimentation that bottlenecks came to light: lack of trained engineers, scientists and managers, inexperienced users, a general lack of a technical basis for economic and social development. A related result of the continuous change of policies and regulations is a dynamic but also very uncertain institutional environment. Weak institutions do not contribute to the problem of reducing high uncertainty caused by technology, competition or the market (Krug and Polos, 2004) because – for instance – property rights are not clearly defined (Lau, Lu, Makino, Chen and Yeh, 2002), which particularly is a problem for software firms (Saxenian and Quan, 2005). Another example is the telecommunications market where much uncertainty exists about issues such as 3G standards (assigned by the central state), the opening of the market, and the control and censorship of content.

4.5.6   Indirect Intervention

Basically, as the next sections will show, other important factors in the development of the ICT industry are more or less influenced by state intervention: foreign investment regulation, private capital policy and the educational system. Some of the reforms supported the development of the ICT industry, others inhibited it. First, state intervention in *foreign investment* promoted and attracted many foreign investors. In the early 1990s, the central government changed its foreign policy by offering market access to firms that brought in advanced technology. In 1992, the management of technology imports was transferred to the State Economic and Trade Commission and changed from a system of 'technology import control' to 'scale of funds control'. The central government set the macro-targets – focusing more on electronics, motors and machinery – but responsibility with respect to the management and control of imports was given to enterprises. Second, *human capital* is one of the key assets in high-technology industries such as the ICT industry. The relative weakness – in terms of skilled labour - of China's human capital base has been the reason for many reforms and other types of state intervention. For instance, the State Council's Decision to accelerate scientific and technological progress (1995) also aimed at promoting and developing high technology and the training of workers. Several reforms of the educational system were enacted and directed at enhancing human capital development. Third, state intervention also increased market demand by promoting the use of IT. The Golden Projects in the early 1990s are good examples of how the central government promoted the adoption of IT in banking, furthered the development of telecom and promoted computer networking for foreign trade. Furthermore, the reforms in the *private capital* market slowly allowed private equity and venture capital to develop, which are crucial incentives for the ICT industry.

4.6   FOREIGN DIRECT INVESTMENT: BRINGING THE NEIGHBOURS IN

The development of China's ICT industry is characterised by the strong presence of Hong Kong and Taiwan firms, as well as multinationals, demonstrating the dramatic change in China's foreign trade policy. Indeed, the statistics show that:

1. FDI increased in response to deregulation of markets;
2. FDI is predominantly of Asian origin, with Hong Kong and Taiwan playing the leading roles ;

3.   Foreign firms tend to establish subsidiaries rather than joint-ventures when this became an option;
4.   FDI became a new channel for technology transfer; and
5.   FDI might not be 'really' foreign, leading one to question the extent of technology transfer and the learning of new capabilities.

First, foreign direct investment increased sharply in response to the deregulation of foreign investment policy. The total inflow of foreign capital increased from US$4.5bn in 1985 to US$64bn in 2004. From the early 1990s onwards, the composition of total foreign investment changed. Even though some foreign capital was still from loans or other foreign investments, it has become predominantly direct investment (FDI) (China Statistical Press, 2005). There has been an increase in investment from US$1.7bn in 1985 to US$60.63bn in 2004. There were basically two phases of FDI inflows (Sun, Tong and Yu, 2002; Yi, Zhong, Men and Huang, 2004). The first phase was between 1979 and 1991. In the first half of this phase, FDI was concentrated on particular state-owned traditional industries in the coastal regions. In the second half, access was extended to a limited amount of other industries and some central regions. During this phase, the Open Door Policy was predominantly restricted to the coastal region, foreign investors had limited access to the Chinese domestic market and the range of industries in which foreigners could invest was restricted. In the second phase, opening up was extended to all regions, the pace was accelerated, the domestic market was further opened, and the direction shifted from a regional to an industrial basis. China maintained a strong specialisation in traditional industries (for example clothing), but also started to build up new, technologically advanced industries (for example computer equipment).

Second, foreign direct investment predominantly comes from within the Asian region (Figure 4.2) with Hong Kong, Japan, Taiwan, Korea and Singapore investing approximately 95 per cent of the total here (China Statistical Press, 2005). Hong Kong and Taiwan have been particularly important as foreign players in the Chinese ICT industry. Given the inequality in population, size and resources they play a remarkable role in the development of Chinese ICT.

As shown in the discussion of the computer industry, the role of Taiwan and Hong Kong firms in terms of investment, learning new technologies and getting managerial assistance is substantial. China received almost US$60.63bn in foreign direct investment in 2003. The share of Hong Kong and Taiwan of the total amount is 36 per cent (China Statistical Press, 2005); thus indicating the dominance of two single, small, territories. Furthermore, the amount of trade with Hong Kong and Taiwan is substantial. In 2004, almost 29 per cent of China's Asian trade was with Hong Kong and Taiwan;

which amounted to almost 17 per cent of the world total. It must be noted that Japan remains China's largest trading partner with 27 per cent of China's Asian trade and 16 per cent of China's world total trade. Hong Kong and Taiwan provide China with a large amount of investment and, especially in the case of Hong Kong, support services and technical and management transfers. The proximity of both economies enables mainland Chinese firms to tap into international markets and imitate and learn new capabilities.

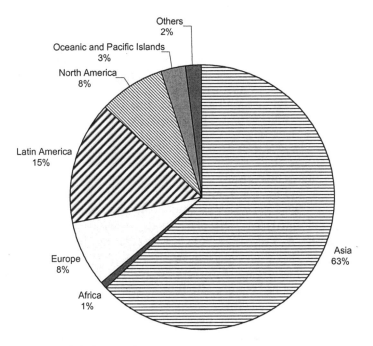

Source: China Statistical Press 2005.

Figure 4.2 Foreign direct investment per region in 2004

Third, the entry mode changed from cooperative enterprises to subsidiaries with a considerably stronger commitment when this became an option. Yi, Zhang, Men and Huang (2004) identified four ways in which FDI enters China: joint-venture enterprises (JVEs), cooperative operation enterprises (COEs), foreign investment enterprises (FIEs) and cooperation development (CD). Until 1992, the total amount of FDI was small and the COE and CD entry modes were dominant. The turning-point is in the early 1990s. From this point onwards the share of foreign investment enterprises increases to almost 50 per cent of total FDI. The share of COE and CD declined when more structural investments were allowed and foreign investors were allowed to make stronger commitments. The development of FDI and types of FDI entry modes is strongly linked to the regulatory reforms regarding foreign firms and national-level political events (Table 4.1). The more rights and opportunities that were given to foreign enterprises, the larger the inflow of investment.

Table 4.1   Reforms in foreign regulation

Phase	Regulatory reform	End of phase
1979–1985	Law of the PRC on Joint Ventures Using Chinese and Foreign Investment	High inflation
1986–1991	PRC Law on Foreign Enterprises	Tiananmen Square Incident
1992–	1990 Amendments to the Joint Venture Law 1991 Income Tax Law for Enterprises with Foreign Capital and Foreign Enterprises 1992 Deng Xiaoping's South China tour	

Fourth, foreign investment – FDI – became a *new* channel for technology imports; to add to the importation of capital and management skills (Wang, Wu and Li, 1998; Zhao, 1995). During the process, localities got more authority and enterprises were given more responsibility through various policy reforms. As Piek (1998: 35) observes 'decentralisation of institutions and lifting of state's monopoly in the foreign sector stimulates domestic enterprises to enter the world market'. For many ICT firms, the increase of foreign investment had positive effects by increasing investments, transfer of knowledge and larger markets.

Fifth, although a very large stock of FDI has entered China, the story is perhaps not as rosy as the figures suggest. FDI per capita is not large, compared to other Asian countries. For example, stock per capita in China is US$160, in Thailand US$320 and in Malaysia US$2000 (Lemoine, 2000). The distribution of FDI is very uneven with a concentration in the coastal provinces (China Statistical Press, 2005). Furthermore, it is unclear to what extent FDI is actually really 'foreign' and, subsequently, to what extent transfer of technology takes place through foreign investment. Graham and Wada (2001) argue that (unspecified) parts of Hong Kong FDI, the largest source of FDI, is in fact of domestic Chinese origin, which is 'round-tripped' through Hong Kong, or Western nations and Taiwan that enters China through Hong Kong intermediaries. Huang (2003) argues that round-tripping of foreign capital was actually promoted by the foreign investment policies of the government which favoured foreign enterprises over domestic enterprises. Furthermore, he finds that China's high reliance on FDI is not healthy because it inhibits the private sector by creating more competition and giving more preferential treatment to such foreign invested firms and protection of SOEs, thereby inhibiting productivity growth. The main problem of round tripped foreign capital is that it does not involve technology transfers and learning of new capabilities, which problematises the benefits of the sharp increase in FDI.

4.7   HUMAN CAPITAL DEVELOPMENT

Human capital is a crucial factor in the development of the ICT industry but seems insufficiently developed for the demands of an emerging ICT industry in China. On the one hand, 'qualified personnel who can monitor technological and other trends, assess their relevance to the prospects for the country and individual firms, and help to develop strategies for reacting to and taking advantage of trends' are needed (Dahlman and Nelson, 1995: 97; see also Mytelka, 2001). On the other hand, strong education is also necessary at the primary and secondary level 'to speed the diffusion and adoption of new technologies, to make local adaptations and improvements on the shop floor, and more generally to increase the awareness and ability to take advantage of technological opportunities' (Dahlman and Nelson, 1995: 97). However, the pre-reform period had left its scars on the educational system. Several observers typified it as insufficient for the development of the necessary human capital (Cheng and DeLany, 1999) and as 'over-centralised' (Mok, 2002). A World Bank study has shown that regulation of the labour market and the skills of employees were the major constraints of the investment climate in China over the past years (Table 4.2, World Bank, 2006; also affirmed by another recent study done by IFC, 2005).

4.7.1   Formal Education: Redefining the Talent Pool for the ICT Industry

In order to expand the ICT industry, more and better qualified academics and skilled workers were needed. While the latter can be trained in-house, the former have to pass the state controlled university system. The challenge was therefore to reform formal education so that it produced more academics, upgraded technical university programmes and opened new programmes, such as management studies. The results so far are mixed. The statistics show that:

1.   basic education is well-developed but access to higher education remains rather limited;

2.   technical education is well-developed whereas management education remains problematic;
3.   the low ratio of students returning from abroad indicates a potential brain drain;
4.   the management and finance of the formal educational system has improved substantially as a result of deregulation.

Firstly, the actual rate of growth of human capital in terms of average years of schooling in the population aged 15–64 has declined in the reform period, as compared to the pre-reform period (Wang and Yao, 2003). It seems that access to secondary and tertiary education is problematic, as indicated by the gross enrolment ratios (Table 4.2). This is a ratio of total enrolment, regardless of age, to the population of that age group that officially corresponds to the level of education shown (World Bank, 2006).

Table 4.2   School enrolment ratios in 2003: international comparison

	United Kingdom	United States	Germany	France	Finland	Korea	China	Japan
primary (%)	101.0	100.3	103.2	105.0	101.7	100.1	113.9	100.7
secondary (%)	157.9	94.1	98.9	107.7	125.9	94.2	68.2	102.5
tertiary (%)	59.0	70.7	N/A	53.6	85.3	77.6	12.7	47.7

Source: World Bank, 2006.

A figure over 100 per cent indicates that there are people enrolled at a certain level that are older than the age group that corresponds to that level. All countries (European, North-American and Asian) have a primary school enrolment ratio of around 100 per cent; this means that the amount of enrolments is as large as the population of the age group that corresponds to that level. However, the secondary and tertiary enrolment rates in China are considerably lower than in all other countries. The statistics show that, compared to other countries, the number of people from the age groups that correspond to the secondary and tertiary level that are actually enrolled is very low. Access to higher education remained limited in the 1990s (Wang and Yao 2003) and still in more recent years: for instance, in 2004 only 12.7 per cent.

Secondly, the figures indicate that engineering, management and literature are attracting the most students and deliver the most graduates (Table 4.3). The reasons for this are harder to find. It is possible that engineering subjects attract the most students because these subjects are often in the spot-light of government policy; for example the 10th Five-Year Plan focuses on engineering and science related topics such as computers, telecommunications and biotechnology. Furthermore, the promotion of high-technology products has increased the socio-political legitimacy of such specialisations. Management studies are also attracting more students: the number of students enrolled in management studies increased by 24 per cent in 2003 and the number of management graduates almost doubled in 2003 (46 per cent).

Table 4.3   Students per major in 2003

	Graduates of higher education	Student enrolment in higher education
Total	1877492	11085642
Philosophy	1196	5974
Economics	88181	604135
Law	110416	560916
Education	117072	592123
Literature	286889	1719230
History	13905	56673
Science	173031	1004506
Engineering	644106	3693401
Agriculture	50057	249671
Medicine	111356	814741
Management	281283	1784272

Source: China Statistical Press, 2005.

However, management studies are still ill-developed and ill-promoted and the absolute number of management graduates remains low. The level of education and management training among Chinese managers continues to be a major concern for foreign invested enterprises (FIEs) even though the situation has improved since the mid-1990s (see for instance, Tsang, 1994).

Thirdly, in order to import superior knowledge in China's economy, a quantity of students is sent abroad every year. At the beginning of the reforms in 1978, official records state that 860 students studied abroad and 248 returned. In 1993, there were already 10,742 students abroad with only 5,128 returning (China Statistical Press, 2005). In 2003, the ratio of students abroad to students returned was even more unbalanced, according to official statistics: 117,307 remained abroad, while only 20,152 returned. If these statistics are correct, one may speak of a trend: more people are going abroad than returning, thus illustrating a so-called 'brain-drain' (Cao, 1996), even though it is impossible to assess the quality of the students that (did not) return. At least half of Chinese students are extending stays or trying to seek permanent residency in foreign countries. The Chinese Embassy in the US estimated that from the 160,000 Chinese students that came to the US in the past 20 years, only 20,000 had returned by 1998. Several scholars point to the seriousness of this problem (Saxenian and Quan, 2005; Zhang and Li, 2001).

Fourthly, the management and finance of the educational system has improved considerably as a result of deregulation. A considerable change is the new two-level management system consisting of central and local governments with the latter as the main management body. The state gave more autonomy to local government and institutions (Mok, 2002). Local government is playing a key role in compulsory education, while central and provincial governments are dominant in higher education. In occupational and adult education, social partners, including industrial organisations, businesses and public institutions, are playing a more important role, suggesting the development of on the job training. Local governments are also increasingly motivated to develop higher education and enhance the relationship between education and regional economic and social development (Mok, 2002).

Furthermore, universities are no longer funded exclusively by the government (Mok, 2002). Calculations from the official statistics of the China Statistical Yearbook indicate that the state's share of educational funding was 84 per cent in 1990 and dropped to 67 per cent in 2000. However, this does not indicate that the government invests less in education but that there is more investment from other sources; the total funds more than doubled every five years, in the last two decades. China received educational funding from UNESCO, UNICEF, UNFPA, UNDP, the World Bank and many other international organisations. Furthermore, the government allowed privately-funded educational institutions and private schooling on other levels. Wang and Yao (2003) show that even though the private financing of education has risen, the distribution is not even and that the distribution of educational funds is even more skewed if one takes private financing into account. Furthermore, it must be noted that China only spent 2.5 per cent of GNP on education in 2001, whereas other developing countries, such as the Philippines, India, South Korea and Singapore spend more than 3 per cent and Thailand and Malaysia more than 4 per cent of GNP of education (UN, 2002).

It is clear that the formal educational system is being upgraded but still remains underdeveloped to meet the needs of the ICT industry. Overall, the size of investment in the formal educational system increased and management improved. There is a wide range of curricula available at various levels of education and more – but still too few – students enter higher education. The large amount of engineers that graduate every year suggests a sound human capital base for high-technology firms. The case study at the end of the chapter illustrated how this can lead to a highly-educated group of technical employees. However, the gross enrolment ratio of students in tertiary education is comparatively low and the quality of education is hard to assess. For instance, the training and education of managers seems ill-developed. Overall, China has a low percentage of college-educated workers and lags behind developed world standards (Heckman, 2005).

4.7.2   On the Job Training: Upgrading Management

On the job training has become an important strategy for developing technical and especially management skills (Xiao and Tsang, 1999). The Decision on the Reform and Development of Adult Education (1987) stipulated that job-related training should get the highest priority as a tool to develop job-specific skills that cannot be provided by the formal educational system. The decision has been implemented in various ways: integrated on the job training, job-related technical drills, short-cycle training classes, thematic lectures and supervised self-study (Xie, 1994).

Data on training in Chinese companies is almost absent, save for some case studies on human resource practices. Cooke's (2002) study on two manufacturing companies show two different approaches. One firm, a beer company, obliged employees to spend 100 hours on training each year to enhance management skills and the production-related skills. The firm had contracts with two universities to provide management training, professional and technical training and further education (for example for shop/office-floor employees). In general, the Chinese State Commission organises several courses and programs for managers and teachers in collaboration with international institutions and organisations (Ding, Fields, and Akhtar 1997). Another firm, a motor company, provided hardly any training, partly because of the low demand for training because there was little innovation and a static workforce. Ding, Fields and Akhtar (1997) study 158 foreign-invested firms in the Shenzhen Municipality investigating human resource management practices of mainly manufacturing industries and some service and trading industries. They found that managers in FIEs in the electronics manufacturing sector received the most training and in the trading business the least. Overall, more than 60–70 per cent of the managers of FIEs in China received training. Of the non-managerial personnel, approximately 50 per cent received training. The major explanation for such high figures is that many FIEs have an obligation to train employees under the Labour Law.

Based on fragmentary information, it is hard to say anything definite about the incentives or constraints arising from on the job training. However, the cases show that such training is often provided by firms and that it is directed at upgrading both management and technical skills. As a building block of human capital, on the job training is important but the commitment of firms to such training is unclear. In the case study at the end of the chapter we see that on the job training is also a way to cut education and recruitment costs.

4.8   PRIVATE CAPITAL ACCUMULATION: WITH THE HELP OF YOUR FRIENDS

When it was said earlier that the development of the ICT industry was accompanied by the emergence of new firms producing new products, then the question is not only where did the competence come from (the question of the educational system) but also where did the capital necessary for establishing new firms come from. China witnessed a large increase in private capital as is shown by the growth of private capital flows (from US$8.107bn in 1990 to US$59.455bn in 2003) and significant increase in savings deposits (from RMB7.12bn in 1990 to RMB103.618bn in 2003). However, an overall increase in private capital does not necessarily mean an increase in private investment. Figure 4.3 shows private investment[10] as a percentage of GDP over the period 1980–1999[11]. There is an overall increase in private investment: from only 3.7 per cent in 1980 to 17 per cent of GDP in 1999. Especially from the early 1990s onwards, the share of private investment in the Chinese economy is growing.

On the one hand, an increase in private capital boosts demands for new products, as was repeatedly the case in the computer hardware and software sectors. On the other hand, it boosts investments. The People's Daily (2003, 2005) reports in several articles that domestic private capital drives the economy. For instance, domestic private capital investment now accounts for 50 per cent of Shanghai's total infrastructure construction industry. Beijing has seen over 60 per cent of housing investments made by private investors. Many transformed Chinese firms under high financial pressures look for outside financing to realise growth and find private equity investors important partners and an important complement to creditors in shaping the incentives of firms.

The private capital market, however, remains underdeveloped. Private equity, especially venture capital, finds it hard to reach firms, even though most of the venture capital is directed at high-tech industries (Batjargal and Liu, 2004). There are no regulations with respect to the legal and organisational structures and would-be investors, mainly local governments, set up limited liability corporations. The Company Law, however, inhibits investments of more than 50 per cent of capitalisation in subsidiaries or other entities, thus preventing firms from investing more than 50 per cent of their assets in other things than cash-equivalent securities (Tenev, Zhang and Brefort, 2002).

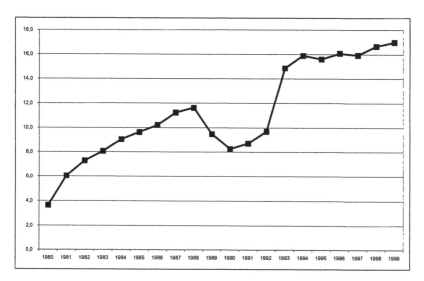

Source: IFC (forthcoming) Stephan Everhart and Mariusz A. Sumlinski. 'Trends in Private
Investment in Developing Countries: Statistics for 1970-2000'

Figure 4.3   Private investments as percentage of GDP in China, 1980–1999

The result is that the 'common' legal form of venture capital firms in advanced economies such as the United States – the limited liability partnership – is thus not recognised (Batjargal and Liu, 2004). The main problem is not that the limited liability partnership is the only possible form venture capital firms should adapt, but 'all venture capital firms are registered and operate as limited liability companies, adding confusion as well as serious risks to the processes by which venture capital firms raise, invest, and manage funds' (Batjargal and Liu, 2004: 159). Furthermore, as Tenev, Zhang and Brefort (2002) observe 'the state still plays a ubiquitous role as fund sponsor, investor and manager.' (Tenev, Zhang and Brefort, 2002: 72), thereby inhibiting risky investments with potentially high returns. Reforms of the legal framework should promote the development of private capital and equity markets, but for the moment they are insufficient. Concluding, the accumulation of private capital is a strong incentive but the development of a private capital market is highly constrained by state intervention. With the private capital market still underdeveloped, the establishment of new firms needs to fall back on traditional, social forms of money raising, such as loans from family members or friends. With most venture capital in the hand of local government agencies, access to capital also depends on successful lobbying and good relations with such agencies.

4.9   MEETING LOCAL DEMAND THROUGH CUSTOMISATION AND COOPERATION: A HANGZHOU ERP SOFTWARE FIRM

The following case is a first exploration of how an ICT firm in China dealt with specific incentives and constraints. The main questions in this case are: what kinds of incentives and constraints had the firm to deal with? And how did the firm manage to benefit from the incentives and mitigate the risks from the constraints? Given the exploratory nature of the study, a case study is the best methodology as it is an empirical inquiry that investigates a contemporary phenomenon within its real-life context, and is often used in contemporary empirical and explorative studies to identify information on how and why certain phenomena occur (Yin, 1989). The analysis relies on an in-depth interview with a manager of 'Firm 6' in the Spring of 2006[12]. The firm is introduced in the first paragraph and the subsequent paragraphs deal with the incentives and constraints.

4.9.1   Background

Firm Six is a small, privately owned software development firm with 20 employees in Hangzhou. Firm Six develops ERP[13] software and cooperates with other firms on joint software projects. Hangzhou is the capital of Zhejiang Province, one of the most advanced and richest provinces in China[14]. The customers of the firm are both state and non-state owned business customers. When Firm Six started its operation the biggest challenge was to attract these customers. Being a new firm in a new industry, it was hard to get a piece of the pie. Over the years, Firm Six's customers increased, as did their demand for software products and services. The demand of both state and non-state owned business customers is increasing but there are no significant changes in demand and the customers are loyal to the firm. Most of the work is done in relatively large project teams (8–10 persons) and 90 per cent of the employees are skilled workers with an engineering degree. Of all the employees, about 20 per cent have a management function and 10 per cent of the employees are temporary workers (part-timers). The organisation of work is straightforward: the majority of employees work exclusively on software development; and the firm's decisions are kept in the hands of the management.

4.9.2 Competition

Competition is becoming stronger but the firm does not see any problems arising from this. *On the one hand*, there is no real threat since competitors do not often introduce new, competitive products and it is extremely hard to copy the firm's products/services because of the highly customised nature of the work: software involving the customer to a great extent and customer-specific investments and innovations. Many software firms face the serious risk of software piracy, but Firm 6's highly customised client-involved work offsets these risks. Competitors do offer substitute products but they are merely integrated combinations of other products. *On the other hand*, there is no foreign competition. Even though there are a lot of foreign firms in Hangzhou and foreign investment in the industry is large, Firm six is not affected by increased foreign pressure. There are basically two reasons for this: first, they localise production in Hangzhou, addressing the specific needs of firms in Hangzhou; and second, the work is extremely customised making it hard to imitate or provide substitutes.

4.9.3 State support

The firm enjoys the benefits of a local government which supports the ICT industry and does not intervene very much in the operations of the firm. Hangzhou is well known for two things: tourism and light industry. The policy of the government in Hangzhou is focused on the developed of light industry and especially promotes its ICT industry, focusing on telecommunication services, software and some equipment manufacturing. The interviewee revealed a reasonable confidence that legislation will protect the firm. The legal requirements are straightforward and there have been no significant changes that affected the firm. A good relationship between the firm and the local government enables it to learn about state policy changes quickly, reducing the risks of uncertain institutional changes. There are almost no specific requirements from state agencies, banks or any other institution regarding any of the firm's decisions and no restrictions on the use or development of the firm's key resources, such as labour, land and capital.

4.9.4 Location and Zhejiang University

The firm enjoys a positive business environment due to the high concentration of ICT firms in Hangzhou. The interviewee told us that there are not many other firms in the software industry offering the same products and services that could serve as examples. There are many success stories but also many failures: these enable the firm to learn and cope with the risks of being a new firm in a new industry.

Furthermore, the firm cooperates with Zhejiang University, a leading technology university in China, for the development of R&D capabilities. Innovation at Firm Six is incremental – due to the nature of their client-involved decision making – and often occurs in cooperation with the university. Furthermore, new employees are easily recruited from the university even though the firm prefers in-house training of employees because it lowers costs. In-house training is facilitated by a project team approach to software development and peer training.

The case shows that the firm benefited from several of the incentives identified in this chapter, such as increased market demand, strong engineering education, preferential policies and geographic concentration of the ICT industry. With a local market, cooperation with Zhejiang University and the (local) government and customisation of products and services, it devised strategies to build a strong human capital base, cope with increased local and foreign competition, and changing institutional requirements. The firm meets local demand through cooperation and customisation.

4.10 DISCUSSION AND CONCLUSION

The remarkable growth of China's ICT industry calls for explanation. This analysis shows that the state intervened both directly and indirectly in order to mobilise greater resources in the ICT industry:

1. Investment: FDI, venture capital, private savings
2. Human capital: formal and informal education, foreign expertise
3. Entrepreneurship: knowledge sharing, arm's length regulation and new SOEs

Firstly, an increase in foreign investment inflow, a growing – although still very limited – venture capital market and an increase in private savings as a result of deregulation of foreign and capital policy have boosted investment and competition. Whereas the central government sets the overall targets, individual firms are increasingly in control of the management of foreign capital inflow, coming predominantly from Hong Kong, Taiwan and Japan. The accumulation of private capital in combination with the increasing reputation of the ICT industry's products and services in the domestic market have boosted private investment. *Secondly*, the government attempts to upgrade China's human capital base through a thorough reform of the formal educational system and increased emphasis on on the job training in combination with imported foreign expertise. The overall investment in the formal educational system has increased but it remains too weak to supply the demand for innovation in the ICT industry. *Thirdly*, one of the major goals of state intervention was the promotion of entrepreneurship. The state's arm's length approach to regulation and promotion – often direct subsidisation – of specific ICT initiatives has created many incentives for entrepreneurs. Furthermore, the state's knowledge sharing initiatives, involving R&D institutes, banks and technology zones, has resulted in new forms of profit-oriented SOEs; collective or collective-private enterprises subordinate to specific R&D institutes.

In sum, there are basically five factors that shape the operations of firms in China's ICT industry: overall economic growth; direct and indirect state intervention; increased foreign investment inflow; development of human capital; and the accumulation of private capital. Each of these factors gives rise to specific incentives and constraints (Table 4.4) that shape the operations of firms in China's ICT industry. The identification of these incentives and constraints and their sources adds to our understanding of the forces with which ICT firms in China have to deal. A case study of a local ERP software firm in Hangzhou based on an in-depth interview shows that the firm met local demand through cooperation and customisation, thereby coping with competition, China's low human capital base and changing institutional requirements. The case thus illustrates how one individual firm managed several constraints and benefited from several incentives.

It would be interesting to explore how firms actually dealt with and used these incentives and constraints. The case study in this chapter is a first exploration but a further structural exploration of the various sectors and firms in the ICT industry would be insightful. Chinese ICT firms must have developed certain competences to deal with the uncertainties of the business environment, use the incentives appropriately and cope with the constraints. The building of relationships with relevant partners (such as the state or a foreign partner) and the development of an appropriate human resource system indicate this. How such competences are built, maintained and used needs to be further explored.

Table 4.4   Incentives and constraints

Factor	Incentives	Constraints
1. Economic growth	Market demand (domestic and foreign); Increased income per capita; Investment opportunities; Upgrading information infrastructure; Being a new industry	Increased competition; Uncertain economic environment
2. State intervention	Promotion of entrepreneurship; New SOEs: => role of governance mechanism; Preferential policies for High-tech industries; Geographic concentration	Direct control over specific sectors; Zones as institutional control devices; Preferential treatment hinders normal market process: => inhibiting risky investments => state-chosen 'innovative' firms
	Indirect intervention in factors 3–5	
3. Human capital development	Strong in engineering and science education; Increased involvement of local governments; Diverse sources of funding; Increase in investments; On the job training: => upgrading both technical and management skills	Limited access higher education; Weak management education; Potential 'brain drain'; Low number of educated personnel
4. Private capital accumulation	Overall growth of private capital; Increased demand and investment; Direction of venture capital to ICT industry	Underdeveloped private capital market: => no regulation with respect to legal and organisational structures => investments over 50% of capitalisation are inhibited => unclear regulation with respect to venture capital
5. Foreign investment inflow	Technology transfer; Capital accumulation; Importing management skills Hong Kong / Taiwan: => learning: technical and management skills => imitation => investment => trade	Competition from foreign firms; Uneven distribution of investments; Possibly inhibiting private sector; Round-tripped foreign investment

NOTES

1. Of the three chosen ICT sectors, telecom operators must negotiate the most state intervention. However, the analysis also deals with telecom equipment producers who deal with far less intervention. The purpose of the analysis is to identify all factors that promote or inhibit growth in all the sectors in the ICT industry. All of the following statistics are derived from China Statistics Yearbook on High Technology Industry (2003) and China Software Industry Association (2003).
2. Besides Nokia, Motorola and Siemens, Alcatel and Ericsson are other foreign investors in telecommunications.
3. 'Foreign PC makers' refers to all non-Mainland Chinese PC makers; even though the PC makers are predominantly from Hong Kong and Taiwan.
4. The East Asian growth economies of South Korea, Taiwan, Hong Kong and Singapore are often referred to as 'tigers'.
5. Even though these aggregate forces also have consequences for individual industries within the economy, such as the ICT industry.
6. One notable exception is the recent IFC (2005) description of the players and the markets, which is highly informative even though it is descriptive in nature.
7. For an informative overview of the early history of China's computer industry, including both software and hardware, see Zhang and Wang (1995). For an overview of China's telecommunications industry see Fan (2006) and Mu and Lee (2005).
8. To some extent this is also a result of the Silicon Valley fever that became prevalent in the 1980s in both developed and developing countries (Wang, Wu, and Li, 1998).
9. Many different forms of ownership co-exist in the zones: state-owned; collectively owned; privately owned; joint-stock; overseas-invested and others. They have in common that 1. they receive a certain favourable treatment from the government, 2. most of them are spin-offs from research institutes or universities and 3. the majority operates in the information technology industry (White, Gao, and Zhang, 2002).
10. Private investment is defined as the difference between total gross domestic investment and consolidated public investment.
11. These data are obtained from the IFC data set 'Trends in Private Investment in Developing Countries:Statistics for 1970–2000' and do not include more recent years.

12. Firm Six interviews were carried out by the author in the Spring of 2006 in Hangzhou, China. Due to our confidentiality agreement, I refer to the firm as 'firm 6'.
13. Enterprise Resource Planning
14. This makes Hangzhou not representative for the rest of China, but does make it a city at the forefront of economic development in China.

REFERENCES

Adams, F. and I. Davis (1994), 'The Role of Policy in Economic Development: Comparisons of the East and Southeast Asian and Latin American Experience', *Asian Pacific Economic Literature*, **8** (1), 8–26.

Aldrich, H.E. and C.M. Fiol (1994), 'Fools rush in? The institutional context of industry creation', *Academy of Management Review*, **19** (4), 645–70.

Batjargal, B. and M. Liu (2004), 'Entrepreneurs' access to private equity in China; the role of social capital', *Organization Science*, **15** (2), 159–72.

Berthelemy, J.-C. and S. Demurger (2000), 'Foreign direct investment and economic growth: Theory and application to China', *Review of Development Economics*, **4** (2), 140–155.

Borensztein, E. and J.D. Ostry (1996), 'Accounting for China's Growth Performance', *American Economic Review*, **86**, 225–228.

Bowman, Micheal J. (1996), 'Training on the job', in Albert Tuijnman (ed.) *International Encyclopaedia of Adult Education and Training*. Oxford: Pergamon, pp. *69–75*.

Brizendine, T. (2002), 'Software Integration in China', *The China Business Review*, **29** (2), 26–31.

Cao, X. (1996), 'Debating "Brain Drain" in the context of globalization' *Compare*, **26** (3), 269–85.

Chang, Gordon G. (2001), *The Coming Collapse of China*, New York, NY: Random House.

Cheng, H. and B. DeLany (1999), 'Quality Education and Social Stratification: The Paradox of Private Schooling in China', *Current Issues in Comparative Education*, **1** (2).

China Software Industry Association (2003), 'Annual Report of China Software Industry', Beijing: China Software Industry Association.

China Statistical Press (2005), *China Statistical Yearbook (2005)*, Beijing: China Statistical Press.

China State Statistical Bureau (2003), *China Statistical Yearbook on High-Technology Industry*, Beijing: State Statistical Bureau.

Chinese Academy of Sciences (2006), 'High-Tech Industry Development', http://english.cas.ac.cn/eng2003/page/T46.asp, 12 April.

Chow, G. (1993) 'Capital Formation and Economic Growth in China', *Quarterly Journal of Economics*, **108**, 809–42.

Chung, C. (1999), 'IT industry in China', Taipei: Chung-Hua Institute for Economic Research.

Chuang, Y.-C. and P.-F. Hsu (2004), 'FDI, trade and spillover efficiency: evidence from China's manufacturing sector', *Applied Economics*, **36**, 1103–1115.

Cooke, F.L. (2002), 'Ownership change and reshaping of employment relations in China: A study of two manufacturing companies', *Journal of Industrial Relations*, **44** (1), 19–39.

Dahlman, C.J. and J.-E. Aubert (2001), 'China and the Knowledge Economy: Seizing the 21st century', Washington, DC: The World Bank Institute Development Studies.

Dahlman, Carl and R.R. Nelson (1995), 'Social Absorption Capability, National Innovation Systems and Economic Development', in Bon Ho Koo and D. Perkins, *Social Capability and Long Term Economic Growth*, Basingstoke: Palgrave Macmillan, pp. 82–122.

Dedrick, Jason and K. Kreamer (1998), *Asia's Computer Challenge: Threat or Opportunity for the US and the World?*, New York, NY: Oxford University Press.

DeWoskin, J.K. (2001), 'The WTO and the Telecommunications Sector in China', *China Quarterly*, **167**, 630–654.

Ding, D.Z., D. Fields and S. Akhtar (1997), 'An empirical study of human resource management policies and practices in foreign-invested enterprises in China: the case of Shenzen Special Economic Zone', *International Journal of Human Resource Management*, **8** (5), 596–613.

Economische Voorlichtingsdienst (2006), 'China', Dutch Ministry of Economic Affairs, http://www.evd.nl/info/landen/land.asp?land=chn, 12 April 2006.

Elek, A. (1994), 'An Open Economic Association in the Asia Pacific: a Conceptual Framework for Asia Pacific Economic Cooperation', Paper Presented to Australian, Indonesia and Japanese Approaches Towards APEC, Australian National University.

Fan, P. (2006), 'Catching up through developing innovation capability: evidence from China's telecom-equipment industry', *Technovation*, **26** (3), 359–368.

Feeser, H.R. and G.E. Willard (1990), 'Founding Strategy and Performance: A Comparison of High and Low Growth High Tech Firms', *Strategic Management Journal*, **11** (2), 87.

Feinstein, Charles and C. Howe (1997), *Chinese Technology Transfer in the 1990s*, Cheltenham: Edward Elgar.

Gabriele, A. (2002), 'S&T policies and technical progress in China's industry', *Review of International Political Economy*, **9** (2), 333–73.

Garnaut, Ross (1990), 'The market and the state in economic development: some questions from East Asia and Australia, The 1990 Shann Memorial Lecture, University of Western Australia', in Muhamed A.B. Siddique (ed.), 1993, *A decade of Shann Memorial lectures and the Australian Economy 1981–90*, Western Australia: Academic Press International.

Gereffi, G. (1999), 'International trade and industrial upgrading in the apparel commodity chain', *Journal of International Economics*, **48**, 37–70.

Graham, E.M., and E. Wada (2001), 'Foreign Direct Investment In China: Effects On Growth And Economic Performance', Working Paper No. 01-03, Institute for International Economics.

Gu, S. (1996), 'The emergence of new technology enterprises in China: A study of endogenous capability building via restructuring', *Journal of Development Studies*, **32** (4), 475–505.

Gu, Shulin (1999), *China's industrial technology: Market reform and organizational Change*, London: Routledge.

Harwitt, E. (2004), 'Spreading Telecommunications to Developing Areas in China: Telephones, the Internet and the Digital Divide', *China Quarterly*, **180**, 1010–1030.

Heckman, J.J. (2005), 'China's human capital investment', *China Economic Review*, **16**, 50–70.

Hendrischke, H. (2004), 'The Role of Social Capital, Networks and Property Rights in China's Privatization process', in B. Krug (ed.), *China's Rational Entrepreneurs: The Development of the New Private Business Sector*, London: RoutledgeCurzon, 97–118.

Hendrischke, H. (2003), 'How local are local enterprises? Privatization and translocality of small firms in Zhejiang and Jiangsu', *Provincial China*, **8** (1).

Hobday, Micheal (1995), *Innovation in East Asia: The challenge to Japan,* Cheltenham: Edward Elgar.

Howe, Christopher, Y.Y. Kueh and R. Ash (2003), *China's Economic Reform: a Study with Documents*, London: RoutledgeCurzon.

Hu, Z.F. and M.S. Khan (1997), 'Why is China Growing So Fast?', *IMF Staff Papers*, **44**, 103–131.

Huang, Yasheng (2003), *Selling China: Foreign Direct Investment during the Reform Era*, New York, NY: Cambridge University Press.

International Data Corporation (2001), 'China Software Market Overview, 2000–2005', Beijing: International Data Corporation.

International Finance Corporation (forthcoming) 'Trends in Private Investment in Developing Countries: Statistics for 1970–2000', Constructed by Stephan Everhart and Mariusz A. Sumlinski. IFC Economics Databases.

International Finance Corporation (2005), 'The ICT Landscape in the PRC: Market Trends and Investment Opportunities', Washington, DC: International Finance Corporation.

Keister, L.A. (2004), 'Capital structure in transition: The transformation of financial strategies in China's emerging economy', *Organization Science*, **15** (2), 145–158.

Kreamer, K. and J. Dedrick (2001), 'Creating a Computer Industry Giant: China's Industrial Policies and Outcomes in the 1990s', Irvine: Center for Research on Information Technology and Organizations.

Krug, Barbara and L. Polos (2004), 'Emerging markets, entrepreneurship and uncertainty', in Barbara Krug (ed.), *China's Rational Entrepreneurs: The development of the new private business sector*, London: RoutledgeCurzon, pp. 72–96.

Krugman, P. (1994), 'The myth of Asia's miracle', *Foreign Affairs*, **73** (6), 62–78.

Lall, S. (1994), 'Industry Policy: the Role of Government in Promoting Industrial and Technological Development', *UNCTAD Review*, Geneva: UNCTAD.

Lau, Chung-Ming, Y. Lu, S. Makino, X. Chen and R. Yeh (2002), 'Knowledge Management of High-Tech Firms' in Anne S. Tsui and C. Lau (eds), *The Management of Enterprises in the People's Republic of China,* Dordrecht: Kluwer, 183–210.

Lardy, N.R. (1995), 'The Role of Foreign Trade and Investment in China's economic transformation', *The China Quarterly*, **144** (December 1995), 1065–1082.

Lemoine, F. (2000), 'FDI and Opening up the Chinese Economy', *CEPII Working Paper 2000–11*, Paris: Centre d'Etudes Prospectives et d'Information Internationale.

Liang, Guoyong (2004), *New competition: foreign direct investment and industrial development in China*, PhD dissertation, Rotterdam: Erasmus University Rotterdam.

Lu, Qiwen (2000), *China's leap into the information age*, Oxford: Oxford University Press.

Meng, Q. and M. Li. (2002), 'New economy and ICT development in China', *Information Economics and Policy*, **14**, 275–95.

Mok, K. (2002), 'Policy of decentralization and changing governance of higher education in Post-Mao China', *Public Administration and Development*, **22**, 261–73.

Mu, Q. and K. Lee (2005), 'Knowledge Diffusion, Market Segmentation and Technological Catch-up: The Case of Telecommunications Industry in China', *Research Policy*, **37** (6), 759–783.

Mytelka, L. (2001), 'Promoting Scientific and Technological Knowledge for Sustainable Development', paper for the Third UN Conference on Least Developed Countries, Round Table: Education for All and Sustainable Development in LDCs, Brussels.

Nee, V. (1992), 'Organizational Dynamics of Market Transition: Hybrid Forms, Property Rights, and Mixed Economy in China', *Administrative Science Quarterly*, 31, 1–27.

People's Daily (2003), 'China's Domestic Private Capital Drives Economy', 12 June, Beijing: People's Daily Online.

People's Daily (2003), 'Private Sector Gets Full Access to 'Restricted Areas'', 9 March, Beijing: People's Daily Online.

People's Daily (2005), 'Private sector in E. China province invests 1.2 bln yuan in state R&D program', 23 November, Beijing: People's Daily Online.

Piek, Hanna (1998), *Technology Development in Rural Industries: A Case Study of China's Collectives*, London: Intermediate Technology Publications.

Qian, Y. (2000), 'The Process of China's Market Transition (1978–1998): The Evolutionary, Historical, and Comparative Perspectives', *Journal of Institutional and Theoretical Economics*, **156** (1), 151–171.

Redding, S. Gordon (1990), *The Spirit of Chinese Capitalism*, Berlin and New York: Walter de Gruyter.

Rodrik, D. (1994), 'Getting interventions right: How South Korea and Taiwan grew rich', *Economic Policy*, **20**, 55–107.

Saxenian, A. & X. Quan (2005) *Government and Guanxi: The Chinese Software Industry in Transition*. In S. Commander The Software Industry in Emerging Markets Cheltenham: Edward Elgar.

Shan, W. (1990), 'An Empirical Analysis of Organizational Strategies by Entrepreneurial High-technology Firms', *Strategic Management Journal*, 11 (2), 129.

Sigurdson, J. (2004), 'Regional Innovation Systems (RIS) in China', Working Paper No. 195, Stockholm: The European Institute for Japanese Studies.

Smith, H. (1995), 'Industry Policy in East Asia: A Literature Review', Working Paper No. 1995/9, Department of International Relations, Canberra ACT Australia: Australian National University.

Stiglitz, J.E. (2003), 'Globalization and growth in emerging markets and the New Economy', *Journal of Policy Modeling*, **25**, 505–524.

Sun, Q., W. Tong and Q. Yu. (2002), 'Determinants of foreign direct investment across China', *Journal of International Money and Finance*, **21** (1), 79–113.

Tenev, Stoyan, C. Zhang and L. Brefort (2002), *Corporate governance and enterprise reform in China*, Washington, D.C: World Bank and the International Finance Corporation.

Tsang, E.W.K. (1994), 'Human resource management problems in Sino-foreign joint ventures', *International Journal of Manpower*, **159** (9–10), 4–21.

Tschang, T. and L. Xue (2003), 'The Chinese Software Industry: a Strategy of creating Products for the Domestic Market', ADB Institute Working Paper.

Tschang, Ted and L. Xue (2005), 'The Chinese Software Industry' in Ashish Arora and A. Gambardella (eds), *From Underdogs to Tigers: The Rise and Growth of the Software Industry in Brazil, China, India, Ireland, and Israel*, Oxford: Oxford University Press, 131–67.

Tsui, A.S., C.B. Schoonhoven, M.W. Meyer, M.W. Lau and G.T. Milkovich (2004), 'Organization and management in the midst of societal transformation: The people's republic of China', *Organization Science*, **15** (2), 133–144.

United Nations (2002), 'Prospect Report of IT Application in Asia', New York, NY: United Nations.

U.S. Embassy (2002), 'An Evaluation of China's Science & Technology System and its Impact on the Research Community', Special Report for the Environment, Science & Technology Section, US Embassy: Beijing, China.

Wang, Jici and M.Y. Wang (2002), 'The Trajectory of the Personal Computer Industry' in Micheal J. Webber, M.Y. Wang and Y. Zhu (eds), *China's Transition to a Global Economy*, Basingstoke: Palgrave, 205–225.

Wang, S., Y. Wu and Y. Li. (1998), 'Development of technopoles in China', *Asia Pacific Viewpoint*, **39** (3), 281–301.

Wang, Y. and Y. Yao (2003), 'Sources of China's economic growth 1952–1999: incorporating human capital accumulation', *China Economic Review*, **14**, 32–52.

White, S., J. Gao and W. Zhang (2002), 'China's Venture Capital Industry: Institutional Trajectories and System Structure', International Conference on Financial Systems, Brussels: Corporate Investment in Innovation and Venture Capital.

World Bank (1996), *Managing capital flows in East Asia*, Washington, DC: World Bank.

World Bank (2006), *World Development Indicators*, http://devdata.worldbank.org/dataonline/, 5 June.

Wu, Y. (2003), 'Has productivity contributed to China's growth?', *Pacific Economic Review*, **8** (1), 15–30.

Xiao, J. and M.C. Tsang (1999), 'Human capital development in an emerging economy: The experience of Shenzhen, China: Research Note', *China Quarterly*, **157**, 72–114.

Xie, G.D. (1994), 'Lifelong education in China: New policies and activities', *International Review of Education*, **40** (3–5), 271–81.

Yang, D., Ghauri, P. and M. Sonmez (2005), 'Competitive Analysis of the Software Industry in China', *International Journal of Technology Management*, **29** (1/2), 64–91.

Yi, Z., Zhang, Z., Men, X. and S. Huang (2004), 'Determinants of structural change to sequential FDI across China: A synthesised approach', *Singapore Management Review*, **26** (1), 63–80.

Yin, Robert K. (1989), *Case Study Research: Design and Methods*, Newbury Park, CA: Sage.

Young, A. (1994), 'Lessons from the East Asian NICS: A contrarian view', *European Economic Review*, **38** (3/4), 964–973.

Yuan, G.Z. and J.S. Gao (1992), 'Programs and Plans for the Development of Science & Technology of China', Beijing: National Defense Industry Press.

Yuntin, Dong (2004), 'The Chinese Experience', in Peter Drysdale (ed.), *The New Economy in East Asia and the Pacific*, London: RoutledgeCurzon.

Zahra, S.A. and J.G. Covin (1993), 'Business strategy, technology policy and firm performance', *Strategic Management Journal*, **14** (6), 451–78.

Zhang, G. and W. Li (2001), 'International Mobility of China's Resources in Science and Technology and its Impact', Paris: OECD.

Zhang, Jeff X. and Y. Wang (1995), *The emerging market of China's computer industry*, London: Quorum Books.

Zhao, H. (1995), 'Technology imports and their impacts on the enhancement of China's indigenous technological capability', *Journal of Development Studies*, **31** (4), 585–602.

5. Enterprise Ground Zero in China

Barbara Krug

5.1 INTRODUCTION

Without private firms there would be no business sector in China. Yet, without entrepreneurs there would be no private firms. Entrepreneurship is also needed when state firms are privatised where new ideas are needed for re-combining productive factors, searching for new products or more efficient techniques.

Yet which kind of economic activities are best organised via competitive firms and which ones are being left to market exchange or state provision does not follow purely 'technical' considerations. Instead aside from investing in an organisational form identifiable as a firm, entrepreneurs also need to invest in organisations or institutions which facilitate private exchange between and among investors, business partners, and government agencies. Neither do entrepreneurs form one social group that can be defined by socio-demographic factors, nor is entrepreneurship an 'exogenous' factor. Entrepreneurs emerge as social agents or economic actors when institutional change rewards risk taking, competence and 'good management' (North, 2005). Part of the required institutional change is political as only the political centre can give up state control over resources and comprehensive regulatory power over economic decision making. Another part of institutional change can be seen in the interaction between government agencies, entrepreneurs and the (emerging) markets. Whether the resulting new forms of organising production and exchange outside state control and beyond the reach of the inherited political elite (state and Party cadres) is regarded as informal or illegal, it is still decided by government agencies. In other words, new institutions that might evolve spontaneously as the outcome of the interaction between markets, entrepreneurs and (local) government agencies, need to fulfil two requirements if they should become a feature of the emerging business system: First, in order to facilitate economic transformation they need to contribute to the expansion of private exchange in order to increase allocative efficiency. Second, they need to align economic and political interests in order to ensure the latter's compliance with organisational innovations at and around the firm level. That allocative efficiency in the form of a functioning price mechanism is a meaningless concept so long as competitive markets are missing is self-evident. Instead economic transformation asks for a dynamic perspective where the move toward more allocative efficiency is assessed by the *expansion of markets*, more precisely the expansion of private, voluntary exchange. Ever since North, institutional change facilitating market development is captured by the concept of transaction costs. It is worth stressing that these transaction costs differ from the Williamson-type in so far as the latter refers to relationship or contract–specific costs in a 'market economy'; while the former reflects weak institutions caused in China by missing private property rights and the co-existence of a socialist sector and (nascent) markets.

These considerations shaped the research, the findings of which will be presented in what follows. First, to analyse the emergence of the new business sector in China, it is necessary to focus on entrepreneurship, while firms are regarded as the outcome of institutional change. Whether it is a new firm, i.e. a greenfield investment, or a privatised firm, in both cases entrepreneurship is needed. Second, analysis of the emergence of a business sector needs to include all economic activities around firms, of which business relations between firms, and the relationship between firms and (local) government agencies are the most crucial. The question *which new institutions and organisations (types of firm) emerged in China caused by which factors and to which effect* calls for a special method. Following Greif (1993), this concept can be called *analytical narrative*. With the help of interviews and life histories of firms we 'generated' a pool of information with respect to new organisations and institutions. In a second step, we used the analytical tool kit as developed by New Institutional Economics to assess whether we can economically explain why these organisations and institutions emerged.

5.2   ON METHODOLOGY

The following can best be described as *analytical narrative* in which interviews provide the raw data for theorising on the emergence of a business sector. The basic question was 'How do economic actors perceive and react to opportunities and restrictions when they embark on "private" production and exchange?' The conceptual frame for the research is provided by the insights of Institutional Economics when we ask about incentives offered and restrictions imposed by formal and informal institutions, as well as the individual solutions for the economic problems around the attempt to establish and operate firms. The term Institutional Economics is chosen as a matter of convenience only and certainly does not do justice to all the approaches which turned out to be useful in explaining the behaviour of Chinese entrepreneurs, such as transaction cost economics, contract and organisational theory, New Institutional Economics in its narrow (North) sense or (a part of) evolutionary economics. What these approaches have in common is that they use behavioural assumptions and concentrate on institutions and their development.

The interviewees are managers and owners who attempted and succeeded in establishing a company. In the last two years, representatives of tax bureaus or the financial departments of local governments were added to the list of interviewees. These *'political entrepreneurs', i.e. those in charge of recombining positive and negative incentives at the political level* (Crouch, 2005) are interviewed to gain more insights into the interaction between the new business and the political sector when it became obvious that this interaction is decisive for the emergence of a business environment at the local level.

Taking into account the size and heterogeneity of China, any attempt to offer general findings must fail. *All analysis based on fieldwork or interviews shows a strong local bias limiting the scope, if not quality, of the findings offered[1].* To avoid this kind of over-generalisation, the 'landscape' needs to be described. The term landscape here stands for the location where the interviews were organised and serves (also) as a proxy for the average income level, or different institutional frames. The landscape as described below defines the explanatory power of our findings, i.e. the scope of generalisation. We regard this as a more rigorous attempt to explain economic behaviour in China as such a procedure invites a comparative study in other parts of the country, and eventually a better empirical base for predicting whether China will end up with one integrated business system.

1. *Interviewees*: The interviews occurred during the period 1998 to 2004. As the research focused on private, domestic firms, those companies which turned out to be a joint venture partner, a State Owned Enterprise (SOE), or otherwise dependent (in an accountancy, or profit recording sense) were later excluded. Likewise, the interviews 2003-2004 with representatives of the local and national tax bureaux were also kept separately. Thus, all in all, the findings rely on 104 interviews with managers and owners, plus 15 (hard to separate) interviews with tax authorities.

2. *Location*: The interviews cover three provinces: Shanxi, Zhejiang and Jiangsu with the latter two clearly dominating. In other words: the features of the emerging business system are based on information from one of the richest regions in China.

3. *Size of firms*: Although the interviews cover a broad variety of firms ranging from a job agency ('head hunter'), consisting of the owner and one secretary, to a machine tool firm employing 1,000 employees, the sample is dominated by 'middle scale' firms, those which employ between 25 and 200 People. To classify the firms according to turnover is (still) a problem. In many cases the interviewees either did not know, or were unwilling to disclose the figure.

4. *Age*: The firms are young, and were predominantly established after the mid-nineties, if the date when they were registered is taken as the starting point. They were on average six years old when the interview occurred. As the life history of the firms reveals however, 'Greenfield investment' is rare and concentrated in 'modern' (IT or service-sector) industries in the two southern provinces. Half of the firms grew out of collective firms such as 'township and village enterprises' (TVEs) or developed from independent companies set up by big state firms (SOEs). As a consequence of mixed information there is an arbitrary element in the classification of firms, more precisely about when to regard a firm as non-state (to keep it in the sample).

5. *Industries*: Unexpectedly, we encountered problems with classifying firms according to sector. Questions about the 'core business' often enough could not be answered. In this situation we learned how many firms work in different, unrelated sectors and do not see many advantages from concentrating on one sector. We took a firms *registered* business as our guide here. Unsurprisingly the light industry sector, such as textile and IT played a prominent role in the two southern provinces, while in Shanxi machine tool manufacturing such as bearings and fittings and transport linked industries (trucks, or tyres) dominated.

We are interested in conceptual problems, namely to what extent can the behaviour of Chinese entrepreneurs be explained by Institutional Economics, and the empirical problem, namely to what extent can the behaviour of Chinese entrepreneurs be explained by 'rational' choice and systematic reactions based on economic responses to a changing institutional environment. Therefore the emphasis is on *common* features, i.e. those that can be found in different localities or industries and which seem to indicate 'salient' features in the three locations where the interviews were organised. As said before, our generalisations reflect our experience in three provinces only. Yet, in a dynamic view, our findings could well go beyond provincial boundaries. It is far more likely that a province such as Jiangsu, one of the richest and most developed provinces, will serve as a benchmark that is more likely to be imitated than a relatively backward province such as Gansu or Jiangxi for example.

The remainder of the chapter is organised as follows: After discussing the specific features of the Chinese economic-political environment, which generates the incentives and constraints for entrepreneurship, our analysis will concentrate on four China-specific responses. First, we look at local embeddedness as a means of (informally) protecting investment and business agreements, and mobilising resources. Second, property rights and performance (crop sharing) contracts are examined as a means of mobilising investment and securing a steady input of social capital. Third, we look at governing social capital via (a) the formal institution of local autonomy and (b) the informal institution of networking. Each section starts with a description of a common feature of entrepreneurship in China, followed by a description of how an economic analysis explains observed behaviour, organisational 'innovation' or change.

As Chinese entrepreneurs often enough define themselves as people searching for solutions in the 'present situation', the first step in our analysis is to describe the business environment as seen from the perspective of entrepreneurs.

5.3 THE EXTERNAL ENVIRONMENT: UNCERTAINTY AND THE NEWNESS OF PRIVATE EXCHANGE

In general terms, institutional change in China can be described by the retreat of the Party-State from economic activities by liberalisation, de-regulation, increased foreign trade and the transfer of state-controlled assets to private actors. So far, the reforms follow the general trend in other transition economies. However, three features make Chinese reform policy unique. First, the Chinese Communist Party still claims to (be able to) steer economic and social development. There was no 'regime change' in 1978. Instead, the reforms reveal a process of incremental change that reflects political bargaining between different layers of government or Party organisations rather than an overall development plan. Second, reform did not start with a constitutional guarantee of private ownership. Instead private property rights appear (in 2004) as a *by-product* of the development of a private business sector. Third, enterprise reform started with decentralisation by which resource control and regulatory powers were transferred to 'local' levels of government.

The discussion about the advantages or disadvantages of the incremental Chinese approach (as opposed to the 'big bang' approach of other transition economies) is far from being concluded. Here it suffices to point out that

Chinese entrepreneurship seriously challenges the claim that only private property rights are able to mobilise the investment and commitment necessary for the emergence of a private business sector. Apparently Chinese entrepreneurs have found ways to compensate for the disincentive of missing property rights[2].

Questions about the external environment in interviews with entrepreneurs revealed a number of trends:

1. The institutional environment is not judged by national legislation but by a whole set of laws, both national and local. Moreover, the institutional environment is not judged by proclamations or stipulations but by what is enforced. The overall picture given is one of an environment where regulations differ, change quickly and in unforeseen ways, where informal ways supplement or contradict formal regulations, in short, where the institutional environment differs over time and across the country. Consequently, entrepreneurs will not act as 'institution-takers' (in the sense of price-takers): they will not invest in strategies that help to optimise their response to any given constraint. Instead, it is assumed that the success of entrepreneurship depends on securing information about differences in and changes of regulations (and prices) *ahead of others*. To put it polemically, it is a competition for insider information reflecting the high information rent individual actors can appropriate.

2. Despite a remarkable confidence in the future of reform, entrepreneurs acknowledge political risks. Although entrepreneurs and firms – unlike peasants – seem to be protected against blatant confiscation of assets, they still reckon with indirect forms of confiscation, such as compulsory mergers with (loss-making) collective or state firms or the expropriation of their cash flow by local tax bureaus or individual 'stake holders'. It is the *ad hoc* nature of this kind of state intervention that is perceived as being 'against the rules'. Bad administration is at fault, if not corruption, or regulation as such. Consequently, the success of entrepreneurship is seen as depending on finding ways to protect not only the value of (private) assets but also the operation and expansion of the firm (for a descriptive analysis of the same phenomenon in Russia see Frye, 2002; Shleifer, 1998).

3. Surprisingly the respondents felt much less limited by scarcity of resources, such as technology or infrastructure than the picture on the aggregate level would suggest. This was even the case in Shanxi, which at the time of the interviews lagged significantly behind the national average. Moreover, even when scarcity is mentioned, such as the lack of (venture) capital, managerial talent, or a skilled workforce for a

modern service industry, the reaction is different from what one would expect. Instead of investing in substitutes or alternative courses of action, the reaction is to invest in 'knowing the right people', that is *social capital*. So long as a still huge national and local bureaucracy or other groups control resources such as much needed financial capital, land, or export-licences, shortage appears as a distribution problem. Therefore, 'who you know', or *guanxi* is a very valuable asset. The success of entrepreneurship is therefore linked to being 'networked' and further investing in new networks.

An economic analysis of the external environment – in particular transaction cost and New Institutional economics – allows us to conceptualise the problem: procedural uncertainty caused by the 'newness' of private business operations and the ongoing co-existence of a socialist and market sector. That there is no general knowledge about (excess) demand, price, or income elasticity of demand, let alone systematic research that would help an entrepreneur to calculate the risk of his venture, is no surprise in such circumstances. Yet, the uncertainty in China refers to a much broader set of features, connected with the newness of new business relations (Krug and Polos, 2004).

There is a low general level of expertise in the society at large. There is nobody to imitate, no procedure to copy, expertise cannot be easily learned, and neither can it be bought. In short, it is the newness of an organisational form, such as a private firm that poses the challenge for its founders. The newness implies further, that there is no collective memory about what can go wrong, as there is no past experience for reference. In such a situation, new organisations need to rely on general skills produced outside the organisation such as formal education, or the Party *nomenklatura* system, at least until investment in organisation specific training pays off (Nee, 2000). Second, new organisations need to invent roles and role relations (for new work profiles and new professions), rewards and sanctions, for which no blueprint is available. Third, the new organisations need to build up business and social relations among 'strangers' in the factor and product markets. In sum, the need to compensate for such uncertainties deprives young organisational forms of private entrepreneurship. This in turn lowers their survival chances, if it does not hinder more risk-averse entrepreneurs to start a business at all.

The usual way economies and societies deal with behavioural uncertainty is by creating institutions and organisations that 'streamline' behaviour, by monitoring and sanctioning, or condoning it. In the West, business practices for example depend on contracts, private property rights, the rule of law, the notion of liability and compensation, and the consensus that innovation should be rewarded. In a dynamic view the effect is the following:

> Institutional environments that provide general purpose safe guards relieve the need for added transaction-specific support. Accordingly, transactions that are viable in an institutional environment that provides strong safeguards may be non-viable in institutional environments that are weak - because it is not cost-effective for parties to craft transaction-specific governance in the latter circumstances (Williamson, 1993: 476).

Institutional weakness in the Chinese context means that national legislation and national reform policies work as occasional blueprints only to the extent that they are (rarely) sanctioned effectively enough. Monitoring is infrequent and irregular contributing to rather than mitigating uncertainty (Stark, 1996). To the extent that China is lacking these safeguards, procedural uncertainty translates into risk for which an appropriate premium needs to be calculated. In such a situation, economic agents have a strong incentive to search for (institutional) solutions, which are more advantageous (for at least some of them). While to change the overall framework is mostly outside the control of individual agents and rather depends on the functioning of the political market, the governance of individual transactions (private exchange) is not.

From an economic perspective this explains why Chinese entrepreneurs invest in social capital or good connections with local government agencies. *Social capital, more precisely to find and connect with people in control of scarce resources and valuable information, offers high returns when compared to other forms of capital*[3]. An economic analysis then, further expects that economic actors search for ways that safeguard or improve the functioning of 'social capital'. In order to function, governance structures should not be in conflict, they should offer a 'code' whose violation is connected to a specific sanctioning mechanism. The less economic agents violate the code and the less codes get violated the higher the level of regularity, and predictability. Thus one aspect of entrepreneurship in China can be defined as follows: *entrepreneurship refers to the ability to establish organisations and institutions that can identify and monitor key areas of 'procedural uncertainty' and to search for governance structures and routines which can efficiently cope with the variance in behaviour of local government agencies or potential business partners.*

5.4 ALERTNESS: DETECTING BUSINESS OPPORTUNITIES IN TRANSITION ECONOMIES

Two common features emerge from the interviews. First, entrepreneurship is best characterised by *alertness* (Kirzner, 1985). In market economies, alertness usually refers to radical technical innovation or global change. Successful entrepreneurship therefore, refers to someone 'alert' enough to see where by 'recombining' existing productive forces in a novel way, or identifying options, and (so far) underused resources net returns can be increased (Kirzner, 1985; Schoonhoven and Romanellu, 2001; Teece and Pisano, 1994). In contrast, in transition economies, 'anything sells' at the beginning of the reforms where the situation is still best described as an instance of Kornai's shortage economy (Kornai, 1980). Meticulous searches for novel products is as unnecessary as novel technical innovation so long as market competition is weak. Undoubtedly, this shortage of goods and a comfortable sellers' market position offer a strong incentive to establish firms, i.e. organisations able to produce larger quantities at lower costs than an individual (or small household) could accomplish. Entrepreneurship in this case is less focused on handling market information. Instead firms need to organise inter-firm relations and market-supporting industries and professions. Yet, first of all the political framework needs to design and safeguard institutions which mobilise and safeguard private investment, while rewarding market-conforming human capital.

The literature on entrepreneurship is, of course, not unaware of the link between technical and intra-industry innovation and organisational, or institutional change (Granovetter, 1985; Aldrich and Fiol, 1994). Whether linked to the nation state (national innovation systems: Nelson, 1992), society at large (legitimation: DiMaggio and Powell, 1983; Scott and Meyer, 1992), or in the form of industrial districts, organisational communities (Aldrich, 1999), and networks (Nooteboom, 1999a), all approaches stress the institutional context in which entrepreneurship operates. Thus, there is a consensus that the socio-political environment provides business opportunities in the form of positive incentives and available resources, and limits business opportunities by setting defaults for normative (DiMaggio and Powell, 1983; Aldrich, 1999) or cognitive (Witt, 2000) reasons.

From this perspective, *entrepreneurship refers to the ability to establish organisations that can identify and monitor key resources of 'volatility' and search for governance structures and routines which can efficiently cope with external shocks or the variance in behaviour of potential business partners or government agencies* (see also Casson, 2005: 335). Indeed, as the following will show, entrepreneurs in China purposefully search for such governance structures.

5.5   ENTREPRENEURSHIP AND CORPORATE GOVERNANCE

Seen from the point of view of entrepreneurs, the establishment of firms turns into a search for efficient *corporate governance*. With no blueprint available, it cannot come as a surprise that the emergence of a private business system is accompanied by experimentation and a great number of failures. As the enterprise life histories reveal, these failures remain invisible and outside the statistics. This is because most of them result in a quick recombination of assets, a change of product line, or disappearance in a 'merger' with another company[4]. Despite the high variety of firms and their quick change of organisational form, four common features can be singled out which characterise the existing firms (and the concerns of managers about how to proceed in the future):

1. *Ownership.* Regardless of whether non-state firms have originated in TVEs, SOE spin-offs, academic institutions, or greenfield investments, collective entrepreneurship is caused by the need to bundle resources, in particular social capital and managerial talent, rather than individual entrepreneurship reflecting product or technical innovation. Claims to ownership are negotiated and are not limited to fixed investment at the time of the firm's establishment. Claims to ownership acknowledge social capital and an ongoing commitment once the firm has started operating. Usually firms are regarded as being 'owned' by friends, local government agencies, or networks. *In the start-up period ownership takes the form of non-contested control rights*, while income from ownership remains non-monetary and takes the form of perks, such as use of a company car, subsidised housing or banqueting.

2. *Corporate assets.* Linked to the composition of owners is the definition of corporate assets. In contrast to Western firms, corporate assets in China are not restricted to physical and financial assets (or human capital in the form of patents). *Social capital is regarded as a major, if not the single most crucial corporate asset.* Likewise, corporate assets are not limited to fixed investments but acknowledge ongoing contributions, in particular in the form of managerial talent, political assistance in the form of favourable regulation and taxation, and the sharing of knowledge.

3. *Empowerment and routinisation.* The interviews show further that *incorporating a firm is seen as a means to empower the firm, i.e. to turn the firm into a corporate actor*, which as a legal person becomes the nominal owner of corporate assets and can conclude contracts. Incorporating a firm is also a way to routinise claims to ownership,

which no longer need to be negotiated on an *ad hoc* basis. Finally, incorporating a firm serves the purpose of defining collaterals in order to get access to bank loans. A new trend in the prosperous region in Jiangsu and Zhejiang suggests further forms of routinisation in areas of economic activities still based on informal, social mechanism. One examples is the emergence of 'advisory committees' around firms that ensure that individuals with scarce knowledge or valuable connections can be bound to the firm in a more regular way.

4.   *Boundaries of the firm.* The firms of the interviewed respondents almost all reveal a weak organisational identity. Exceptions were those supplier firms which relied on long term contracts with one company, usually a SOE, such as China Telecom, or a foreign firm. Chinese owners can rarely be regarded as principals of a firm. Ownership shares are a weak predictor of control rights. Firms can also not easily be identified by a core business or sector. As the life histories and ownership compositions reveal, firms are mostly part of a network which via cross-shareholding, long term contracts or merely personnel connections controls several companies in a multitude of industries. To put it differently: networks act often as 'holdings' of multi-market firms, when they choose discrete governance structures for their assets, by establishing independent firms. Although empirical data are missing, there is enough anecdotal evidence not to consider this feature as a local or a transitory phenomenon. *Instead, network by using economic and social mechanism delineate the opportunity set of a firm's economic activities, define corporate assets and therefore ultimately the boundaries of the firm.*

How can one explain the underlying processes, which resulted in the common features as described so far? China's entrepreneurs reacted to the high level of uncertainty and the newness of private business relations in three ways. First, they opted for 'local embeddedness'. Second, they employ incentive contracts as a way to mobilise investment and ongoing commitments. Third, Chinese entrepreneurs opt for an organisational form which allows them to align their social and commercial interests. They enforce business relations in order to harness the value of investment and the value of business relations.

5.5.1   Local Embeddedness

The Chinese reforms started with a large scale decentralisation by which the villages became 'owners' of land. This was to be followed (in the 1990s) by a widespread transfer of physical assets and regulatory power to local (village, county and district) administrative units. Yet, to argue that entrepreneurs in China merely reacted to this is short-sighted. Entrepreneurs regard a locality not merely as a 'bundle of regulatory constraints and ad hoc state intervention'.

Subsequently, from the point of view of entrepreneurs local embeddedness refers to more than the decision to establish a company at one's birthplace. Entrepreneurs do not even regard their birthplace as the resource base of first choice. Instead they will choose that locality that offers a 'hospitable environment', i.e. one with which they are familiar. In such a locality they will:

- Take the local labour market as a given and provide workplaces for the community by relying on a technology by which the greatest number of local labour can be employed;
- Raise capital from 'local' friends or via local institutions and decide on a product that can be sold in the local market or via local distribution channels;
- Search for business information for better functioning in the local market or via local channels;
- Yet they do not feel obliged to limit the scope and scale of their economic activities to the local base. They will leave the local nexus via new investment in new subsidiaries or cross shareholding in other companies (including foreign firms) elsewhere while keeping the 'headquarter' at the place of origin. They will do so when new business opportunities or a more favourable tax and regulatory regime arise elsewhere, or when the local resources base is exhausted;
- Local embeddedness seems to matter less for the younger generation of entrepreneurs, i.e. those who started a business from the end of the nineties onwards. Entrepreneurs made use of markets or market conforming institutions when this became a viable option. Thus, for example when bank loans became available to private firms, entrepreneurs started investing in collateral needed for loans instead of further investing in good relations with representatives of local government agencies in control of 'investment funds'.

In an economic analysis local communities are regarded as the primary social group for collective (political or economic) decision making. How and why they exist is not at the core of this analysis. The question is rather why local communities survive as economic actors and whether they contribute to the performance (or survival) of firms. There is a broad consensus in the economic, sociological and management studies literature that local communities are the social capital producer 'of last resort' generating a valuable asset often enough preceding the generation of financial or human capital; and often enough effective enough to function as a surrogate for absent or ill-functioning markets (Greif, 1993, 1998; Tilly, 2001). The fact that the social capital that local (or ethnic) communities employ is often sufficient for mobilising private exchange beyond a village boundaries – but still embedded in a local (ethnic) group before and without private property rights are established – suggests that local embeddedness is a remnant of history or a phenomenon connected with the 'less' developed world (literature review in Alesina, 2002). Only recently did local communities (re) gain prominence in connection with the debate on multi-layered government (in the EU, see Crouch, 2005), the Comparative Business System literature (Whitley et al., 1996; Whitley, 1999; Hollingworth et al., 1994) and within the literature on networks and local embeddedness (the classic article is Granovetter, 1993, see also review in Uzzi, 1996 and Borgatti and Foster, 2003). It is the last stream of literature which is of interest here. In general *local embeddedness refers to the process by which social relations as structured by a locality shape economic actions.* Though local embeddedness is not a concept that allows the formulation of refutable propositions (Williamson, 1994) it nevertheless draws attention to specific features in economic behaviour. Despite all differences, there is a broad consensus that local embeddedness offers transaction cost advantages. Whether called identity, familiarity or referred to as a sharing of cultural values, local communities are characterised by a low level of opportunism. Yet, there is no 'blind' trust. Beside monitoring and enforcing economic activities, local communities employ enforcement mechanisms for streamlining and standardising economic behaviour. Local communities are self-enforcing organisations to the extent that information impactedness, proximity, reputation and social mechanisms ensure reliability and predictability in private exchange. Trust will contribute to the performance of firms when it facilitates investment and commitment (Nooteboom et al., 1997). The transaction cost advantage in this case is a response to the situation-specific problem of China, namely procedural uncertainty (and liability of newness) (for Russia see Batjargal, 2003; see also Alesina and La Ferra, 2004).

The interviews confirm the findings in the literature: Chinese entrepreneurs react to locally induced transaction cost advantages and employ local embeddedness as a means to overcome the problem of uncertainty and liability of newness. That entrepreneurs are indeed aware of the transaction cost advantage of their home county can be seen in the fact that individuals often enough started being entrepreneurial by going to the big cities to earn cash, to be saved and used as start-up capital back in their hometown. The fact that Chinese entrepreneurship is geographically widespread, and covers rural areas finds it explanation in the transaction costs differential between place of origin and unknown or unfamiliar places.

That at the beginning of economic transformation entrepreneurs need to pool financial resources is self-evident, less attention is however paid to the need to generate and acquire knowledge and business information in order to increase a firm's chances of survival. In the sellers' market situation and at the beginning of the reform neither relative prices, changes in demand, let alone 'exit' of marginal producers are reliable predictors for the relative market position of a firm. As was shown elsewhere (Geertz, 1978) in such a situation of imperfect markets and asymmetric information, bargaining and exchanging information is an effective means to gain valuable business information on both the customer and producer side. Thus, to start a firm within the confines of a locality is a transaction cost mitigating device.

The interviews finally reveal that local embeddedness does not forestall networking beyond the local nexus, or become market coordination. In general, efficient networking does necessitate flexibly switching from strong to weak ties (Granovetter, 1985) to find efficient governance systems for coordinating network activities. Before this point is taken up, the economic activities that are not co-ordinated by social relations but by contracts need to be identified and explained.

5.5.2   Incentive Contracts

The interviews show that incentive (crop sharing) contracts are employed to:

- Reward scarce managerial talent;
- Mobilise capital including social capital around one firm;
- Align the interests of local government agencies with the interest of a firm.

We also learned that:

- The Contract Law from 1994 forces economic actors to employ standardised contracts. These however are regarded as a 'soft' enforcement device only. Accompanying *oral* business agreements on the other hand are regarded as binding;
- 'Trust' and contracts supplement each other. While trust-based social relations are not regarded as a substitute for business agreements, one would not embark on a business relationship with somebody one does not trust;
- Business agreements are regarded as constituting long term relations. Agreements are automatically prolonged so long as no business partner

objects. Conflicts are solved by renegotiation between partners and with the help of a trusted third party from the home base (Jacobs et al., 2004).

Incentive contracts first re-appeared in China when the TVEs transferred 'economic responsibility' to the managers of inherited collective firms. It is worth stressing that 'crop sharing' has been practiced for centuries in the Chinese agricultural sector (Cheung, 1969a). As such, villages (or government agencies) act as leasers and (new) managers as lessees. The contract knows one performance–independent part, i.e. a fixed salary (or rent) and one performance–dependent part. Both partners negotiate the value of the performance–independent part and the sharing parameter of the innovation rent (and risk) (Krug, 1997; Li and Rozelle, 2003; Dong et al., 2002, 2004). As was shown elsewhere (Cheung, 1969; Stiglitz, 1974) the sharing parameter allocates risk. When for example the manager can claim more than 50 per cent then he gets more than the half of profit, yet also has to carry the burden in case of losses. The sharing parameter at the same time also allocates the innovation rent. In the example given above the manager would get more than a half of the profit that can be attributed to product, process or organisational innovation.

With villages being risk-averse or under-estimating the potential for innovation at the inherited technological level, these contracts were crucial for generating the first 'affluent class' in China (Goodman, 1994). As the interviews further reveal, not least for tapping the household savings of managers and binding them to the firm, managers were encouraged in a second step to convert their performance-depending part of income into 'options' for ownership shares. At the latest, when the firms got incorporated managers could call on their options and if needed raise additional money to acquire 50 or more per cent of the company. These stories are supported by other fieldwork allowing the conclusion that this kind of management-buy-out is the dominant form of privatising TVEs – and might explain the above average economic performance of the TVEs, at a time when they were still officially registered as a collective (i.e. state controlled) firm (see overview in Li, 2005). Moreover, this kind of incentive contract is also widely used in SOEs when they want to privatise part of their production range and amongst private entrepreneurs when they want to secure the long term commitment of a manager.

A special form of an unwritten crop-sharing agreement is the way in which the new corporate governance acknowledges the different kinds of capital, crucial for the establishment and operation of a firm, namely financial, human and social capital. To secure the ongoing collaboration of those in control of scarce (market or political) information, valuable business contacts, or technical knowledge incentive agreements are designed to acknowledge a claim of ownership. Without immediately binding contracts the owners of social capital, as quasi-owners, can rely on compensation in the form of 'dividends' (or access to the cash flow of a firm). Unsurprisingly, the effect of such incentives is high intra-firm consumption, if not corruption which often enough threatens the liquidity of the firm (Shleifer and Vishny, 1993; Shleifer, 1998). Using firms as cash cows is not an uncommon phenomenon in China. Yet, to dismiss this as an indicator of corruption is to miss the point (for example Li, 2005); what matters is that a governance structure is chosen which puts a high premium on the organisational innovation of managers, so helping to transfer ownership to those who have proven to be competent.

As information, resources, and knowledge are still linked to official positions in the Party and other administrative systems, it cannot come as a surprise when firms 'offer' incentive contracts to government agencies or individuals, thus making no difference between an individual, institutional, or public 'shareholder'. The Chinese development of corporate governance serves as a warning not to dismiss 'public' ownership as a political phenomenon too quickly, or to regard such ownership as a constraint which limits a firms in its competitive behaviour.

In short, in an economic analysis, the use of contracts cannot come as a surprise. *Crop sharing contracts are a powerful institution as they offer incentives to innovate while spreading the risk* (Cheung, 1969; Stiglitz, 1974). The difference to the standard analysis is that in China contracting is less transaction-specific than responding to the high transaction cost generated by the procedural uncertainty and liability of newness. Thus, the economic analysis would expect that the sharing parameter as well as the relative weight of the performance independent part of the salary (or income) will reflect different degrees of uncertainty (and risk) in different parts of China.

Contracts are employed for mobilising capital, and for aligning interests between the business partners. This is in sharp contrast to that literature (for example Williamson, 1994) where contracts are an *ex post* device for limiting opportunism, yet more in line with the literature on 'hybrids' (Powell, 1990) which also stresses the aspect of co-operation rents and aligning of interests. Once more the form of 'contracting' reflects the external environment. Whether contracts are embedded in (local) networks, markets or a national judiciary seems also to follow transaction cost considerations. The interviews reveal that legal enforcement is dismissed by almost all entrepreneurs as being too costly, and often counterproductive to the environment of trust on which effective networking depends. Market discipline as a way to secure contract compliance on the other hand, is seen as a valuable alternative to the effect that most entrepreneurs regret that markets are still not functioning well enough. In short, Chinese entrepreneurs carefully compare the use of the market, the judiciary and (local) networks and will embed the business agreement in that organisational form that offers enforcement most effectively or at lowest cost.

5.5.3 The Governance of Social Capital

So far it has been shown that entrepreneurs attempt to turn social capital into a corporate asset by offering private property rights or incentive contracts to those in control of 'good connections', information, competence or regulatory power. The entrepreneurs further start by choosing the place that offers a lower level of procedural uncertainty thanks to proximity, familiarity, and social sanctioning mechanisms. Such a niche-strategy must limit scope and scale of entrepreneurship once local resources are exhausted. Thus, as mentioned before entrepreneurship in a dynamic view needs to establish *organisations and institutions that can identify and monitor key areas of 'procedural uncertainty'* and to search for *governance structures and routines which can efficiently cope with the variance in behaviour of local government agencies or potential business partners.*

Unlike the literature's claim that family (objected to already by Pistrui et al., 1999) or culture (in the form of *guanxi*, see for example Park and Luo, 2001; Peng and Luo, 2000; Peng, M., 2001; Peng, Y., 2004) is the backbone of entrepreneurship in China, the interviewees refer to two other institutions both of which offer a broader resource base and superior governance regime: local autonomy and networking.

5.5.4 Local Autonomy

The reforms, i.e. the liberalisation of markets and accompanying de-regulations only partly succeeded in de-bureaucratising the economy (Nee, 2000). Entrepreneurs and firms are still restricted by (too) many regulations and the need to negotiate with local government. It needs to be stressed that only by interviewing entrepreneurs did we learn about the institution of tax contracts which are negotiated between economic actors and government officials. As later interviews with representatives of the tax administration and financial departments of local government agencies confirmed, the Chinese version of *tax farming* refers *to tax contracts between the lower and higher level of government agencies, and between economic actors and local government agencies.* Tax farming (see Chapter 6) makes local governments the claimant of marginal tax revenue. After the local administrative units have fulfilled their obligation to transfer tax revenue to the national coffers and higher administrative units, they can keep (a part of) 'surplus' tax revenue. In other words local governments directly profit from increasing income in their jurisdiction. Therefore they have an interest in accommodating the needs and demands of entrepreneurs.

Another rather unusual feature of the Chinese financial system is the mix between formal rules and informal negotiation. Both together constitute 'local autonomy' whose economic interpretation follows the summary of our talks as seen from the perspective of entrepreneurs or the emerging business community:

- Institutional change as formulated at the national level appears in different forms of local government. In each case, local governments claim to follow national legislation or directives, but implementation, with very few exceptions, is locally formulated. Further, with the exception of national tax administration, economic actors seldom deal directly with representatives of the central state. Instead under the specific Chinese system of so-called dual leadership, local governments are asked to implement national legislation according to local circumstances, for which purpose they coordinate their local policies with higher administrative levels, such as counties, districts, prefectures and provinces. As a result, there is no 'state' or even 'local state' as such. Instead economic actors deal with a variety of local governments all referring back to central policies for their legitimisation, but differentiated in their policies along horizontal and vertical lines.
- Which 'local state' forms the nexus of bureaucratic regulation depends on the location of firms rather then registration. Firms can be registered at the township, county, district or provincial level, depending on local industrial settlement policies and sometimes the size of firms. Yet, in the end it is the physical site of the firm which determines the level of government acting as 'local state'. Generally speaking enterprises in rural areas are tied to a township, enterprises in urban areas are tied to a city district.
- Decentralisation not only transferred regulatory power 'downwards', the tax farming system further offers the financial means to execute local policy. By making tax authority partially negotiable among levels of local government, but also between local government agencies and the business community, and conferring dominant 'land ownership rights' to local governments, contributed not only to the geographical inequality of income differences but also to the emergence of different business environments. In particular local governments in regions that experienced increasing land prices grew out of central budgetary control and can afford to lower overall taxes (and fees), while local

government agencies in the *hinterland* relying (again) on financial transfers from the centre have less leeway to design an industrial policy – according to local conditions (see Chapter 6).

- Local policy formulation, from the perspective of entrepreneurs, can be seen in industrial settlements, regulations, taxation (and subsidisation), and in investment in complementary infrastructure and land management.
- Local financial incentives to enterprises are offered as a mix of formal and informal incentives. Only by including the informal side of taxation and subsidisation does one learn that entrepreneurs are responsive to specific taxes or tax rates. Formal tax rates by themselves remain ineffective as an allocative or sanctioning mechanism since entrepreneurs bargain for the (minimum) overall tax burden corrected by the value of appropriable subsidies, favourable land lease contracts (or land prices), or quicker access to valuable information or other bureaucratically controlled input.
- That firms are tied to a local jurisdiction does not imply that they are immobile. They can and will move out and establish subsidiaries (or invest in other firms) in other locations. They can also invest in other industries that offer lower taxation and less regulation.

It is hard to find another case that resembles the Chinese form of political and financial decentralisation. In particular the co-existence of a national tax system based on national legislation and implemented by national bureaucracy, and tax-farming linked to (different) layers of government unsupported by legislation that separates the tax base and mandatory tasks is rather unique. The economic analysis on Fiscal Federalism was therefore an eye-opener for those who (still) modelled the Chinese state as a black box, assuming that the central leadership controls everything. Particularly insightful and confirmed by later developments is Qian (Qian et al., 1995) who demonstrates the extent to which Chinese style federalism has shaped the privatisation of assets and introduced the notion of jurisdictional competition, which outlines these structures for the very early stages of privatisation.

The general literature on Chinese central – local relations either neglects the interaction between different layers of local governments (Wong, 1991; Wong et al., 1995), or argues for a 'corporatist' model (Walder, 1995; Oi, 1995). Neither explains how the (new) interaction between entrepreneurs and political agents functions, nor allows for a dynamic view.

The interviews suggest modelling the interaction between entrepreneurs and local government agencies as local autonomy. Indeed, following Greif (1993) this interaction can be regarded as a *constrained co-operation game* between local government agencies and managers (entrepreneurs) as those two groups, which control the resource base of a locality. Both share an interest in growing the local resource base, as each benefits from overall growth. Therefore both groups have an incentive to co-operate. Entrepreneurs can convert their 'demand' for asset protection, contractual security, valuable business information or favourable taxation and public investment or corporate governance into a corresponding supply at low costs. In return local government agencies can expect tax revenues and tax compliance. The co-operation is however constrained by the incentive to increase the share of the co-operation rent for each of the two groups to the detriment of the other. Entrepreneurs can move taxable activities outside the local jurisdiction, while local government agencies can invent new taxes, fees, or land prices. The tax farming system in an economic interpretation is then the means to flexibly and frequently re-negotiate the sharing of state-private co-operation, while jurisdictional competition forces both to search for effective policies which ensure the competitiveness of the locality. Local autonomy depends on a 'weak' central state, a condition certainly met in China's economic and financial sector (Wong, 1991; World Bank, 1995, Brean, 1998). Nevertheless, both partners can mobilise support 'from above' in the negotiation game. Local government agencies can ask higher administrative levels for additional regulation; entrepreneurs can use networks which go beyond the local nexus for promoting their interests.

In short, Chinese entrepreneurs identified key areas of procedural uncertainty in local (rather then national) jurisdiction. They contribute, if not insist on a mode of governance, i.e. tax farming contracts between individual tax payer and local government agencies, by which both partners can align their interest and better cope with the business and political risks in the external environment.

It is worth mentioning that this economic interpretation is a step in the direction of modelling local autonomy, formulating refutable hypotheses, embarking on a comparative analysis – and thereby increasing the explanatory power of the concept while better coping with China's heterogeneity.

The second new institution, and the one dominating business relations in China is networking. Though often enough overlapping, this is different from local autonomy. First, networks may but do not necessarily, include representatives of the (local) state. Second, social capital generated at the local level and manifest in a predictable business environment is non-transferable, while networks are an institution that allows entrepreneurs to embark on and govern inter-firm relations irrespective of the original local nexus.

5.5.5 Networking

From the point of view of Chinese entrepreneurs, networks and networking are as ubiquitous as they are elusive. Networking is a way of doing business that is seldom questioned and whose functioning remains unscrutinised. It is rather by listening to Chinese entrepreneurs talking amongst themselves that one can learn the specificities. This can be cautiously summarised as follows (an insightful analysis of this is offered in Chapter 8):

1. Without networking nothing gets done. Networking is seen as a requirement for better coping with both the bureaucracy and the market. The claim that networking makes the market work more efficiently points less to cultural values but to the information problem (asymmetric information) nascent markets are still characterised by.
2. Networks are not clubs (or guilds). There is no fixed number of members nor is the identity of all members necessarily known. Networks can also not be defined by what they 'produce' or by their location. Entrepreneurs are not worried about the lack of organisational form, nor do they regard networks as being at the core of corruption *per se*. Instead they point to the effectiveness of networks which generate mobility by overcoming the fragmented markets of local jurisdictions.
3. Yet in most, if not all, cases do networks form the backbone of a firm which becomes visible at *vital events* such as the liquidation of a firm, mergers and acquisitions, linking up to foreign companies, the incorporation of a firm, or use of net profits. A network member seems to be somebody whose claim to participate in the decision making process is left uncontested.
4. The functioning of networks is not restricted to co-ordinating business relations. Instead, networks offer a platform for sharing hard to exchange knowledge, for learning what can go wrong and what 'good practices' are, and for agreeing on certain routines. The effectiveness of such meetings has to be seen in context of the 'liability of newness' which turns entrepreneurship and management into a 'craft' to be learned by experience.
5. The governance of networks remains unscrutinised by most network members. To ensure compliance, entrepreneurs refer to the need to build up and maintain a reputation for being honest and competent since the network can de-activate all business relations with the non-complying member, and exclude them from useful knowledge sharing, if not ostracise them (or their family).

In short, networks are an elusive organisational form whose origin, functioning, and economic consequences have led to a lively debate in the 1990s with a quickly mushrooming literature (see the impressive overview in Borgatti and Foster, 2003). Simultaneously, the argument that networks are steered by cultural norms and that their economic behaviour deviates from (rational) behaviour gained momentum yet was mainly restricted to cultural studies and the management literature (Lui, 1996; Luo, 1997; Tong and Yong, 1998; Tsang, 1998; Lovett et al., 1999; Park and Luo, 2001; Peng, 2004).

In an economic analysis whether the network originates in cultural values (or not) matters less then its functional value and in its ability to shape economic behaviour. In the Chinese version, networks are a social mechanism for co-ordinating economic activities in which *mutual trust, affinity, norms of reciprocity and reputation limit moral hazard* (Jacobs, et.al., 2004; Redding, 1996; Hendrischke, 2004; Bian, 2001; Yang, 1994, 2002). Networks emerge when economic actors individually or by collective consensus opt to use this form of social mechanism. Though primary groups, such as the family, classmates, colleagues or friends, form the hard core of networks the scale and scope of the networks is not limited to a predefined pool of trustworthy and likeable people. To change from one business relation or from one network to another is seen as neither a breach of contract nor a breach of loyalty. Subsequently, the sanctions for doing so remain low. When a business relationship no longer offers expected returns, it is 'de-activated' but not ended in the sense that both partners remain socially connected as friends, colleagues, or family members. If enough individual actors do so then a network stops functioning as a mechanism for co-ordinating economic activities, yet retains its social functions. Likewise, entry to a network works via social acceptance as trustworthy and competent, judged by the fact that an outsider is doing business with one network member.

In an economic interpretation, individual economic actors will embark on networking when they expect it to produce 'comparative advantages' which they can appropriate or at least consume. In this sense a network functions like a 'collective good', which can best be described as a reduction of the relational risk in business deals. Therefore, networks, like contracting, contribute to the emergence of markets when thanks to a lower premium for relational risk, prices confer better or more market information such as scarcity, marginal costs or quality (Batjargal and Liu, 2002; Bengt, 1988; Lechner and Dowling, 2003). In a dynamic interpretation two other features stand out: First, underperforming networks are not driven out of the market. Instead, they turn into *dormant* (Kuilman, 2005) organisational forms, whose social capital or other assets can be re-activated (at low cost) should relative prices and rates of return change. Second, networks are subject to *diffused competition* (Hannan and Carroll, 1992), i.e. less steered by changes in prices (or marginal costs) of producers than by changes in attention or interest on the demand side.

The effectiveness of a network is therefore ensured by competition, reputation of a network, the fact that one network member vouches for any new one, and the repertoire of social mechanisms by which networks can sanction moral hazard. As in the case of local autonomy, *networks are seen as an institutional solution for identifying key areas of procedural uncertainty, namely ill-functioning markets and weak national legislation while offering a mode of governance, i.e. reciprocity, enforced by network sanctioning, for better coping with the business and political risks in the external environment.*

In general, economic actors in China (or any other transition economy) face the choice of either doing something alone, *embarking on economic activities together with others*, or asking government agencies to provide those goods and service private economic actors find too expensive or risky to organise (Powell, 1990; Coleman, 1988; Greif, 1993). Our analysis points to Ostrom's Jointly Owned Resources (Ostrom, 1990), which concentrate on co-operation rent beyond the most general statement that with ill-functioning markets and shrinking co-ordination by the old state sector, private collaboration offers a high co-operation rent (Grabher and Stark, 1997b; Nee and Stark, 1989; Stark, 1996, 1998; see also Boisot and Child, 1988, 1996 and the interesting empirical study by Uzzi, 1997). While the causes for networking seem to be straightforward, the effects point to a 'hybrid' form of institution which is situated somewhere between a market surrogate (Qian, 2002), a collective actor (Krug and Mehta, 2004), a corporatist state (Walder, 1995; Oi, 1995), and a business community (Ghemawat and Karna, 1998). On the one side, networks contribute to allocative efficiency as individual entrepreneurs have to compete for scarce network controlled resources and to the extent that networking facilitates jurisdictional competition. On the other side, there is increasing (price) competition due to 'excess production' and supply setting incentives to embark on rent-seeking and (local or sectoral) protectionism. Finally, more empirical research is needed to clarify whether standardisation of business practices is driven by investment that rewards the best working institution and organisational form, thus contributing to the integration into one national market, or whether networks are a feature that is more than 'hybrid' but will lead to a business environment characterised by different business systems.

5.6   CONCLUSION

What kind of business sector can we expect knowing how entrepreneurs respond to the environment:

1. Unsurprisingly, *productivity increasing innovation in China comes from new entry-firms.* However, new entry firms are not necessarily established to last. Innovation centres on organisational and institutional rather than technical innovation and aims at first empowering firms so that they become corporate actors, and second increasing the efficiency of inter-firm business relations. *Intra- and inter-firm relations will be governed by a mix of incentive contracts and embedded trust-safeguarding institutions such as local communities, networks or coordinated by local autonomy.*
2. The mortality of firms reflects network considerations rather than market discipline. *Networks will close down firms irrespective of profitability if new business opportunity offers higher returns which can be realised by disassembling the assets of the existing firm and recombining such freed resources in another firm.* The mortality of firms reflects also the networks' response to asymmetric information (about markets) and (political) risks.
3. As networks enjoy discretionary power to decide the organisational form of a firm, new firms might reflect a network's decision to establish discrete governance structures for their assets, i.e. an independent firm instead rather than a big vertically integrated one. Uncertainty and risk diversification will make them opt for a number of independent small multi-market companies situated in different locations. *As a consequence, the new business sector will see a multitude of different middle scale multi-market (Ghemawat and Khana 1998) incorporated firms connected via networks which must not be registered as owners or share holders.*
4. The individual firms are characterised by a weak organisational identity, weak boundaries and no well-defined core business. The residual control rights will be held by networks and not necessary owners;

A dynamic view questions what transitory organisational forms are, and whether they can be expected to survive further economic transformation. That the relative value of social capital and therefore networking will decline is not hard to see. On one side, due to learning affects, routines will emerge which can be imitated at low costs. On the other side less uncertainty and increasing competition will destroy the comfortable sellers' market position that most firms enjoy at the moment. In that situation firms need to aim for price competition and technical innovation both asking for supplementary investment which then will cause a change in corporate assets and ownership.

Some final remark on the lessons that can be drawn from the study of entrepreneurship and the Chinese business sector for an analysis of institutional change:

1. Reforms to be successful need to increase allocative efficiency and need to align the interests of the old elite, i.e. (state) bureaucracy and party officials (Nee, 2002) with their own. To insist on using an ideal type of a market system as a benchmark leaves no room for analysing institutional change that result in transitory institutions or hybrid forms of governance. Yet, we need to know more about these 'hybrids', their causes and effects in order to identify those which might survive, so adding to the variety of forms of capitalism (Qian, 2002).
2. The analysis suggests to distinguish between two forms of transaction costs, the Williamson (contract, or relation specific) type where a market economy is regarded as given, and transaction costs which are the direct consequence of weak (market compatible) institution. Identifying the different forms of transaction costs, which lead to different types of 'hybrid' organisations, is a necessary requirement for much needed comparative studies between different transition economies or different localities within China: outlined already by Williamson (2000) himself.
3. China can contribute to a debate best summarised as 'primacy of property rights' versus 'primacy of exchange relations'. Economic historians (see contributions in Bates, 1998) have been joined by post-colonial economists, and development studies scholars. The latter studies also offer empirical support to the hypothesis that institutions facilitating and safeguarding private exchange can mobilise investment and commitment – a feature usually (exclusively) linked to private property rights (LaPorta et al., 1997: Acemoglu et al., 2001).

NOTES

1. The best-know example is Hofstede and Hofstede though in his case the bias is not linked to one location but to one firm, namely IBM. See Hofstede and Hofstede (2005).

2. Known also as the Grabbing Hand – Helping Hand controversy. For the first hypothesis, see Shleifer and Vishny (1998). For the corporatist approach, see Oi (1995) and Walder (1995). See also Hoff and Stiglitz (2002).
3. Social capital, networks or embeddedness are often hard to distinguish as all three concepts refer to 'social ties'. In what follows social capital is seen as a resource which like other forms of capital – financial or human – once invested generates 'utility' or tangible returns (Lechner and Dowling, 2003; Johannisson, 1988; Hitt et al., 2002.
4. See below the section on networks.

REFERENCES

Acemoglu, D., S. Johnson and J.A. Robinson (2001), 'The Colonial Origins of Comparative Development: An Empirical Investigation', *American Economic Review*, 91, 1369–13401.

Aldrich, Howard (1999), *Organizations Evolving*, London: Sage.

Aldrich, H. and M. Fiol (1994), 'Fools rush in? The institutional context of industry creation', *Academy of Management Review*, **19**, 645–670.

Alesina, A. (2002), 'The size of Countries: Does it Matter?', *Journal of the European Economic Association*, 1 (2-3), 301–316.

Alesina, A. and E. La Ferra (2004), 'Ethnic Diversity and Economic Performance', *Journal of Economic Literature*, XLIII, 762–800.

Bates, R.E.A. (ed.) (1998), *Analytical Narratives*, Princeton, NJ: Princeton University Press.

Batjargal, B. (2003), 'Social capital and entrepreneurial performance in Russia', *Organisation Studies*, 2004, 535–556.

Batjargal, B. and M.M. Lin (2002), 'Entrepreneur's Access to Private Equity in China: The Role of Social Capital', William Davidson Institute Working Paper No. 453, Ann Arbor, MC: University of Michigan Business School.

Bian, Y. (1997), 'Bringing Strong Ties Back In: Indirect Connection, Bridges, and Job Search in China', *American Sociological Review*, 62, 266–285.

Boisot, M. and J. Child (1996), 'From fiefs to clans: explaining China's emerging economic order', *Administration Science Quarterly*, 41, 600–628.

Borgatti, St. and P. Foster (2003), 'The Network Paradigm in Organizational Research: A Review and Typology', *Journal of Management*, 29, 991–1013.

Brean, D.J.S. (ed.) (1998), *Taxation in Modern China*, New York, NY: Routledge Press.

Casson, M. (2005), 'Entrepreneurship and the theory of the firm', *Journal of Economic Behavior & Organization*, **58**, 327–348.

Cheung, S.N.S. (1969a), The Theory of Share Tenancy, Chicago, IL: University of Chicago Press.

Cheung S. (1969), 'Transaction Costs, Risk Aversion, and the Choice of Contractual Arrangements', *Journal of Law and Economics*, **12**, 23–42.

Coleman, J.S. (1990), *Foundations in Social Theory*, Cambridge, MA: Harvard University Press.

Crouch, Colin (2005), *Capitalist Diversity and Change. Recombinant Governance and Institutional Entrepreneurs*, Oxford: Oxford University Press.

DiMaggio, P.J. and W.W. Powell (1983), 'The Iron Cage Revisited: Institutional Isomorphism and Collective Rationality in Organizational Fields', *American Sociological Review*, **48**, 147–160.

Dong, X., P. Bowles and S.P. Ho (2002), 'The determinants of employee ownership in China's privatized rural industry: Evidence from Jiangsu and Shandong', *Journal of Comparative Economics*, **24**, 181–201.

Dong, X., L. Putterman and B. Unel (2004), 'Enterprise Restructuring and Firm Performance: A Comparison of Rural and Urban Enterprises in Jiangsu Province', William Davidson Institute, Working Paper No. 668, Ann Arbor, MC: University of Michigan.

Frye, T. (2002), 'Capture or Exchange? Business Lobbying in Russia', *European Asia Studies* (forthcoming).

Frye, T. and A. Shleifer (1997), 'The Invisible Hand and the Grabbing Hand', *American Economic Review* (Papers and Proceedings), **87**, 354–358.

Geertz, C. (1978), 'The Bazaar Economy: Information and Search in Peasant Marketing', *American Economic Review*, **68**, 28–32.

Ghemawat, P. and T. Khana (1998), 'The Nature of Diversified Business Groups: A Research Design and Two Case Studies', *Journal of Industrial Economics*, XLVI, 35–61.

Goodman, David S.G. (1994), 'The People's Republic of China: The Party-State, Capitalist Revolution and New Entrepreneurs', in David S.G. Goodman and R. Robinson (eds), *The New Rich in Asia: Mobile Phones, McDonalds and Middle Class Revolution*, London: Routledge, pp. 225–245.

Grabher, G. and D. Stark (1997), 'Organizing Diversity: Evolutionary Theory, Network Analysis, and Post-Socialism', *Regional Studies*, **31**, 533–544.

Granovetter, M. (1985), 'Economic Action and Social Structure: The Problem of Embeddedness', *American Journal of Sociology*, 91, 481–510.

Granovetter, M. (1993), 'The Strength of Weak ties: A Network Theory Revisited', *Sociological Theory*, **1**, 201–233.

Greif, A. (1993), 'Contract Enforceability and Economic Institutions in Early Trade: The Maghribi Traders Coalition', *American Economic Review*, **83**, 525–548.

Greif, A. (1998), 'Self-enforcing Political Systems and Economic Growth: Late Medieval Genoa', in R.E.A. Bates (ed.), *Analytical Narratives*, Princeton, NJ: Princeton University Press, 23–63.

Hannan, Michael and Glenn Carroll (1992), *The Dynamics of Organisational Populations*, Oxford: Oxford University Press.

Hendrischke, Hans (2004), 'The Role of Social Capital, Networks and Property Rights in China's Privatization Process', in Barbara Krug (ed.), China's Rational Entrepreneurs. The Development of the New Private Business Sector, London: Routledge, pp. 97–118.

Hofstede, Geert and Gert Jan Hofstede (2005), 'Cultures and Organizations: Software of the Mind', New York, NY: McGraw-Hill.

Hollingworth, John R., P.C. Schmitter and W. Streeck (1994), 'Capitalism, Sectors, Institutions, and Performance', in John R. Hollingworth, P.C. Schmitter and W. Streeck (eds), *Governing Capitalist Economies. Performance and Control of Economic Sectors*, New York and Oxford: Oxford University Press, pp. 3–16.

Jacobs, Gabriele, F. Belschak and B. Krug (2004), 'Social Capital in China: the Meaning of Guanxi in Chinese Business', in Barbara Krug (ed.), *China's Rational Entrepreneurs: The Development of the New Private Business Sector*, London: Routledge: pp. 166–188.

Kirzner, Israel M. (1985), *Discovery and the capitalist process*, Chicago, IL: University of Chicago Press.

Kornai, J. (1980), *Economics of Shortage*, Vol. I and II, Amsterdam: North Holland.

Krug, Barbara (1997), 'Privatisation in China: Something to learn from?', in Herbert Giersch (ed.), *Privatisation at the Turn of the Century*, Berlin: Springer, pp. 269–293.

Krug, Barbara (2002), 'Norms, Numbers and Hierarchy', *The American Journal of Economics and Sociology*, 61, 555–562.

Krug, Barbara and L. Polos (2004), 'Emerging Markets, Entrepreneurship and Uncertainty: The Emergence of a Private Sector in China', in Barbara Krug (ed.); *China's Rational Entrepreneurs. The development of the New Private Business Sector*, London: Routledge, pp. 72–96.

Kuilman, Jeroen (2005), *The Re-Emergence of Foreign Banks in Shanghai: An Ecological Analyis*, Ph.D. Dissertation, Rotterdam: Erasmus University.

LaPorta, Rafael, F. Lopez-de Silanes, A. Shleifer and R.W. Vishny (1998), 'Law and Finance', *Journal of Political Economy*, 106, 1113–1155.

Lechner, Christian, and M. Dowling (2003), 'Firm networks: external relationships as sources for the growth and competitiveness of entrepreneurial firms', *Entrepreneurship & Regional Development*, 15, 1–26.

Li, David D. (1996), 'Ambiguous Property Rights in Transition Economies: The Case of the Chinese Non-State Sector', *Journal of Comparative Economics*, 23, 1–19.

Li, H. and S. Rozelle (2003), 'Privatizing Rural China: Insider Privatization, innovative contracts, and the performance of township enterprises', *The China Quarterly*, 176, 981–1005.

Li, P.P. (2005), 'The Puzzle of China's Township-Village enterprises: The Paradox of Local Corporatism in a Dual Track Economic Transition', *Management and Organization Review*, 1, 197–224.

Lovett, S., L.C. Simmons and R. Kali (1999), 'Guanxi versus the Market: Ethics and Efficiency', *Journal of International Business Studies*, 30, 231–247.

Lui, Tai Lok (1996), 'A Brief Note on Guanxi', in Gary G. Hamilton (ed.), *Asian Business Networks*, Berlin: Walter de Gruyter & Co., pp. 385–398.

Luo, Y. (1997), 'Guanxi: principles, philosophies, and implications', *Human Systems Management*, 16, 43–51.

Nee, V. (1992), 'Organizational Dynamics of Market Transition: Hybrid Forms, Property Rights, and Mixed Economy in China', *Administrative Science Quarterly*, 31, 1–27.

Nee, V. (2000), 'The role of the state in making a market economy', *Journal of Institutional and Theoretical Economics*, 156, 66–88.

Nee, Victor and D. Stark (eds) (1989), Remaking the Economic Institutions of Socialism: China and Eastern Europe, Stanford, CA: Stanford University Press.

Nee, Victor and S. Su (1996), 'Local Corporatism and Informal Privatization in China's Market Transition', in J. McMillan and Barry Naughton (eds), *Reforming Asian Socialism: The Growth of Market Institutions*, Ann Arbor, MC: University of Michigan Press.

Nelson, Richard R. (1992), *National innovation systems: A comparative analysis*, New York, NY: Oxford University Press.

Nooteboom, B. (1999), 'Innovation, learning and industrial organizations', *Cambridge Journal of Economics*, 23, 127–150.

Nooteboom, Bart (1999a), 'The Triangle: Roles of the Go-Between', in S. Gabbay and R. Leenders (eds), *Corporate Social Capital*, Dordrecht: Kluwer Academic Publisher, pp. 341–355.

Nooteboom, B., H. Berger, N.G. Noorderhaven (1997), 'Effects of Trust and Governance on Relational Risk', *Academy of Management Journal*, 40, 308–332.

North, D.C. (1984), 'Transaction Costs, Institutions, and Economic History', *Journal of Institutional and Theoretical Economics*, 140, 7–17.

OECD (2005), *Governance in China*, Paris: OECD Publications.

North, D. C. (2005) *Understanding the Process of Economic Change*. Princton: Princton University Press.

Oi, J.C. (1995), 'The Role of the Local State in China's Transitional Economy', *The China Quarterly*, 144, 1132–1149.

Ostrom, Elinor (1990), *Governing the Commons*, Cambridge: Cambridge University Press.

Park, S.H, and Y. Luo (2001), 'Guanxi and Organizational Dynamics: Organizational Networking in Chinese Firms', *Strategic Management Journal*, 22, 455–477

Peng, M.W. (2001), 'How entrepreneurs create wealth in transition economies', *The Academy of Management Executive*, 15, 95–108.

Peng, M.W. and Y. Luo (2000), 'Managerial Ties and Firm Performance in a Transition Economy: The Nature of a Micro-Macro Link', *Academy of Management Journal*, 43, 486–501.

Peng, Y. (2004), 'Kinship Networks and Entrepreneurs in China's Transitional Economy', *American Journal of Sociology*, 109, 1045–1074.

Pistrui, D., W. Huang, D. Oksoy, J. Zhao and H. Welsch (1999), 'The Characteristics and Attributes of New Chinese Entrepreneurs and Their Emerging Enterprises', *Business Forum*, 24, 31–38

Powell, W.W. (1990), 'Neither Market nor Hierarchy: Network Forms of Organizations', *Research in Organizational Behaviour*, 12, 295–313.

Qian Yingyi (2002), 'How Reform worked in China', Berkeley, CA: University of California, Center for Economic Policy Research.

Redding, S.G. (1996), 'The Distinct Nature of Chinese Capitalism', *The Pacific Review*, 9, 426–440.

Schoonhoven, Claudia B. and E. Romanellu (2001), 'Emergent Themes and the Next Wave of Entrepreneurship Research', in Schoonhoven, Claudia B. and Elaine Romanellu (eds), *The Entrepreneurship Dynamic*, Stanford, CA: Stanford University Press, pp. 383–408.

Scott, W.R. and J.W. Meyer (1992), 'The Organization of Societal Sectors', in John W. Meyer and W. Richard Scott (eds), *Organizational Environments: Ritual and Rationality*, Newbury Park, CA: Sage, pp. 129–153.

Shleifer, A. (1998), 'State versus Private Ownership', *Journal of Economic Perspectives*, 12, 133–150.

Shleifer, Andrej and R.W. Vishny (1993), 'Corruption', NBER Working Paper No. 4372, Cambridge, MA: National Bureau of Economic Research.

State Statistical Yearbook of the People's Republic of China (2004), Oxford: Oxford University Press.

Stark, D. (1996), 'Recombinant Property in East European Capitalism', *American Journal of Sociology*, 101, 993–1027.

Stark, David (1998), *Post-socialist Pathways: Transforming Political and Property in Eastern Europe*, New York, NY: Cambridge University Press.

Stiglitz, J.E. (1974), 'Incentives and Risk Sharing in Sharecropping', *Review of Economic Studies*, 61, 219–255.

Stiglitz, Joseph E. (1991), 'Government, Financial Markets, and Economic Development', Cambridge, MA: National Bureau of Economic Research.

Tabellini, Guido (2005), 'Culture and Institutions: Economic Development in the Regions of Europe', CESifo working paper No. 1492.

Teece, D.J. and G. Pisano (1994), 'The Dynamic Capabilities of firms: An Introduction', *Industrial and Corporate Change*, 3, 537–556.

Tilly, Charles (2001), 'Welcome to the Seventeenth Century', in Paul DiMaggio (ed.), *The Twenty-First-Century Firm. Changing Economic Organization in International Perspective*, Princeton and Oxford: Princeton University Press, pp. 200–207.

Tong, C.K. and P.K. Yong (1998), 'Guanxi bases, Xinyong and Chinese business networks', *British Journal of Sociology*, 49, 75–96.

Tsang, E.W.K. (1998), 'Can guanxi be a source of sustained competitive advantage for doing business in China', *The Academy of Management Executive*, 12, 64–73.

Uzzi, B. (1996), 'The sources and consequences of embeddedness for the economic performance of organizations: the network effect', *American Sociological Review*, 61, 674–698.

Uzzi, B. (1997), 'Social Structure and Competition in Interfirm Networks: The Paradox of Embeddedness', *Administrative Science Quarterly*, 42, 35–67.

Walder, A.G. (1995), 'Local Governments as Industrial Firms: An Organizational Analysis of China's Transitional Economy', *American Journal of Sociology*, 10, 263–301.

Whitley, Richard D. (1999), *Divergent Capitalism: The Social Construction and Change of Business Systems*, Oxford: Oxford University.

Whitley, R., J. Henderson, L. Czaban and G. Lengyel (1996), 'Trust and Contractual Relations in an Emerging Capitalist Economy: The Changing Trading Relationships of Ten Large Hungarian Enterprises', *Organisation Studies*, 17, 397–420.

Williamson, Oliver E. (1985), *The Economic Institutions of Capitalism*, New York and London: Macmillan.

Williamson, O.E. (1993), 'Calculativeness, trust and economic organization', *Journal of Law and Economics*, 36, 453–86.

Williamson, O.E. (1994), 'The Evolving Science of Organization', *Journal of Institutional and Theoretical Economics*, 149, 36–63.

Williamson, O.E. (2000), 'The New Institutional Economic: Taking Stock, Looking Ahead', *Journal of Economic Literature*, 38, 595–613.

Witt, U. (2000), 'Changing cognitive frames – changing organizational forms: An entrepreneurial theory of organizational development', *Industrial and Corporate Change*, 9, 733–755.

Wong, Christine P., C. Heady and W.T. Woo (1995), Fiscal Management and Economic Reform in the People's Republic of China, Manila: Asian Development Bank.

Wong, C.P.W. (1991), 'Central-Local Relations in an Era of Fiscal Decline: The Paradox of Fiscal Decentralization in Post-Mao China', *The China Quarterly*, 128, 691–715.

World Bank (1995), *China: Macroeconomic Stability in a Decentralised Economy*, Washington, DC: World Bank.

6. China's Emerging Tax Regime: Local Tax Farming and Central Tax Bureaucracy

Ze Zhu and Barbara Krug

6.1 INTRODUCTION

Economic transformation asks not only for less state appropriation of resources, it also asks for a change of the *means* by which the state does so. Generally speaking, there are four ways to generate budgetary revenues: first, exploitation of state owned/controlled resources; second, taxation of assets and income or trade flows; third, forced loans on economic agents and finally, *seigniorage*, i.e. printing money. Given their commitment to stability, the Chinese government is forced to rely on the first three revenue sources. Yet, privatisation and un-competitiveness of state-owned firms reduce government revenue from the state sector; while revenue from forced loans, i.e. compulsory transfers of the firms' cash flow and compulsory saving of private households, declines following price and wage liberalisation. Subsequently, state expenditure depends increasingly on taxation, which needs to be revised to comply with the reform course.

This shift in state revenue sources draws attention to the fact that *transition economies need to establish market conforming taxation*. Three aspects can be singled out. First, new tax codes need to include the re-emerging private sector, such as firms or investors, and foreign companies. Second, a new system of intergovernmental transfers needs to replace the old planning bureaucracy allowing for decentralisation. Third, a new tax bureaucracy needs to be established. In contrast to the European transition economies, which right from the beginning copied tax codes from neighbouring countries (or the EU), China opted for incremental reform of its tax system. In other words, one component of economic transformation is the change in the country's *public finance*.

While traditional public finance theory (see, for instance, Musgrave, 1959, 1969) propagating rational financial systems concentrates on the effectivity of taxation (and spending) with respect to well-defined goals, public choice literature treats the state as a Leviathan (Brennan and Buchanan, 1980) and sees fiscal federalism (Oates, 1972; Olson, 1969) as institutional remedy. The trade off between rational taxation versus small government (expenditure) was taken up again in the discussion of institutional change in transition economies, where two opposing hypotheses define the conceptual and empirical discussion, namely the 'Grabbing Hand' hypothesis (Frye and Shleifer, 1997; Shleifer and Treisman, 1999) pointing to the risk that the Leviathan will survive economic transformation (the Russian case), and the 'Helping Hand' hypothesis (Oi, 1992; Walder, 1995) stressing the benefit of continuing state intervention during the transformation period (the China case). The China specific dimension of this debate centres around three features: local autonomy; local diversity; and tax farming.

6.1.1   Local Autonomy

Descriptive analysis of China's fiscal reform since 1978 concludes that fiscal decentralisation, whether intended or not, generated local autonomy. Some studies attribute China's success to a market-preserving federalism that empowers local governments and offers them positive incentives for promoting local economic growth (Montinola et al., 1995; Weingast, 1995; Qian and Weingast, 1996, 1997; Qian and Roland, 1998). For example, *local state corporatism* (Oi, 1992, 1994, 1995) describes the local government as a business corporation which mobilises resources *ad hoc*, offers preferential tax policy, or brokers bank credit as a means to insure profitability of its tax base. Such a form of corporatism, based on loosely coupled coalitions (Nee, 1992, 1998) between local government agencies and the emerging private sector, leads to minimised upward tax transfers and facilitates privatisation from below (Naughton, 1994). Then the industrial base of a locality can be added to the local tax base.

In the case of Township and Village Enterprises (TVEs), local governments act as quasi-owners when they claim residual profit and as quasi-tax-legislators when they levy taxes on TVEs provided these are registered as firms 'outside the planned economy'. Subsequently, this institutional setting not only secures local property rights in a weak market setting and uncertain institutional environment (Weitzman and Xu, 1994; Chang and Wang, 1994; Li, 1996), but also gradually releases resources from state control accompanied by a shift of revenue sources from direct expropriation of profit or cash flow to taxation of firms in the non-state sector.

6.1.2 Local Diversity

Characterised by a severe principal-agent problem between the central government as the principal and local units as agents, fiscal decentralisation must also lead to local diversity (Krug, 2004a; Krug and Hendrischke, 2003; Hendrischke, 2003). First, the central government grants different 'degrees' of independent decision-making to different local government agencies (Bird and Chen, 1998) as in the case of Special Economic Zones. Second, different local government agencies react differently to the same central policy guidelines according to different local conditions, such as size, geography, history and resource endowments (Krug, 2004b; Hsu, 2004). Third, jurisdictional competition forces local governments to generate competitive advantages by offering preferential taxation and subsidies to its tax base (Walder, 1995, 1996). Fourth, an alliance between firms and local government agencies facilitates escaping national legislation, if not manipulating national tax legislation (Wedeman, 2003; Shirk, 1993; Wank, 1996; Chen and Rozelle, 1999)[1].

6.1.3 Tax Farming

One unexpected component of decentralisation was the introduction of tax farming in general. A tax farming system is connected to the pre-modern states of England and France (Kiser, 1994; Kiser and Kane, 2001; O'Brien, 1988; Weir, 1989; White, 1995; 2004)[2]. It was only after the Glorious Revolution in the former and French Revolution in the later that a centralised tax bureaucracy developed in both countries in response to changing transaction costs, and the expansion of financial markets, which offered an alternative means for financing state budgets. An economic analysis of this change argues that two factors influence institutional choice: the monarch's (state's) attitude toward (economic or political) risk and the incentives necessary to compel lower administrative units to act as tax agents on behalf of the monarch. With respect to the incentive structure, three different forms of tax systems can be singled out, usually described as contractual arrangements between the central state and local agents: a *rent-based*, a *wage-based* and a *(crop) sharing contractual arrangement* (Stiglitz, 1974; Sappington, 1991; Allen and Lueck, 1995). The first refers to a lump sum contract-type where the central state 'farms out' tax authority to local governments in return for a guaranteed (low risk) fixed sum. By doing so, local tax agents become the residual claimant on tax revenue. The second wage-based arrangement refers to a professional *bureaucracy*, which in return for a share of the national budget, fixed wages and promotion within the state bureaucracy 'selflessly' implements central policy without bearing individually or organisational risks. The third form follows *crop-shared contracts* in which both central as lesser and local governments as lessee share economic risk productivity gains in tax administration (cropping sharing contract).

While in the socialist era, China had a Weberian-style bureaucracy, it started experimenting with tax farming in the 1980s to be followed (in the 1990s) by a widespread (tax) sharing system and the re-introduction of a bureaucratic system. This unusual phenomenon of different tax systems co-existing, calls for empirical analysis. Does that kind of institutional choice follow arguments offered by the analytical concepts? Or which other factors that prompted institutional change can be singled out:

1. Normative considerations, such as taxing 'equal activities equally'?
2. Distributional considerations, most prominently the problem of regional disparities?
3. Economic considerations, such as standardisation gains or transaction costs in monitoring and enforcement?
4. Political considerations such as conflicting interests between the central and local government agencies, or setting incentives that ensure local government agencies comply with the reform course?

As will be shown in what follows the different reforms aimed mostly for a mixture of all these motives. However, in the end, economic and political considerations prevailed.

A second set of questions refers to the present state of affairs: What is the effect of the tax reform in 1994? How did the local governments react? What is the *status quo* of the tax system at the local level at the lowest governmental level, the township? What can we say about the *de facto* as opposed to the *de jure* tax system?

In order to analyse local autonomy and local diversity caused by taxation (tax farming), and to answer the questions above, it is necessary to explore not only recent developments. Such an analysis needs also to *endogenise* formal and informal elements in actual tax policy. For this reason findings from fieldwork undertaken in Zhejiang and Jiangsu province in 2004 and 2005 will be included in the part that deals with the actual functioning of the tax system at the township level.

Here follows a descriptive analysis of the different reforms since 1978 stressing the causes and effects of institutional change with respect to local autonomy and local diversity (Sections 6.2 and 6.3). Then a *status quo* analysis of the present tax system (Section 6.4) serves as an introduction to the analysis of how the present tax system, local autonomy and local diversity interact – formally and informally – at the lowest layer of government in China (Section 6.5). This is done in order to illustrate the difference between the intended functioning of the tax system and the actual interplay between taxation and the emerging market sector. The paper ends with a summary of the empirical results and a general assessment of China's tax system (Section 6.6).

6.2 REBUILDING TAX CODES: SHIFTING GOVERNMENT REVENUE

In the pre-reform era three categories of indirect taxes[3], i.e. the industrial and commercial tax, tariff and the agriculture tax, were levied in China[4]. State-owned enterprises (SOEs) were subject to the industrial and commercial tax in addition to the compulsory transfer of 'profit' and cash flow. Tax revenue (1978: 46 per cent) and profit remittance (1978: 51 per cent) were the two dominant resources of total revenue (MOF, 2005). To increase productive efficiency while avoiding privatisation, the reforms introduced first a 'contract responsibility system' (*chengbao zeren zhi*) to be followed by a 'tax-for-profit' scheme (*li gai shui*) in 1983 and 1984. Both reforms acknowledged the SOEs as independent economic actors entitled to part of profit which they could allocate internally to working capital, investment, wages, and bonuses without state intervention as long as they fulfilled the contract quota. The share of after tax profit and the tax rate were subject to individual negotiations between the firm and the responsible state agency and varied according to enterprise size, sector and *ad hoc* situation. It quickly turned out that in response to fuzzy property rights the SOE managers channelled undisclosed profit into their private pockets by establishing joint ventures with TVEs or by outsourcing production to new private firms rather than reinvest in productivity increasing change. That asset-stripping eroded the state sector's profitability further and ended in a sharp increase of loss making SOEs. Yet, with a state sector still not liable to a hard budget constraint (Kornai, 1986), the underperformance of the state sector directly translated into higher government expenditure in the form of subsidies or loans necessary to 'bail out' the bankrupt SOEs. The situation was further aggravated when the non-state sector started to out-compete the SOEs further reducing the latter's profit remittance and tax contribution. In 1985 already, subsidies for SOEs were eleven times higher than the revenues from SOEs (MOF, 2005). Facing such eroding revenue base the central government had incentive enough to search for a new broader tax base, namely one that included foreign enterprises and all forms of joint ventures.

Thus, direct (income) taxation made its re-appearance in China, which foreign enterprises, joint ventures, SOEs, collective enterprises and individuals became subject to. Simultaneously the reform of indirect taxes started with introducing VAT for twelve categories of products, (such as machinery, and steel, but also consumer goods, such as bicycles, electric fans, or sewing machines) with rates between 6 and 16 per cent. Other economic transactions were taxed by product (270 items) subject to a flat rate varying from 3 to 60 per cent in 1984. Such a diversified tax structure increased the monitoring and enforcement cost for tax collection and administration considerably. Unsurprisingly, the 1994 reforms abolished the product tax, expanded VAT to all manufactured products with a standard rate of 17 per cent (and a reduced rate of 13 per cent for necessities), and levied a business tax on the service industry but kept the consumption tax on eleven categories of goods[5]. Since then a total of 29 taxes have been levied on turnover, income, resources, property and behaviour (Table 6.1)[6]. Now, indirect taxes are the major revenue source of the Chinese state. In 2003, VAT, consumption tax, business tax and custom duties added up to 69 per cent of total tax revenues, in which VAT alone provided 36 per cent of the total (SAT, 2003).

After all, the reforms of 1994 support the assumption that tax changes can (and will) follow transaction costs considerations, i.e. monitoring, collecting and enforcement costs when indirect taxes were introduced. As is pointed out elsewhere, indirect taxation allows concentrating on a few taxable assets thereby offering lower collection costs than a system that aims at assets or income of all (potential) tax payers (Kiser and Kane, 2001; Ardant, 1975). China's WTO entry in 2001 prompted further changes in order to comply with international standards. Foreign (15 per cent income tax) and domestic (25 per cent income tax) firms would no longer be treated differently by the tax authorities (Mui and Jia, 2002). The scope of VAT would be expanded to cover a broader range of products. A new social security and property tax are aimed at better coping with challenges created by the economic transformation, including employment insecurity and greater disparities in wealth.

All in all, the institutional changes within the tax systems reflect the attempt to define a tax base and establish tax codes compatible with a market economy. The description also shows that transaction costs played a major role when it came to designing and re-designing the tax base, and tax rates.

6.3   TAX FARMING: POSITIVE INCENTIVES AND LOCAL AUTONOMY

Fiscal decentralisation in China refers to taxation and intergovernmental fiscal relations, i.e. the allocation of revenue and expenditure across different government levels, based on a decentralisation of regulatory powers or agreed upon transfers. The inherited centralised fiscal system relied on local government agencies to collect revenues for transfer to the national treasury. In return, the central government assigned (expenditure) items financed basically by re-transferring revenues to local budgets. Labelled as 'eating from the big pot (*chi da guo fan*)' local agencies had neither an incentive to promote the local economy, nor did they have the leeway to do so.

Table 6.1   China's tax codes after 1994

	Taxes
National tax	Consumption tax, Tariff, Income tax on FIEs and FEs [a], Vehicle acquisition tax
Local tax	Business tax [b], Agricultural tax, Tax on special agricultural produce, Animal husbandry tax, Resource tax [c], Urban and township land usage tax, Occupied farmland tax, Real estate tax [d], Urban real estate tax [d], Land appreciation tax, Urban maintenance and construction tax [e], Deed tax, Vehicle and vessel usage license tax, Vehicle and vessel usage tax, Vessel tonnage tax, Slaughter tax [f,] Banquet tax [f], Orientation adjustment tax on investment in fixed asset [g]
Shared tax	Value-added tax (VAT), Enterprise income tax [h], Individual income tax, Stamp tax

Notes:
a. Enterprises with foreign investment (FIEs) refer to Chinese-foreign equity joint ventures, Chinese-foreign contractual joint ventures and wholly foreign-owned enterprises; Foreign enterprises (FEs) refer to foreign companies, and other economic organisations that are not Chinese legal entities, but operate in China. The tax rate on is 33 per cent of which 30 per cent are allocated to the central, and three per cent to the local government.
b. Business taxes on railway, headquarters of banks or insurance companies go to the central government.
c. The resource tax on ocean and petrol companies goes to the central government.
d. Domestic enterprises and Chinese citizens are subject to the real estate tax while FEs, FIEs and foreigners are subject to the urban real estate tax, with different tax rates.
e. Urban maintenance and construction tax of the Railway Administration, the headquarters of banks and insurance companies go to the central government.
f. To be abolished (Guofa 1994. No.7).
g. To be abolished (Caishuifa 1999, No.299).
h. Income tax of SOEs subordinate to the central government, local banks, foreign-funded banks and non-bank financial institutions are allocated to the central government.

Source: State Administration of Taxation, PRC, www.chinatax.gov.cn.

To redress this problem, the reforms started with transferring fiscal authority, i.e. the power to tax, to local governments. Several experiments were carried out, such as a 'fixed overall revenue sharing rate' in Jiangsu province in 1977, 'dividing central, local and central-local sharing revenue' in Sichuan province in 1979 and a 'fixed lump sum transfer' in Guangdong and Fujian province in 1979, later (1980–1993) expanded to six types of contract arrangements (Oksenberg and Tong, 1991; Wong, 1991; 1992). It is worth mentioning that these fiscal arrangements are modifications of tax contracting analytical models described earlier[7].

Empirical fieldwork suggests that the rental-based model quickly emerged as the dominant form. In this kind of tax contracting, the central government negotiates a fixed share of revenue (in absolute terms, or as a ratio) leaving the local government the *de facto* residual claimant of revenue. From the local perspective, disposable revenues were directly linked to economic growth and/or the attractiveness of the local economy for investment from outside (other jurisdictions or foreign companies). Yet, as suggested in the economic analysis of tax farming, three unintended consequences emerged. First, the principal-agent problem remains unresolved: local governments profit from asymmetric information; hiding the correct information (if not falsifying tax reports) is an easy way to minimise the amount of tax revenue to be transferred to the contract partner. Second, renegotiable contracts include an element of uncertainty in local budget planning as well as in anticipating budgeting across localities. With the length of contracts and the sharing formulas re-negotiable, future budgetary revenue depends less on economic trends but rather on the relative power positions of the contract partners. Contract arrangements vary also with respect to sharing rates, time period, or spatial factors, when some provinces, regions, or localities are granted special licences from the central government. Third, as all 'agents' share the interest to minimise upward transfers and manipulate the tax base, the state's financial base is eroded even further. Whether the trend is measured as total government revenue per GDP, or central revenue as a share of total government revenue during the 1980–1993 period, the result is the same: the ratio of total government revenue to GDP fell from an already low 26 per cent in 1980 to 13 per cent in 1993. The share of the central revenue to total government revenue fell from 41 per cent (1984) to 22 per cent (1993) (Figure 6.1).

The introduction of tax farming reflects three aims of the Chinese government: first, to mobilise local support for the implementation of the reform course; second, to link the self-interest of local government agencies to the economic performance of their local jurisdictions; and third, to offer enough flexibility in the tax system that widely differing local conditions can be accommodated.

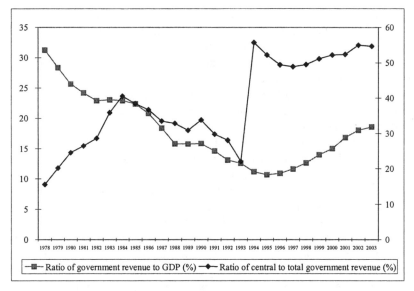

Figure 6.1   Ratio of government revenue to GDP and central to total government revenue

6.4   TAX SHARING: BUREAUCRATISING TAX ADMINISTRATION

In the face of shrinking revenue the central government attempted to re-centralise tax authority in the reforms of 1994 by building up a central tax bureaucracy regarded to more effectively implement tax collection. Yet, not much unlike the monarchs in Europe before them (Kiser and Kane, 2001) the central government had to accept that local autonomy is not easily disposed of. The Tax Sharing System (*fen shui zhi*) (Wong, 1997; Wong et al., 1995) aimed at replacing locally negotiated tax farming with a unified national system of taxation. Aside from the re-centralisation effort, the change was expected to address three further issues. A unified tax system would ensure equal taxation for equal transactions and tax base. A higher share of central revenue would ensure that distributional effects could be mitigated, as the system of local autonomy had no provision (and no incentive) for inter-provincial transfers. A third intention, namely the abolishment of extra- and off-budgetary revenue sources will be dealt with separately.

The newly introduced tax sharing system does not refer to a separation of tasks between different layers of government to which specific sources of revenues (taxes) are allocated as in 'Western' models of multi-layered government, such as federalist states or the EU for example. Instead, the tax revenue (and not tax legislation) are divided in such a way that some taxes are exclusively assigned to the central level, some are assigned exclusively to the local level, and some taxes are shared between both levels according to a fixed ration. It is worth stressing that this category of local revenues includes fees and other kinds of revenue which are manipulated by local governments. As Table 6.1 illustrates these local taxes encompass a variety of fees and taxes, which reflect the willingness and ability to tap local resources when they concentrate on the taxation of relatively immobile factors rather than following an economic policy of generating competitive advantages for a locality[8]. At first sight the tax sharing system seems to follow international practice in the sense that the two largest revenue sources, namely VAT and income tax, are divided between the central and local level (see Table 6.2). That revenues from tariffs go directly to the national coffer is also common. On the other hand the socialist legacy can be seen in the fact that the income taxation of foreign firms remains a concern of the central government.

Table 6.2   Central–local taxes: sharing formulae

Shared Taxes	Central	Local
VAT	75%	25%
Enterprises income tax [a]	50%(2002) 60%(2003)	50%(2002) 40%(2003)
Individual income tax [b]	50%(2002) 60%(2003)	50%(2002) 40%(2003)
Stamp tax	94% of taxes on security transaction	6% of taxes on security transaction Other stamp taxes

Notes:
a. Before 2002 the 'corporate income tax' on domestic enterprises was a local tax, afterwards it became a shared tax.
b. Taxes on capital gains go to the central government. Before 2002 the personal income tax was a local tax, afterwards it became a shared tax.

Source: Certified Public Accountant (CPA) Committee, Ministry of Finance (MOF), *Taxation laws*, (Beijing: Zhongguo Jingji Chubanshe, 2003)

To better cope with the monitoring and enforcement problem, the tax administration was split into two separate bureaucracies, each with a distinctive line of command. The national tax bureau (*guoshuiju*, NTBs) subordinate to the State Administration of Taxation (SAT), (defined as a ministry since 1993), was put in charge of central and shared taxes[9]. While the SAT is autonomous with respect to central taxes, its role changes when it comes to local taxes administered by local tax bureaus (*dishuiju*, LTBs), the second tax bureaucracy. As stipulated by the law, the SAT and local government 'jointly' supervise the LTBs, which in the case of the SAT limits its role to operational guidance (*yewu zhidao*) and comment on nominations for tax personnel to the provincial LTBs (Figure 6.2). In other words, LTBs, in particular below the provincial level, are *de facto* subordinate to local governments leaving the institutional architecture of local autonomy unchanged.

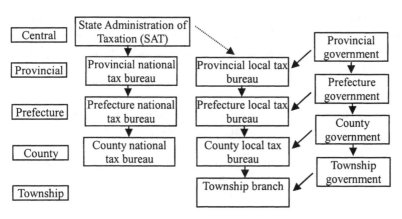

Notes:

a.   The hierarchy of taxation administration is corresponding to government administrative structure.

b.   The black line refers to vertical leadership.

c.   The dashed line refers to operational guidance.

*Source:*State Administration of Taxation, PRC, www.chinatax.gov.cn.

Figure 6.2   Structure of taxation administration

Aside from the introduction of computer based monitoring devices, a system of merit-based recruitment and systematic government training (0.4 million national and 0.35 million local tax officials in 2002 alone) are seen as the first necessary steps for shifting toward a bureaucratic tax system at all levels of government. At the same time, the personnel deployment policy, which asks for out of place-of-origin appointments and job rotation, is seen as a means to prevent corruption. This follows stricter legislation as stipulated in the *Law on the Administration of Tax Collection* (1995) and the amendment to the *Criminal Law* which explicitly addresses the problem of tax collection and dereliction of duty on taxation (1997).

While generally successful in consolidating central state control[10], a more detailed analysis shows that the system was rather ineffective in establishing rational unified tax codes and tax bureaucracy. Tax farming is still the dominant institutional architecture at the lower level of the state political and administrative system. Once more transaction cost considerations and the need to compromise politically with local politicians and agencies prevail in institutional choice.

6.5   THE STATUS QUO OF THE TAX SYSTEM

It is worth emphasising that all reforms in the last three decades were directed toward the provincial level, while sub-provincial government agencies were rarely mentioned. General recommendations, such as 'promoting' local initiatives (*fangquan rangli*) or 'adjusting' for local conditions (*yindi zhiyi*) left the provinces with considerable leeway to modify central policy. Thus, for example, the 1994 reform merely stipulates that provinces improve sub-provincial fiscal administration without giving further directions. This apparent neglect should be interpreted as a political compromise where rich provinces (in particular) and/or sub-provincial government agencies saw their discretionary powers re-confirmed in return for compliance with other parts of the reform programme. The creation of a national tax bureaucracy outside the reach of 'local' control is a good example of this.

6.5.1   Ad Hoc Non-Tax Levies

One of the most striking differences between the Chinese and international tax systems are the so-called extra-budgetary revenues (EBRs) and off-budgetary revenues (OBRs), two devices inherited from the socialist past yet in the 1990s re-invented for ad hoc taxation, and for legitimising income from commercial activities (Wong, 1997, 1998; Fan, 1998; Eckaus, 2003).

Extra-budgetary revenues (EBRs) originated in 1950 as a means to locally finance specially earmarked local expenditures. It includes three major parts: 1) government funds and surtaxes, such as agriculture surtax, and education surtax, levied on the income, consumption, profit or turnover base; 2) a hold up of special funds of SOEs, such as depreciation, major repair, and innovation funds; and 3) locally self-raised funds and administrative fees, such as road construction funds, public utility fees, road tolls, and tuition fees[11]. OBRs on the other hand are public 'voluntary' contributions made by individuals, firms or Overseas Chinese, various unregulated fees, and lately, profits from TVEs, and revenues from land sales (Fan, 1998). Lacking uniform procedures with respect to computation, base, rate, or frequency means that in fact, EBRs (or OBRs) are quasi-taxes. Their ambiguous legal status adds support to the notion of strong local autonomy in today's fiscal system (Wong, 1998).

EBRs and OBRs were hardly worth mentioning if they had not been hijacked by local governments in the 1990s to legitimise new revenue sources. As previously mentioned, local governments have no tax legislation power and are only entitled to collect 'local tax' legislated by the national government whose total amount cannot but add to a minor fraction of local budgets (Table 6.3). Yet, driven by local self-interests and disposable revenue maximisation, local governments are motivated to search for additional revenues sources whether entitled to do so or not. They sell state assets, invest in business activities, apportion mandatory contributions to local projects, issue local bonds, or levy illegal service charges, the proceeds of which are listed as EBRs and OBRs in order to suggest legitimate revenue sources. As will be shown later (tables 6.4 and 6.5) the revenues from commercial activities for which there is no precedent in the socialist era became the largest source for local income in particular in the rich East. Profits (or dividends) or local taxes on TVEs, as well as proceeds from land deals and real estate management can increase the independence of local government agencies. EBRs and OBRs are used to legitimise revenue maximisation, which is further evidence of local resistance to central budgetary control.

EBRs and OBRs remain a controversial issue. Some analysts stress the negative influence on economic stabilisation, state redistribution capacity and fiscal administration (Wong, 1998; Lee, 2000), while others emphasise its positive outcome in the form of local wealth as measured in the provision of local public goods and services, such as school or heath care (see Fan, 1998). In some places, such as the less-developed inland regions, arbitrary EBR or OBR extraction has led to rural protest and violence (Bernstein and Lü, 2003; Tsui and Wang, 2004). On the other hand, in coastal and developed provinces, the advantages of EBRs or OBRs are seen in the ability of local government agencies to quickly respond to local public needs, if not as a starting point for more civil participation in local policy formation (as demonstrated in Fan's field research of 1998).

Table 6.3   Tax collections by authorities

Collection Authority	Items
National tax bureaus (NTBs)	Consumption tax, VAT, income tax on enterprises [a], Income tax on FIEs and FEs, stamp tax on security transaction, vehicle acquisition tax
Local tax bureaus (LTBs)	Business tax, individual income tax [b], resource tax, urban and township land usage tax, urban maintenance and construction tax, real estate tax, urban real estate tax, land appreciation tax, vehicle and vessel usage license tax, vehicle and vessel usage tax, slaughter tax, banquet tax, other stamp taxes
Customs	Tariff, VAT (collected by Customs), consumption tax (collected by the Customs), vessel tonnage tax
MOF/LTBs [c]	Agricultural tax, tax on special agricultural produce, animal husbandry tax, deed tax, and occupied farmland tax

Notes:
   a.   The local tax bureau collects corporate income tax of those domestic firms established before 1 January 2002. The SAT collects the same tax of younger firms. The SAT also collects the Corporate income tax on central government owned SOEs, ministry of railway, headquarters of banks, and ocean and petrol companies.
   b.   Individual income tax became a shared tax in 2002 but is still collected by the local tax bureau.
   c.   Before 1996, Ministry of Finance (MOF) collected occupied farmland tax, deed tax, agricultural tax, tax on special agricultural produce and the animal husbandry tax, to be replaced bay local tax bureaus.

Sources: Certified Public Accountant (CPA) Committee, Ministry of Finance (MOF), *Taxation laws*, (Beijing: Zhongguo Jingji Chubanshe, 2003); State Administration of Taxation, PRC, www.chinatax.gov.cn.

6.5.2   Complicated Intergovernmental Transfer System

There is still no procedure for coordinating intergovernmental transfers between the five layers of the administrative hierarchy (central, provincial, prefecture, county and township). The present tax sharing system only deals with the central-provincial level and leaves considerable discretionary power for sub-provincial transfer practices. Diversity within the sub-provincial intergovernmental transfer system is unavoidable. The 1994 reforms did not tackle the problem; to the contrary it became even more complicated by adding the new transfer modes of national taxation.

Under the previous tax farming system, local governments transfer the contracted lump-sum amount, a progressive sharing ratio on incremental revenue, or a fixed sharing ratio of overall revenues (or a combination of all these). In return, the central government re-transfers subsidies to the provinces according to the agreed upon fixed amount, earmarked purposes or *ad hoc* appropriation of local budget surpluses (*jiesuan*) at the end of the fiscal year. Aside from the former negotiable transfer system, the present reforms introduced the rule-based transfer for the national taxes supervised by the SAT. For instance, local governments are entitled to the re-transfer of 25, 40 and 40 per cent of the VAT, corporate and individual income tax respectively.

In other words, the tax farming nature of sub-provincial intergovernmental relations is kept unchanged. Superior layers of government farm out taxation to lower layers. Such a tax contract describes the agreed upon share of tax revenue to be transferred to the superior level as well as the agreed upon provision of public services invested and operated by the lower level. Negotiations between different levels of local governments on transfer and re-transfer of revenue became a constant feature of local intergovernmental relations. Regardless of which version of tax contracting is chosen, two systematic features dominate the effects: First, as a 'lessee' and residual claimant, each agency at the lower level attempting to maximise discretionary revenue will shift expenditures for public services upwards while manipulating the tax base to minimise upward transfers (Tsui and Wang, 2004); Second, as will be seen presently, effective tax rates do not reflect tax legislation; they are rather the outcome of intergovernmental tax contracting, and the unsolved principal agent problem, or reflect the ingenuity of sub-provincial government agencies in finding new revenue generating sources.

6.5.3 Dual Tax Administration System

As said earlier, two tax systems co-exist in China. One is defined by national legislation which stipulates the tax base, tax rates, procedures by which taxes are enforced, and how total revenue is shared between the central and local budgets (consolidated at the provincial level). The other one is characterised by provincial and sub-provincial discretion and tax contracting, *ad hoc* taxation, and unspecified procedures. This dual tax system has major implications. First, firms can calculate the effective tax rate only *ex post* when the exact local rates and fees are known. This makes, second, the local government agencies the ultimate authority in defining effective tax rates. Third, local government agencies facing different (financial) needs and/or different political leverage in tax contracting will differ in their revenue generating policy, subsequently contributing to the diversity of the local business environment. Finally, the national treasury or central government has only limited ways of controlling overall taxation. The most recent reform focused only on the revenue and central-provincial sharing side and cut off the link to the government spending. Moreover, the 'tax-for-fee' reform launched in 2000 attempted to put an end to the practices of sub-provincial government agencies using *ad hoc* fees (Yep, 2004) and aimed at tighter budgetary control, yet also on limiting the overall tax burden for overcharged peasant households, i.e. distributional purposes. Since local governments were obliged to generate even more revenue sources by embarking on commercial activities, the effect was minimal, if not counterproductive.

6.6   TOWNSHIPS M AND L: BUDGETS AND INTERGOVERNMENTAL TRANSFER

China has an atypical system of taxation where different jurisdictions overlap and procedures are left unspecified, or burdened with a political rhetoric that confuses even the technical side of tax collection. How does this system work in practice? With only little information available at the local, i.e. prefecture, county and township level, data needed to be generated before a systematic analysis could be attempted. We decided to focus on the lowest level of the political and administrative hierarchy, namely the township, as this is the government agent, which meets the tax payer (in most cases firms)[12]. On the factual side, we wanted to know how the dual tax system affects local budgets, and how intergovernmental transfers contribute to local revenues. On the behavioural side, we wanted to know how the effective tax rate for firms is calculated, how much disposable income townships have and how they make use of their disposable funds. Finally, we expected that the answers to these questions would shed more light on the problem of diversity and local autonomy. The interviews conducted between 2003 and 2005 cannot answer all these questions. Instead of offering general interpretations, we decided to present two case studies, which, to the best of our knowledge, offer the first complete picture of budgets and budgetary procedures in two townships, called M and L[13].

6.6.1   Revenues

The budgets of the two townships presented in Table 6.4 and Table 6.5, offer different pictures which is partly caused by different ways to categorise revenue items. Township M classifies all revenue into two categories only, namely budgetary revenue and extra-budgetary revenue, while Township L is much more specific. In the latter case revenues are listed as budgetary revenue, budgetary fund revenue, earmarked fund revenue and 'other revenue' (Table 6.4). This practice confirms the findings from the World Bank (2002: 64) that there is no standard procedure for reporting revenues at the local level.

After reclassifying the revenue items (in Table 6.5), it becomes clear that Township M depends much more on taxation (45.2 per cent of total financial revenue) and extra-budgetary revenues (22.3 per cent) than Township L (24.4 per cent and 11.6 per cent, respectively). To put it differently, the category of 'other revenue' is essentially revenue from commercial activities, such as land deals, TVE shareholding and other business activities. It contributes 32.5 per cent of total revenue in Township M, yet 64 per cent in Township L, in turn suggesting that the latter is more entrepreneurial. It is worth emphasising the returns from TVEs (dividends or profit) contribute 9.9 per cent of total revenue compared to the proceeds from land sales plus local tax on transaction, which add up to 53.6 per cent of total revenue, in Township L!

6.6.2   Intergovernmental Transfer

Information about intergovernmental transfer of taxes is not published but needs to be generated by interviewing three to four groups of economic agents: representatives of the national and local tax administration, representatives of the local government, and firms. Instead the transfers follow the bargaining between government agencies, and between the township and firms. The interviews in Township M suggest three features that characterise transfer practice at the township level.

1.   Township M has to share revenue with four superior government layers: local (county level); prefectural; provincial; and national. Interaction between these different layers of government agencies is partly statutory, i.e. based on legislation, and partly resulting from previous negotiations. At the time of the interview, seven transfer modes were employed. Aside from the standardised sharing rules supervised by the SAT, a negotiated sharing of 'excess' tax income, as for example more revenue from VAT than anticipated in the tax contracts for a budget year (see below). Other sharing formulae address 'approved budgetary expenditure', 'approved budgetary expenditure of financial department', 'other shared tax items', 'subsidy from superior units' and 'remittance to the prefecture level'. Each mode follows distinctive formulae such as quota-based, growth-based, progressive or regressive rates.

Table 6.4   The revenue side of M and L townships' budgets

M Township	Original tax base	L Township	Original tax base
Budgetary revenue	Income, output	**Budgetary revenue**	Income, output
Bonus remittance of taxes		Bonus remittance of taxes	
Fixed remittance of taxes		Fixed remittance of taxes	
Earmarked subsidy		Earmarked subsidy	
Extra-budgetary revenue		**Budgetary fund revenue**	
Surcharges to taxes for education	Income, output	Surcharges to taxes for rural education	Income, output
Fee for garbage collection	user	Surcharges to taxes for education	Income, output
Fee for sewage disposal	user	**Earmarked fund revenue**	
Fee for public security	p.c., per firm	Profit of TVEs	
Fee for public utility	user	Fee from administration agencies	User, p.c.
Water rates	user	Water conservancy construction fund	p.c., per firm
Fee for family planning	p.c.	Proceeds of education-assets-sale	
Banking interests		Other subsidy	
Other subsidy		**Other revenue**	
Proceeds of land-sale		Proceeds of land-sale	
Fee for land transaction		Fee for land transaction	
Other		Other	

Note: User charges asked by those units that provides the service, i.e. usually public utilities, are not fees in budgetary terms but charged by the providers directly (Eckaus, 2003, 78).

Source: *Respondent 24 & 26 (2004).*

Table 6.5   Composition revenue, 2003: M and L townships

Items	M (%)	L (%)
Total financial revenue	100	100
Budgetary revenue	45.23	24.40
Thereof		
Bonus remittance of taxes	31.90	18.20
Fixed remittance of taxes	12.78	4.58
Earmarked subsidy	0.55	1.62
Extra-budgetary revenue	22.28	11.65
Thereof		
Surcharges to taxes for education	4.08	5.44
Fees charged by administration agencies	6.51	1.63
Other	11.69	4.58
Other revenue	32.49	63.95
Thereof		
Proceeds of land-sale	26.99	44.58
Fees for land transaction	5.24	8.98
Profit of TVEs or governmental investments	0.03	9.85
Other	0.69	0.54

Source: Respondent 24 and 26 (2004).

For instance, in the tax contract for 2003, M Township agreed to collect 120 million RMB in VAT and consumption tax on behalf of the SAT. The actually collected amount added up to 160 million, which was not allocated according to the usual 75:25 percentage formula between the centre and the local units. Instead, Township M is entitled to a bonus based on the 40 million of 'excess' revenue. The calculation follows a 'progressive' rate: 12 per cent bonus for the first 12 per cent of the excess revenue (1.73 million), 15 per cent bonus for the following 12-15 per cent of excess revenue (54 thousand) and 18 per cent bonus for any excess beyond 15 per cent (3.94 million). The total amount of the thus calculated bonus added up to RMB6.2m considerably lower than the RMB10m the local tax agencies would have been entitled to, if the usual tax sharing formula had been applied (Table 6.6).

2.   Superior government agencies, such as the province, prefecture or county can and will press for a sharing formula which squeezes the township of the tax income generated here. All that is needed is a document written on an official letterhead (*hongtou wenjian*). This form

of state capture (Hellman, 1998) can be illustrated by the way the bonus on VAT collection is allocated to different layers of government. For instance, Township M was entitled to a due share of 3.88 per cent of total VAT and consumption tax generated in the township. Yet, Suzhou city, superior to Township M, appropriated 0.6 per cent, leaving M with 3.28 per cent. Even worse, for 2004 Suzhou increased 'its' share to 1.6 per cent, which would cut Township M's share to 2.06 per cent (Table 6.6).

3.   In Jiangsu province, out of the 25 per cent that goes to local units from consumption taxes, 50 per cent is claimed by the provincial government, 16 per cent is claimed at the prefectural level, 6.8 per cent remains at the county level, and only 27.2 per cent remains in the township. Likewise, of the total tax revenue collected by Township M in 2003, 40 per cent went to the central budget, 27 per cent to the provincial budget, 10 per cent to the prefecture budget, 5 per cent to the district (county) budget and 18 per cent to the township budget. Unsurprisingly, the local government officials in Township M 'lament being sacrificed for superior officials'. They, as most other townships, must search for alternative revenue sources. These are usually off-budgetary activities.

6.6.3   Expenditures

Only after looking at both revenue and expenditure can the complete picture of financial flows around the local tax system be seen. One major reason why expenditure needs to be integrated into the analysis of intergovernmental transfers and local budgets is the fact that tax farming between the township and the tax payer shows up on the expenditure side. As said before, the township cannot change or modify tax legislation, while at the same time having a strong incentive to cultivate a wealthy tax base, if not to expand the tax base by attracting additional investment. Thus, the tax contracts between the township and individual firms do not prescribe lower tax rates, for example. Instead tax rebates or exemptions, bonuses, grants, subsidies, or awards are negotiated which promise *ex post* reimbursement for taxes paid. These rebates are usually listed as means for supporting the local economic sector.

Thus for example, L Township grants all firms established since 2001 a three-year exemption (via *ex post* reimbursements from local budget) from VAT, enterprise income tax and business tax. Likewise, firms investing more than ten million RMB in technological innovation enjoy a three-year tax refund. These refunds show up on the expenditure side of the Township L (Table 6.7) under industry and transportation items in 2003, reaching 38 million RMB at 20.9 per cent of Township L's total financial expenditure. In addition to tax preferential treatment, Township L invested 46 million RMB (25.6 per cent of total expenditure) in infrastructure and 65 million RMB (35.9 per cent of total expenditure) in education to improve the investment environment. Land prices are another are of interjurisdictional competition, which at a discounted rate can be used for attracting investment. As Township L claims it was this policy that enabled them to attract 83 new established enterprises in 2003, of which 40 enterprises were from other localities.

Table 6.6   *A case of state capture: sharing VAT and consumption tax revenue M township (2003–2004 in mil. RMB)*

No.	Item	2003	2004[a]	Remarks
1	VAT and consumption tax	160	210	Total tax revenue collected.
2	Revenue target	120	160	Total tax revenue collected in last year.
3	Growth part above revenue target	39	49	3=1–2
4	Share based on 0–12% part of growth part	1.73	2.31	Shared ratio 12%; 4=2*12%*12%
5	Share based on 12–15% part of growth part	0.54	0.72	Shared ratio 15%; 5=2*(15%-12%)*15%
6	Share based on above 15% part of growth part	3.94	4.66	Shared ratio 18%; 6=(3-2*15%)*18%
7	Township entitlement to share	6.21	7.69	7=4+5+6
8	Remittance to prefecture level	0.96	3.36	8=1*remittance ratio (0.6% 2003, 1.6% 2004)
9	Actual shred revenue	5.25	4.33	9=7–8
10	Actual shared percentage (%)	3.28%	2.06%	10=9/1

*Note:*Predicted figure based on revenue task 2004.

Source: Respondent 24 (2004).

To sum up, tax farming at the lowest administrative level defines the *effective tax rate* for firms, i.e. by far the largest taxpayer. The effective tax rate can be calculated only *ex post*, as the rate depends on reimbursement in the following year. Jurisdictional competition between lower level government agencies exists and thrives; yet alimented by local returns from commercial activities of government agencies rather than by 'tax design'.

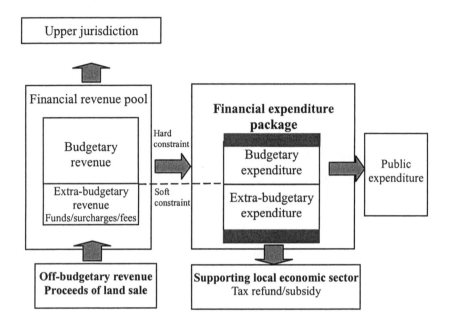

Note: The shadow part of expenditure refers to extra expenditure of actual amount.

Figure 6.3   Financial revenue and expenditure at township level

Intergovernmental transfer is renegotiable and enables agencies (in particular, the middle-layers of government, such as prefecture and county) to appropriate a share of tax revenues. At the township level, tax administration and tax policy cannot be separated. Despite all the technical formulae used within the tax sharing process, the budget procedure at the township level follows three rather straightforward steps. The township first estimates the total amount needed to fulfil the mandatory tasks, keeping the agreed upon commitments to different groups (such as firms) and the money needed to run the local government. In a second step, the township negotiates the volume of tax revenue to be transferred and re-transferred with all other local government agencies. As the township knows the range of transfers and re-transfers from past experience, it can anticipate a deficit or surplus. The township will simultaneously, in a third step, search for additional revenue sources outside the bureaucratic tax system. In short, *the township is not forced to adjust expenditure to revenue available, but adjusts revenue to expenditure planned and contracted.* The system implies further that the more the central state attempts to harden the budget constraint the more entrepreneurial townships will become, by embarking on business activities outside the reach of bureaucratic control.

Table 6.7   The expenditure side of L township's budget, 2003

Items	Amount (million RMB)	Per cent
Total financial expenditure	181	100
Agriculture	4	2.5
Industry and transportation	38	20.9
Infrastructure	46	25.6
Education	65	35.9
Culture	8	4.5
Health	3	1.9
Social	4	2.4
Administration	10	5.4
Other	2	0.9

Source: Respondent 26 (2004).

6.7   CONCLUSION

China's tax system is unique. We don't know of any other case where a national tax bureaucracy and local tax farming co-exist. It would however be misleading to interpret this co-existence as a case where the socialist legacy prevails. To the contrary, the institutional change in taxation is the deliberate response to the political and economic development in China's economic transformation.

First, aside from the rhetoric, the *reforms were driven by transaction cost considerations* and political compromises. Each reform step reveals the search for a broader tax base, and enforcement mechanisms, which increase administrative efficiency. Second, reforms to the tax system *serve as a means to better align the interests* of different government agencies. Unlike other countries where taxation defines hard (budget) constraints and state enforcement agencies, China's tax system offers positive incentives for its tax agents which in return for compliance to the national tax codes (if not the whole reform programme) are entitled to residual tax revenue. Third, tax farming harnesses local autonomy. *It offers townships a resource base outside central control.* It is worth stressing that local autonomy in China is not the consequence of a constitutional separation of power, but the consequence of decentralisation, i.e. the transfer of regulatory power to local agencies, and the transfer of resources that enable local jurisdictions, such as the township, to finance local policy. Fourth, unsurprisingly then, tax farming must contribute to diversity in economic outcomes as well as diversity in the institutional architecture at the local level. It is hard to find evidence which would support the Grabbing Hand or state seizure hypothesis (Northrup and Rowan, 1963; Fry, 2002) on the one hand and the Helping Hand or state capture hypothesis (Hellman, 1998) on the other hand, which claims that over time the central state will increasingly appropriate more resources in the case of the former; or that the alliance between the business community and local government agencies will over time subvert the institutional architecture to better serve their own self-interest. Both would imply the emergence of informal (if not illegal) organisations and institutions, while the tax farming bargaining game is part of the official tax system. From this point of view, local *tax farming can be seen as an ex ante device for limiting, if not even legitimising, ex post opportunism* (of the tax agents). Finally, jurisdictional competition seems to work, limiting overall taxation. This does not mean however that China can expect a corporatist state with as many local business and tax systems as townships or counties. As the interviews indicate, imitation of good (tax) practices in neighbouring localities will lead to at least regional convergence of the *de facto* tax systems, if not tax practices.

NOTES

1. There is a measurement problem. With the notable exception of World Bank (2002), most studies stop at provincial level (see Wong, 1991, 1992, 1997; Wong et al., 1995; World Bank, 1990, 1993, 1995; Brean, 1998; Ma, 1995; Oksenberg and Tong, 1991; Chung, 1995; Lee, 2000; Tsui and Wang, 2004; OECD, 2005) due to the lack of statistical data to the effect that a systematic analysis across provinces, prefectures, counties (districts) and townships is missing.
2. The French, as in the tax farming system of Imperial China, 'farmed out' tax authority not only to lower administrative levels but also to private persons.
3. Except the urban real estate tax.
4. A total of 13 taxes were levied after 1973 which were industrial and commercial tax, consolidated industrial and commercial tax, industrial and commercial income tax, tariff, cattle transaction tax, bazaar transaction tax, urban real estate tax, vehicle and vessel usage license

tax, vessel tonnage tax, slaughter tax, agricultural tax, animal husbandry tax, and deed tax.

5. Consumption tax encompasses 11 tax items and often enough serves as an educational tax discouraging the consumption or use of luxury products, such as cigarettes, liquor, cosmetics, jewellery, firework, gasoline, diesel oil, car tyre, motorcycle, and cars.

6. In fact, total tax items are 26 not 29 because inheritance tax, security transaction tax and fuel tax are not levied yet.

7. Rich provinces may keep a certain portion of incremental revenue based on a preset shared ratio or formula while those poor provinces received subsidies and grants from the central government.

8. This is known in public finance as the Ramsey Rule (1927): immobile factors are more vulnerable to tax as the exit option can be considered at high costs only.

9. The shared tax would be retransferred to local government based on the shared ratio.

10. The ratio of total government revenue to GDP increased from 13% in 1993 to 19% in 2003. The share of the central government revenue to total revenue in 2003 (55%) is about two times of that in 1993 (22%), as shown in Figure 6.1.

11. Major changes in the composition of extra-budgetary revenue in 1993 and 1997 excluded the innovation fund, the major repair fund and government funds.

12. The following findings form part of the larger research project on local autonomy. Both authors want to thank Hans Hendrischke for generously providing us with some findings from his interviews on 2004 and 2005.

13. Close to Suzhou, Jiangsu province, Township M covers 34 square kilometres with population of 53,000 in 2003. Township L is located at 15 kilometres away from Hanghzou, capital of Zhejiang province and covers 43 square kilometres with population of 60,000 in 2003.

REFERENCES

Allen, D.W. and D. Lueck, (1995), 'Risk Preferences and the Economics of Contracts', *American Economic Review*, **85**, 447–451.

Ardant, Gabriel (1975), 'Financial Policy and Economic Infrastructure of Modern States and Nations', in Charles Tilly (ed.), *The Formation of National States in Western Europe*, Princeton, NJ: Princeton University Press.

Bernstein, Thomas P. and Xiaobo Lü, X. (2003), *Taxation without*

Representation in Contemporary Rural China, Cambridge: Cambridge University Press.

Bird, Richard M. and Duan-jie Chen (1998), 'Intergovernmental Fiscal Relations in China in International Perspective', in Donald J.S. Brean (ed.), *Taxation in Modern China*, NY: Routledge Press.

Brean, Donald J.S. (ed.) (1998), *Taxation in Modern China*, New York: Routledge Press.

Brennan, Goeffrey and James M. Buchanan (1980), *The Power to Tax: Analytical Foundations of a Fiscal Constitution*, Cambridge; NY: Cambridge University Press.

Campbell, J. (1996), 'An Institutional Analysis of Fiscal Reform in Postcommunist Europe', *Theory and Society*, **25**, 45–84.

Chang, C. and Y. Wang (1994), 'The Nature of The Township-Village Enterprises', *Journal of Comparative Economics*, **19**, 434–52.

Chen, H. and S. Rozelle (1999), 'Leaders, Managers, and the Organization of Township and Village Enterprises in China', *Journal of Development Economics*, **60**, 529–557.

China Statistical Yearbook (2004), Beijing: China Statistics Press.

Chung, J.H. (1995), 'Studies of Central-provincial Relations in People's Republic of China: A Mid-term Appraisal', *China Quarterly*, **142**, 487–580.

Eckaus, R. (2003), 'Some Consequences of fiscal reliance on extrabudgetary revenues in China', *China Economic Review*, **14**, 72–88.

Fan, Gang (1998), 'Market-oriented Economic Reform and the Growth of Off-Budget Local Public Finance', in Brean, Donald J.S. (ed.), *Taxation in Modern China*, NY: Routledge Press.

Frye, T. (2002), 'Capture or Exchange? Business Lobbying in Russia', *European Asia Studies* (forthcoming).

Frye, T. and A. Shleifer (1997), 'The Invisible Hand and the Grabbing Hand', *American Economic Review Papers and Proceedings*, **87**, 354–358.

Goodman, D.S.G. (2000), 'The Localism of Local Leadership: Cadres in Reform Shanxi', *Journal of Contemporary China*, **9**, 159–183.

Grandy, C. (1989), 'New Jersey Corporate Chartermongering, 1875–1929', *Journal of Economic History*, **49**, 677–92.

Hellman, J.S. (1998), 'Winners Take All: The Politics of Partial Reform in Postcommunist Nations', *World Politics*, **50**, 203–234.

Henderischke, H. (2003), 'How local are local enterprises? Privatisation and translocality of small firms in Zhejiang and Jiangsu', *Provincial China*, **7**, 27–39.

Hsu, S.P. (2004), 'Deconstructing Decentralization in China: fiscal incentive versus local autonomy in policy implementation', *Journal of Contemporary China*, **13**, 567–599.

Kiser, E. (1994), 'Markets and Hierarchies in Early Modern Tax Systems: A Principal Agent Analysis', *Politics and Society*, **22**, 284–315.

Kiser, E. and J. Kane (2001), 'Revolution and State Structure: The Bureaucratisation of Tax Administration on Early Modern England and France', *American Journal of Sociology*, **107**, 183–223.

Kiser, E. and X. Tong (1992), 'Determinants of the Amount and Type of Corruption in State Fiscal Bureaucracies: An Analysis of Late Imperial China', *Comparative Political Studies*, **25**, 300–331.

Kornai, Janos (1986), 'The Soft Budget Constraint', *Kyklos*, **39**, 3–30.

Krug, Barbara (ed.) (2004a), *China's Rational Entrepreneurs: The Development of the New Private Business Sector*, London: Routledge Press.

Krug, Barbara (2004b) 'Introduction: New Opportunities, New Sector, New Firms', in Krug, Barbara (ed.), *China's Rational Entrepreneurs: The Development of the New Private Business Sector*, London: Routledge Press.

Krug, B. and H. Hendrischke (2003), 'China Incorporated: Property Rights, Privatisation, and the Emergence of a Private Business Sector in China', *Managerial Finance*, **29** (12), 32–45.

Lee, P.K. (2000), 'Into the Trap of Strengthening State Capacity: China's Tax-Assignment Reform', *China Quarterly*, **164**, 1007–1025.

Li, D.D. (1996), 'Ambiguous Property Rights in Transition Economies: The Case of the Chinese Non-State Sector', *Journal of Comparative Economics*, **23**, 1–19.

Ma, J. (1995), 'Modelling Central-local Fiscal Relations in China', *China Economic Review*, **6**, 105–136.

Ministry of Finance People's Republic of China (2005), www.mof.gov.cn, Beijing: Ministry of Finance People's Republic of China

Montinola, G., Y. Qian and B.R. Weingast (1995), 'Federalism, Chinese Style: The Political Basis for Economic Success in China', *World Politics*, **48**, 50–81.

Mui, M. and I. Jia (2002), 'China Reforms for the World Stage', *International Tax Review*, **1**.

Musgrave, Richard A. (1959), *The Theory of Public Finance*, NY: McGraw-Hill.

Musgrave, R.A. (1969), *Fiscal Systems*, New Haven and London: Yale University press.

Naughton, B. (1994), 'Chinese Institutional Innovation and Privatisation from Below', *American Economic Review*, **84**, 266–70.

Nee, V. (1992), 'Organizational Dynamics of Market Transition: Hybrid Forms, Property Rights, and Mixed Economy in China', *Administrative Science Quarterly*, **37** (1), 1–27.

Nee, V. (1998), 'Norms and Networks in Economic and Organizational Performance', *American Economic Review*, **88** (2), 85–9.

Northrup, H.R. and R.L. Rowan (1963), 'State Seizure in Public Interest Disputes', *Journal of Business*, **36**, 210–227.

O'Brien, P. K. (1988), 'The Political Economy of British Taxation, 1660–1815', *Economic History Review*, **41**, 1–32.

Oates, Wallace E. (1972), *Fiscal Federalism*, New York: Harcourt brace Jovanovich.

OECD (2005), *Governance in China*, Paris: OECD Publications

Oi, J.C. (1992), 'Fiscal Reform and the Economic Foundations of Local State Corporatism in China', *World Politics*, **45**, 99–126.

Oi, Jean C. (1994), *Rural China Takes Off: Incentives for Reform*, Berkeley: University of California Press.

Oi, J.C. (1995), 'The Role of the Local States in China's Transitional Economy', *China Quarterly*, **144**, 1132–1149.

Oksenberg, M. and J. Tong (1991), 'The Evolution of Central-Provincial Fiscal Relations in China, 1971–1984: The Formal System', *China Quarterly*, **125**, 1–32.

Olson, M. Jr. (1969), 'The Principle of "Fiscal Equivalence": The Division of Responsibilities among Different Levels of Government', *American Economics Review*, **59**, 479–87.

Qian, Y. and G. Roland (1998), 'Federalism and the Soft Budget Constraint', *American Economic Review*, **88**, 1143–62.

Qian, Y. and B.R. Weingast (1996), 'China's Transition to Markets: Market-Preserving Federalism, Chinese Style', *Journal of Policy Reform*, **1**, 149–85.

Qian, Y. and B.R. Weingast (1997), 'Federalism As a Commitment to Market Incentives', *Journal of Economic Perspectives*, **11**, 83–92.

Qian, Y., and B.R. Weingast (1997), 'Federalism as a Commitment to Market Incentives', *Journal of Economic Perspectives*, **11**, 83–92.

Ramsey, F.P. (1927), 'A contribution to the Theory of Taxation', *Economic Journal*, **37**, 47–61.

Sappington, D.E.M. (1991), 'Incentives in Principal-agent Relationships', *Journal of Economic Perspective*, **5**, 45–66.

State Administration of Taxation (2003), www.chinatax.gov.cn, Beijing: State Administration of Taxation

Shirk, Susan L. (1993), *The Political Logic of Economic Reform in China*, Berkeley, CA: University of California Press.

Shleifer, Andrei and Daniel Treisman (1999), *Without a Map: Political Tactics and Economic Reform in Russia*, Harvard, MA: MIT Press.

Stiglitz, J.E. (1974), 'Incentives and Risk Sharing in Sharecropping', *Review of Economic Studies*, **61**, 219–255.

Tsui, K. and Y. Wang (2004), 'Between Separate Stoves and a Single Menu: Fiscal Decentralization in China', *China Quarterly*, **177**, 71–91.

Walder, A.G. (1995), 'Local Governments as Industrial Firms: An Organizational Analysis of China's Transitional Economy', *American Journal of Sociology*, **101**, 263–301.

Walder, Andrew G. (ed.) (1996), *China's Transitional Economy*, Oxford: Oxford University Press.

Wedeman, Andrew H. (2003), *From Mao to Market: Rent-Seeking, Local Protectionism, and Marketization in China*, Cambridge: Cambridge University Press.

Weingast, B.R. (1995), 'The Economic Role of Political Institutions: Market-Preserving Federalism and Economic Development', *Journal of Law and Economic Organization*, **11**, 1–31.

Weir, D.R. (1989), 'Tontines, Public Finance and Revolution in France and England, 1688–1789', *Journal of Economic History*, **49**, 95–124.

Weitzman, M. and C. Xu (1994), 'Chinese Township Village Enterprises as Vaguely Defined Cooperatives', *Journal of Comparative Economics*, **18**, 121–145.

White, E.N. (1995), 'The French Revolution and the Politics of Government Finance, 1770–1815', *Journal of Economic History*, **55**, 227–255.

White, E.N. (2004), 'From Privatised to Government-administered Tax Collection: Tax Farming in Eighteenth-century France', *Economic History Review*, **57**, 636–663.

Winch, Donald and Patrick K. O'Brien (ed.) (2002), *The Political Economy of British Historical Experience, 1688–1914*, Oxford: Oxford University Press.

Wong, Christine P.W. (ed.) (1997), *Financing Local Government in the People's Republic of China*, Hong Kong: Oxford University Press.

Wong, Christine P.W, (1998), 'Fiscal Dualism in China: Gradualist Reform and the Growth of Off-budget Finance', in Donald J.S Brean (ed.), *Taxation in Modern China*, NY: Routledge Press.

Wong, Christine P.W., Christopher Heady and Wing T. Woo (1995), *Fiscal Management and Economic Reform in the People's Republic of China*, Manila: Asian Development Bank.

Wong, Christine P.W. (1991), 'Central-Local Relations in an Era of Fiscal Decline: The Paradox of Fiscal Decentralization in Post-Mao China', *China Quarterly*, No. 128, 691–715.

Wong, C.P.W. (1992), 'Fiscal Reform and Local Industrialization: The Problematic Sequencing of Reform in Post-Mao China', *Modern China*, **18**, 197–227.

World Bank (1990), *China: Revenue Mobilization and Tax Policy*, Washington, DC: World Bank.

World Bank (1993), *Budgetary Policies and Intergovernmental Fiscal Relations*, Washington, DC: World Bank

World Bank (1995), *China: Macroeconomic Stability in a Decentralised Economy*, Washington, DC: World Bank.

World Bank (2002), *China National Development and Sub-national Finance: A Review of Provincial Expenditures*, Washington, DC: World Bank.

Yep, R. (2004), 'Can "Tax-for-fee" Reform Reduce Rural Tension in China? The Process, Progress and Limitations', *China Quarterly*, **177**, 42–71.

Zhu Ze and B. Krug. (2006), 'Is China a Leviathan?' *ERIM Report Series*, ERS-2005-087-ORG, Rotterdam: RSM Erasmus University, Erasmus Research Institute of Management (ERIM).

7. Narratives of Change: Culture and Local Economic Development

David S.G. Goodman

7.1 INTRODUCTION

Outside of the People's Republic of China (PRC) and its various discourses of nationalism, culture is not much favoured as an explanatory device to account for economic change in that country. To the extent that cultural explanations are sought and found in the academic literature the field is largely left to business studies, particularly business management. Those who offer advice on how to do business in China often refer, if in different ways, to the mysteries of Chinese culture (Collins, 2006). In particular much is made of the practice of relying on 'special relationships' (关系 [*guanxi*]).

Indeed, research on 'culture' in the context of the spectacular development of the economy of the PRC during the last thirty years seems to have focussed, often to the exclusion of all else, on the phenomenon of *guanxi*. The term was incorporated into the social science literature on contemporary China in the late 1970s and early 1980s, initially with respect to politics (Pye, 1982; Jacobs, 1980). Now, it is said that *guanxi* is a specifically Chinese cultural construct without which no business can be undertaken successfully in China (Hayes, 2005; Chen and Chen, 2004; Gold, Guthrie and Wank 2001; Luo, 2000) [1]. This focus is problematic not simply because it over-essentialises Chinese society and culture, but also because it hinders consideration of other more meaningful interpretations of the role of culture in explaining both economic development generally and more specifically the development of businesses in the PRC.

This is not the place to undertake a full-scale critique of Pye's earlier formulations on *guanxi* or indeed later developments in the literature. It is clearly the case that business people in China do talk about the need to 拉关系 '*la guanxi*' (to 'pull' or 'rely on special relationships') and 走后门 '*zou houmen*' ('go through the back door') to get things done. To the extent that there is a vocabulary for these practices then it might be possible to argue that the culture expresses itself in particular ways. All the same, to claim that *guanxi* and associated practices are uniquely Chinese for this reason may be doing considerable disservice to social science more widely. Many societies have specific vocabularies for similar practices – think '*protectsia*' in Israel and '*influenza*' in Italy, not to mention 'Masonic' networks in the UK. Most societies have developed similar practices to govern social interactions at some time or another when there is an absence of rules and regulations, when the rule of law is weak or has broken down, or when new regimes are being established, as Charles Tilly pointed out in contemplating the emergence of so-called new forms of entrepreneurship, 'Welcome to the 17th Century!' (Tilly, 2001).

There are essentially three difficulties attending any search for cultural explanations of change in China: culture can be a broad and often a somewhat imprecise concept; the scale of China makes for difficulties in the unit of analysis; and the assumption of historical continuity may be somewhat attenuated. The definition of 'culture' is almost necessarily contested. In practice, the term is applied to a range of concepts including not only the articulation, representation and manifestation of social distinctiveness, but also to the values, attitudes and constructs of a specific society and even the whole of that specific society itself. It may even apply to the attributes of a specific society, or even a section of that society. In China, for example, before the modern era the term 文化 (*wenhua*, culture) referred not simply to (a high level of) education but specifically to the ability to read and write Chinese characters. Those who had culture, who were educated in this way were part of civilisation, those who did not were 'barbarians'. This range of definitions and meanings is of course not very helpful to inquiry. The danger in approaching the idea so broadly is that if everything is 'culture' then effectively nothing is, as the concept loses analytical purchase and operationality.

At the same time, 'culture' cannot but help be somewhat imprecise. While it is always tempting to regard culture as either a resource, finite and tangible, or as a secret ingredient that transforms social and historical background into action (perhaps through some black box explanation) these views are of course misleading. Moreover, culture is neither an organic nor genetic trait of either groups or individuals. Culture is a social construct, occasionally codified (at specific historical moments, such as the birth of new regimes) but more usually a matter of discussion, subject to constant negotiation.

Scale is always important when considering China. 1,300 million people on a large land mass cannot be readily compared, let alone, equated in any sense, with 60 million who live on a small island off the coast of Mainland Europe, or even the relatively homogenous 80 million German speakers in the dominant European economy. China is a continental system which contains a large number of different social and cultural practices. Its 34 provincial-level jurisdictions are most usually country-sized by the standards of the rest of the world (Goodman, 1997). Even in a single province there is often a large variety of first languages, as well as a variety of birth, marriage and death practices, not to mention cuisines. In Guangdong Province alone, there are six major language groups; and five in North China's Shanxi Province, with almost every one of the province's 100 counties having well-recorded language variations. There may be homogenising elements in society and culture that result from and accompany economic growth and development, but as with the economy there is essentially still a low level of integration (Keng, 2001; Keng, 2006; Goodman, 2002). Of course, this is not to argue that there is no such thing as Chinese culture, but rather that it is a concept of more limited usefulness than might immediately appear to be the case. There are commonalities in terms of the state and statecraft, and by extension through the education system to high culture, especially writing and painting. On the other hand, other social interactions, notably family structures, music, material cultures, food and drink, and business practices are significantly more localised.

The various discourses of modern Chinese nationalism all make much of the equation between the PRC and a historic China. Today's PRC is said to be the inheritor of Chinese culture from the Chinese imperial system (Fitzgerald, 1994). Much is made of the Confucian Tradition, which in large measure is taken to be the definition of Chineseness. In addition, while modern Chinese nationalism assays an ethnic distinction between the Han Chinese and other inhabitants of the PRC, it simultaneously also attempts to recognise all inhabitants of the PRC as Chinese in the sense of citizens of China, all of whom are said to have historically been subject to the Confucian Tradition. The difficulty is that those different (and sometimes conflicting) notions of Chineseness are modernist ideas shaped by initially European understandings of sovereignty and identity which the Imperial system and the Confucian Tradition did not share (Dikotter, 1997; Chih-yu, 2002; Guo, 2003). Moreover, they are all still less (roughly) than a 100 years old. Before 1900 those who lived in the area we now call China referred to it by the name of the ruling dynasty rather than as any form of the 'Middle Kingdom' [2] and to themselves as subjects of the dynastic ruler. The apparent form of an ethnic descriptor was not adopted until the the twentieth century neologism of 汉人 (*Hanren* or Han) adopted in a deliberate reference back to the Han Dynasty (206 BCE to 221 CE) long recognised as a 'Golden Age.'

The antidote to essentialisation about Chinese culture is to approach explanation at a more local level. A recognition that there are local accounts of social and economic change that both help motivate behaviour and provide legitimation for specific forms of activity provides a more convincing framework for understanding the role of culture in both the evolution of the economic environment and business development. The argument has been presented elsewhere that an emphasis on local culture and identity encourages business participation and (through targeting of specific historical examples) provides reassurance generally for moves towards commercialisation in China's transitional economy (Goodman, 2004).

The evidence from an examination of town and village enterprises (TVE) and their enterpreneurs in Taiyuan, provincial capital of Shanxi; of Islamic Salar entrepreneurs in Xunhua (Qinghai Province); and of women entrepreneurs in Qiongshan, Hainan[3] suggests that local culture also plays a role in determining the manner of business development, especially structures of ownership, management and operation, as well as to some extent the kinds of economic activity that are developed. Each community has its own narrative of change that explains to each individual where they fit into the community and where their community fits into the wider world. This is not to argue that firms and entrepreneurship should not be seen in terms of networks of special relationships, for they are clearly important to each and every operation. Rather it is to emphasise that the culturally distinct aspects of economic development are deeper in the background, more long term, and without question more local.

7.1.1 TVE Entrepreneurs in Taiyuan

Taiyuan is the provincial capital of Shanxi Province: a heavy industrial centre in North China since the 1920s, as well as a resource rich area of the interior centred on coal. The city had a population at the end of 1998 that was 2.96 million out of a provincial total of 31.72 million people. At that time, its GDP per capita was 10,971 *yuan*, over twice the provincial average of 5,072 *yuan*[4]. Shanxi's role in China's political economy is determined not only by its dominance of the coal, coke, aluminum and specialist steels industries, but also by the Chinese Communist Party's deep social roots in the province, that resulted from its mobilisation there during the Sino-Japanese War of 1937–1945 when the province hosted the three major front line areas of national resistance (Breslin, 1989; Goodman, 2000). During the Mao-dominated era of modern China's political life, many of the models for socio-cconomic experimentation were located in Shanxi, including most notably, the Dazhai Production Brigade. Deng Xiaoping was based in the province's southwest during 1938–1945 and many of his allies in the development of the PRC's reform program from the late 1970s on were from Shanxi. Taiyuan is where these social, economic and political influences meet and are writ large.

Not least because of its interior location, Shanxi was necessarily slower to embrace the agenda of 'reform and openness' adopted nationally by the

Chinese Communist Party (CCP) at the end of 1978. Nonetheless, in 1992 Shanxi adopted economic and social restructuring in earnest with dramatic effect: after 1995 Shanxi's annual rate of GDP growth consistently outperformed the national average (*Provincial China*, 1998). The new 'Overtaking' strategy was designed not simply to achieve growth but also to transform the structure and practice of the provincial economy. Its focus was on the development of infrastructure for industry and communications, in particular to the goal of becoming a major energy provider – coal, coke and electricity – to the rest of the country. Where previously the province had exported its raw materials elsewhere (despite inadequate communications), now processing was to be locally based.

A crucial part of the new strategy was a provincial cultural development strategy, which emphasised both the importance of local identities within Shanxi and the province's central role in the shaping of China's culture as a whole. Much was made of Shanxi's place at the centre of (and sometimes the generator of) Chinese culture and tradition, as well as its role in the birth of the CCP regime through resistance to Japan (Goodman, 1999). Equally, the focus on local identity and self-help could not have been stronger. In 1993, the leader of Shanxi Province, Hu Fuguo, in his speech to the Provincial People's Congress broke dramatically with the tradition of political discourse established since the mid-1950s when he emphasised his local perspective:

> I was born in Shanxi, grew up in Shanxi, lived and worked in Shanxi for 44 years. Shanxi is my home, and the Shanxi people raised me as a son of peasants. As the saying goes "Home influences are hard to change, home feelings hard to forget". I have never been able to forget the affection of the people at home. My own fate and that of my home are firmly bound together (Hu, 1996a).

Later, he moved on more dynamically in his speech to the 7th Shanxi CCP Provincial Congress in January 1996:

> It has been nearly half-a-century since the Liberation. What reason do we have to see our people live such a poor life? Shanxi enjoys rich natural resources and our people are kind-hearted and hard-working. How can we continue to let them live in poverty ? Shanxi people made enormous contributions to the nation during the revolutionary war and subsequent socialist construction. How can we reward them with such poverty? How can we allow our people to enter the 21st century in the shackles of poverty? (Hu, 1996b).

These statements and the shaping of a provincial cultural development strategy provided the legitimacy for a rapid change in the province's economic structure, reflected overwhelmingly and positively in both the attitudes and actions of TCE entrepreneurs interviewed in Taiyuan[5].

Coal clearly dominates the economy has it has done since the early twentieth century – approximately 20 per cent of the provincial economy was derived from extraction and processing in the late 1990s and a further 20-25 per cent was derived from coal-related industry[6]. The new development strategy targeted specialist steels and aluminium, energy and coal derived materials. In particular, it led to the development of a township and village enterprise-based processing and consumer goods industry, especially in coal-derived and coal-industry-supporting activities. By the late 1990s this sector accounted for 33 per cent of provincial GDP from a virtual standing start (*Touzi daokan*, 1996). According to state statistics, a significant feature of change has been the well-above average expansion of the private sector of the economy, which on a provincial basis was second only to Zhejiang Province in its share of GDP (*Statistical Yearbook in Provincial Perspective*, 1997). Indeed, within Shanxi itself there was suspicion that the real figure for the size of the private sector was considerably higher, with many private entrepreneurs masquerading for political reasons as part of the local government economy (Jia, 1998).

The heavy-industry focus to local economic development, particularly centred on coal and its by-products (including chemicals and plastics) is hardly remarkable given Shanxi's resource base. More surprising perhaps is the extent to which change has taken place within a framework of inherent political conservatism. Taiyuan has been a party-state dominated city jurisdiction since before 1949 and so it has remained. Unlike economic change in Zhejiang or Jiangsu, where it was sometimes an advantage to be seen apart from the institutions of the party-state (Goodman, 2006), in Taiyuan participation at a high level was an entrepreneurial requirement. TVE entrepreneurs either had to start off with a solid background in the party-state or, if they had previously been on the outer and energised by the calls of the Overtaking Strategy, they had to be prepared to take on a role (and often a leadership role) in the party-state locally.

By 1998 there were estimated to be about 51,813 enterprises in Taiyuan, whose metropolitan area includes a sizeable rural hinterland, of which 21,810 were service enterprises and 5,306 were state sector enterprises[7]. Taiyuan's pre-reform local power elite with its foundations in both heavy industry and earlier communist traditions has certainly been a major source for the local 'new rich'. At the same time, it has also been possible for previously less politically privileged entrepreneurs to be socially mobile, especially within the services sector. However, these are not two economically or socially distinct groups: economic and social change has been driven by a series of strategic alliances – between capital and knowledge, between the local power elite and the previously politically excluded, and between the private and the public.

Taiyuan's entrepreneurs in the late 1990s came from a bewildering array of companies whose official designations often effectively masked their status as having either owners or managers. Not all managers are managers, particularly in the collective local government sector where some are owners; and ownership is more usually mixed than the official categorisation of the economy into state, collective, private and foreign-funded sectors implies. Indeed, ownership and management are probably less important signifiers of activity than entrepreneurship, especially as the latter is now required even of state sector enterprise managers. Formally, the state sector is the planned part of the economy; the collective sector is the unplanned part of the state economy, with enterprises owned by the workers in the company (mainly in urban areas) or by a locality (mainly in rural areas); and the private sector is that for owner-operators. However, in practice with reform these distinctions have become increasingly less meaningful as explanations of economic structures and activities (Nee, 1992; Goodman, 1995).

With change it has become possible to identify five categories of TVE entrepreneurs, differentiated by organisational context, the major source or sources of investment, and by the scale of activity: rural entrepreneurs, private entrepreneurs, joint venture managers, private enterprise managers, and owner-operators. Table 7.1 provides information on the scale and size of the different kinds of enterprise (as indicated by the size of average fixed assets and net profits) which were identified in interviews with TVE entrepreneurs. A comparison is also provided with local state sector enterprises which indicate very clearly the smaller scale of TVE operations.

Table 7.1   *Average fixed assets and profits after tax for different categories of enterprise by sector, million yuan per annum, Taiyuan,1999*

	Fixed assets	Net profits
Rural enterprises	26.54	4.10
Private enterprises	42.31	7.52
Foreign-funded joint ventures	52.23	3.22
Owner-operator Enterprises	6.77	317
State sector enterprises	1,583.91	22.29

The rural enterprises include collectives and stock companies established by townships, villages, and districts in Taiyuan's rural and suburban areas. Although originally fairly small-scale and village-based, often growing out of former agricultural machinery workshops, shops and restaurants, many took advantage of the rural sector's preferential economic regulation to develop sizeable industrial concerns, especially in mining and associated activities. The growth of rural enterprises was particularly spectacular in suburban areas where villages were able to benefit from their rural status as well as access to markets and technical inputs. In Taiyuan for example, one former suburban village ceased farming, having sold its land to the municipality and invested the returns in building one of the city's biggest department stores, which it now operates. Rural entrepreneurs were most likely to be local residents, and frequently former local officials, who mobilised the locality behind the particular idea that led to the development of the enterprise. Many had been the village head in name or in fact, and were members of the CCP, if not branch officials.

Technically the desgnation of a foreign-funded joint venture could apply to any other kind of enterprise that brought in investment from outside the PRC, including Hong Kong. There are about a 100 of these in Taiyuan, with half sourced from Taiwan or through Hong Kong. Most are large and developing versions of private or state sector enterprise, though there are also a few rural collectives and social unit–owned companies that have transformed themselves into joint ventures. Joint venture managers in Taiyuan anecdotally are seen to be rather ostentatious. Certainly they come overwhelmingly from 'good' political backgrounds with parents who have worked at a high level in the party-state; have often been state officials themselves; have a high level of education; and are usually members of the CCP.

The designation 'private enterprise' applies to those which have either become designated as collective enterprises through cooperation with local government or which have become share-based companies, but where the original individual entrepreneur remains in the senior management position. Private enterprise was initially sanctioned by the CCP during the 1980s as small-scale economic activities such as retail and service provision which were more efficiently provided in this way according to market needs. There was virtually no thought given to individual enterprise development and indeed when small-scale private entrepreneurs started to accumulate and wanted to reinvest in new areas, and especially wanted to become small-scale industrialists, they found themselves without access to bank loans, or the additional labour, machinery and land that they required (Young, 1989). In consequence, private entrepreneurs wanting to expand or to develop into new areas have usually cooperated with local government, villages, townships or occasionally with state sector enterprises to form new companies. In contrast, as Table 7.1 indicates, owner-operator enterprises remain fairly small-scale.

Owner-operators are either those who own and run the entire economic infrastructure of a private sector enterprise, or those who run businesses based on village, local government, state or collective sector ownership of capital where the operation of the enterprise is then contracted out. Elsewhere in China, owner-operators are frequently characterised as young, poorly educated, and the previously economically and politically excluded (White, 1998; Young, 1991). In Taiyuan this was certainly somewhat the case during the 1980s. However, in the 1990s whilst many owner-operators remained young, private enterprise also began to attract considerable numbers of university graduates whose parents were more from the establishment – either as state officials or members of the CCP – than from the socio-economic periphery.

The final category of new entrepreneurs were the managers of the larger private enterprises. There are some extremely large-scale private enterprises, which are the size of large-scale state sector enterprises. The Antai International Enterprise Group Company, led by Li Anmin, which is based in and dominates Jiexiu County, to the south of Taiyuan is one of those. Founded originally on coke production in the 1980s it has now expanded into a range of coal industry by-products, fashion and textiles, and owns its own trains. It has also built its headquarters in Taiyuan: an enormous skyscraper which is the city's second tallest building, after the People's Bank of China. As with the managers of joint venture firms, private enterprise managers are likely to be well-educated, with experience working in the party-state and to be CCP members themselves.

As these comments suggest, the CCP has remained central to the processes of social and economic change in Taiyuan. However, in keeping with changed national priorities, the CCP's processes and mobilisatory techniques to ensure that centrality were inclusionary and accommodative rather than ideologically driven. The social role of the CCP in the formation of new enterprises is perhaps the most dramatic: the children of party-state officials and state sector managers moved on in disproportionate numbers to become TVE entrepreneurs during the 1990s. They almost certainly built on their parents' associations within the party-state to the extent that those who were small-scale owner-operators often did not see an immediate need to become members of the CCP themselves. Table 7.2 summarises information about the social and political relationships between entrepreneurs, their parents, and the party-state.

There would appear to have been two predominant career paths for Taiyuan's new TVE entrepreneurs: they were either members of the party-state at local levels who had taken the lead in developing economic initiatives and enterprises; or they were individuals who having become successful entrepreneurs were then recruited to the CCP. The relatively high proportion of owner-operators outside the CCP, though still not large, reflects the process of incorporation. Owner-operators were generally younger entrepreneurs with small-scale operations who as they became more successful would become private entrepreneurs, at which stage if they were not already CCP members it would be more likely for them to be invited to join, particularly where they were children of CCP members themselves.

Table 7.2   Entrepreneurs and the party-state, percentage in each category of entrepreneur, Taiyuan,1996–99

Category of entrepreneur	Parent in party-state	Entrepreneur worked elsewhere in party-state	Member CCP
Rural entrepreneur	45	59	82
Private entrepreneur	51	61	68
Joint venture manager	43	76	80
Private enterprise manager	52	76	87
Owner-operator	47	22	41

The CCP has clearly sought to incorporate most of the more successful owner-operators and private entrepreneurs into the activities of the party-state. Often this has been through recruitment into the CCP, as Table 7.2 indicates, though this technique is not used exclusively. A number of high profile, successful private entrepreneurs (most usually responsible for fairly large-scale enterprises) have quite explicitly not been permitted to join the CCP, even though party branches have been established in their enterprises. Instead they are publicised as 'model entrepreneurs' and become delegates to the Provincial and National People's Congresses, which can certainly be regarded as other forms of membership in the party-state[8].

7.1.2   Salar Entrepreneurs in Xunhua

Generally speaking the various peoples and communities of Qinghai Province, in Northwest China, have been even slower to adapt to the new spirit of economic reform than was the case in Shanxi (Goodman 2004). The exception has been the Salar People of Xunhua County, in the Eastern part of Qinghai. Xunhua has been regarded as the 'homeland' within the PRC of the Salar – an Islamic, Turkic people – since 1955[9]. Though the result of entrepreneurialism here has not been considerable wealth by the standards of

Eastern China, it has been substantial for a county within Qinghai. Growth through the 1990s had resulted in a GDP by 2001 of RMB30m (US$3.75 m). The explanation of this dramatic turnaround in the fortunes of Xunhua would seem to be a product of the Salar's revival of their culture and identity, made all the more remarkable because from 1958 to about 1982 the PRC moved to suppress Salar culture.

Xunhua is a county of 2,100 square kilometres that runs for 90 kilometers along the course of the Yellow River as it moves into Gansu Province, at between 1780 meters above sea level (the low point is exactly where the Yellow River enters Gansu Province) and 4498 meters above sea level. It is a county of mountains and valleys, poorly connected to the rest of China and poorly integrated in itself. Until 1972 there was no paved road into or out of the county. The main communication route was along the Yellow River into the Linxia District of Gansu. There is an extremely fertile strip along both sides of the Yellow River, with a heavy clay soil, where annual yields of 800 *jin* of grain per *mu* are normal. At the same time a large part of the county is barren mountains, referred to by locals as 'the land where nothing lives', and not even suitable, as elsewhere in Qinghai Province for grazing.

In 2001, Xunhua County had about 120,000 people, and just under 30,000 households, living in 147 towns and villages [10]. Xunhua's population is predominantly Salar (62 per cent) though a substantial minority (24 per cent) are Tibetans, largely agriculturalists living in the Tibetan villages at the east of the county. Relationships between the Salar and Tibetans are for the most part close. Most adult Salar speak a fair amount of Amdo Tibetan. Salar refer generally to Tibetans in extremely friendly tones as *ajiou* meaning 'maternal uncle', a term denoting as close a relative as can be without being parent, child or sibling (Ma, Ma and Stuart, 2001), and during the 1950s the two communities cooperated on several occasions in acts of resistance against the PRC. These culminated in 1958 with an outright revolt which led to the suppression of Salar culture until the early 1980s. Large numbers of Salar males were sent to 'Reform through Labour' camps, mosques were closed, and cultural artefacts were removed from Xunhua 'for safe keeping'. Repression only ended with the changed PRC policies towards the so-called 'minority nationalities' including the Salar, during the early 1980s.

PRC-recognised minority nationalities are required to have their own language and their own homeland within the PRC (Harrell, 1994). In the 1950s the Salar became a state-recognised nationality defined through their distinctive Salar language, their homeland in Xunhua County, and additionally their origins as exiles from the Samarkand area in today's Uzbekistan (*Salazu jianshi bianxiezu*, 1982). Exile is not only central to the definition of the Salar; a sense of banishment, of being 'outsiders' is also part of common consciousness in Xunhua County and indeed for the Salar as a whole. In addition, there are various underlying accounts of migration in explanations of Salar identity, including not only their origin but also their interaction with both the Islamic world and Chinese society. Crucially the Salar see themselves as both Muslims and Chinese, preferring to use Chinese for reading and writing, though still retaining the Salar language for speech (and Arabic for religious purposes).

The evidence of the Salar as a people in exile from Samarkand (or indeed anywhere else) is somewhat attenuated at best (Goodman, 2005). Nonetheless, there is no denying its prevalence as a highly active myth of origin. Exile is particularly interesting as part of the definition of Salar identity because unlike other exiled groups there is no imperative to return and no presentation of themselves as victims. On the contrary, interviews with Salar businessmen and community leaders suggest that discourses of exile and migration are now once again in use as instruments of Salar mobilisation and wealth generation. The key economic activities have been the export of labour outside the county, the wool industry, and the production of cloths and clothing with Islamic religious significance.

Religion, language, and Xunhua have been key pillars in the recent elaboration of Salar identity that reinforce feelings of community and solidarity and encourage individuals to economic activism. So too is exile, which helps the Salar believe they have a competitive advantage that comes from not being fundamentally native to the area in which they live and operate, despite having been born and grown up there. They see themselves as being both more mobile than those around them and more dynamic elements in the development of society.

The self-attributed case for Salar exceptionalism, and in particular the link between the nationality's origins in exile, on the one hand, and social and economic activism, on the other, can be seen in the following reports of interviews with local entrepreneurs. They convey the spirit of Salar activism in the development not only of Xunhua, but also of Qinghai and China's Northwest. These vignettes provide evidence of the range of motivations, as well as of activism and leadership to be found among community leaders and business people. In particular, they highlight the ways in which individuals proceeded to activism from an understanding of a special Salar 'outsider' status; emphasised Salar physical mobility and outwardness in outlook; and developed local products, including religious artefacts, for the wider market.

'Ever since I was young I've been an entrepreneur', admitted Manager Ma[11]. His group enterprise now owns a transport company with twelve trucks that shuttle between Qinghai and the Tibet Autonomous Region; and three hotels, one in each of Xunhua, Xining and Ping'an (the Dalai Lama's birthplace just east of Xining). At a young age he was a trader in Qinghai, the Tibet Autonomous Region, Gansu and Ningxia, selling clothes and food products. With the money he generated from these activities in the 1980s and early 1990s he invested in hotels and trucks. When asked about the secret of his success, he referred to the large spirit and high energy levels of the Salar. 'As our history of exile clearly demonstrates' he said 'Salars can suffer a lot and still prosper.' This was a message echoed both explicitly and implicitly by other interviewees.

One was another Ma, this time a village CCP branch secretary, and a long time leader of his village[12]. A peasant in Xunhua until the 1980s, he was one of the first to harnass the opportunities presented as part of the Salar revival to mobilise his fellow villagers to economic goals. His village has limited arable land (less than 0.5 mu per capita) so he encouraged others to engage in economic activities outside Xunhua. 'Our ancestors were forced to leave Samarkand, so we can certainly travel less permanently for work'. In the early 1980s he led a group of villagers from his home and adjacent villages to undertake odd jobs at a copper mine elsewhere in Qinghai, and then to mine gold in Sichuan. Fifty of the village's 215 households have now been running restaurants outside Xunhua for many years. Eighty of the village's households have formed odd job teams that travel outside the county for work in summer and return for winter. In addition, nine of the village's households have been able to afford to buy trucks or buses that shift people and goods around the Northwest. For himself Ma has become fairly wealthy, now has seven sons, and eventually (2001) opened a brick plant.

A similar story was told by another Ma, also a village leader[13]. Since the early 1980s he has led his village's 310 households to such good affect that only three households now live in poverty. Yields are good on the available arable land (1000 *jin* of wheat per *mu*; the village also grows prickly ash and walnuts) but there is precious little workable land. Under Ma's influence and appeals to moving to the work (as opposed to expecting the work to come to it) the village now has twelve private trucks or buses, with about 100 villagers going to work outside Xunhua on a regular basis. There are about 20 households from this village working in Xining, 30 in Golmud and over 30 households responsible for eateries in the coastal cities of the PRC. As Ma pointed out 'historically, we're used to moving about' and 'now [2002] Salar restaurants in coastal cities can bring in about 50-60,000 *yuan* each per year'.

Manager Han has developed one of Qinghai's largest companies, based on the production of wool from sheep and yak, and attributes the success of the company directly to the fact of Salars being 'outsiders' and so therefore willing to always go that step further in making an effort, as well as to new technology[14]. In the 1980s, Manager Han had been the manager of a small state run enterprise in Xunhua engaged in wool production. Through the 1990s he restructured the company, expanded it and turned it into a local collective. Based initially on sheep's wool – in his view 'Qinghai Xunhua sheep, and their wool, are the best' – he then thought to branch out into yak's wool production. He traveled widely throughout north and northwest China to find out about new equipment, which he eventually ordered from Italy. The company became so successful that by 2000 they had moved their headquarters operation to Xining, exporting not only to Italy and Europe, but also to North America. As with many new Salar industrialists, Manager Han's localist discourse leads him not only into providing jobs and economic opportunities for his local community but ensures that he is a major donor to communal causes.

Ma Yitzhak (Yisihake) [15] is an even more large-scale entrepreneur and the effective owner of Qinghai's largest private enterprise, the Xuezhou Sanrong Group, whose Snow Lotus brand is familiar to many cashmere sweater-wearers outside China. This was a village-based company established in the late 1980s as a self-help endeavour led by Ma. Though he is clearly heavily influenced by his Salar background and upbringing, like many others of those interviewed, this is not an inward-looking perspective on the world. His stated goal has been to 'Take Australia's history and economic growth on the sheep's back as a model for Qinghai's development.' [16] He has in his own words, applied 'Salar dynamism to develop pastoral products and build a business in the international market'. The company now exports all over the world and now even imports wool from Australia. Interestingly Ma Yitzhak was quite outspoken in his criticism of officials in Xining whose behaviour in repeatedly telling him that Xunhua was one of the most undeveloped places he found offensive. According to Ma, since 1989 Xunhua's growth had been one of the strongest in China's West, thanks to the Salar. At the same time, and reflectively, he accepted that buildings and technology change faster than people's patterns of thinking.

Another Han is General Manager of a Salar cloth and hat maker company that has taken traditional Salar products to a wider market, largely through automation[17]. The company grew out of a small village factory producing animal products (leather and skins) in the early 1990s. Through bank loans and with local government support Han and his father (who runs the headquarters office in Xining) have been able to expand the business significantly with sales now going all over China, even to non Salar. There is apparently a sizeable and growing market for minority nationality's products. Necessarily because of its output, the factory is a center of community focus. In particular, designs and product ideas are provided from the community. Han's own experience had previously been that of a trader around North and Southwest China, which he said had provided him with a broader perspective than for most people in Qinghai.

Manager Ma runs a chili paste production factory in Gaizi[18]. Chili paste production is a major industry in Gaizi, with three other competing plants, though Manager Ma's is the biggest. He buys in chilis from the nearby five villages and produces three product lines, which are then marketed quite widely in northwest China: Beef Complement, Prickly Ash paste, and Chili Paste. He sees his competition as coming from Sichuan, Anhui and Gansu. According to Manager Ma the secret of the factory's success has been the excellence of the Xunhua chilis, grown on the soil and with the special climate that exists there; and the activism of the local Salar people. At the same time, he recognises that 'chili production is part of poverty' and was driven by a need to do something to help his native village. 'Like our earlier ancestors when they first arrived here, we do our best with the available resources'.

Han Zhanxiao was a quite well-known Salar folklorist before the suppression of Salar customs and practices in the late 1950s[19]. Together with his family he now produces Salar embroidery for ceremonial purposes as well as other Salar musical and secular artifacts. In the 1950s he had been a music folklorist and had left Xunhua for Beijing and the Central Nationalities Institute. After his release from imprisonment at the end of the Cultural Revolution he started work again with the Beijing Folklore Festival which took him around the PRC. By the time he eventually retired and returned to Xunhua in the 1990s he had come to see the 'need for creation and representation of our nationality. I had particularly come to realise this lack after a visit to Inner Mongolia. We need logos and symbols to represent Salar identity to the outside world as well as to ourselves.' One result was the development of his family folklore enterprise.

7.1.3 Women Entrepreneurs in Qiongshan

The third example of the impact of local culture on economic change and business development is the experience of women entrepreneurs in Qiongshan, Hainan. Hainan Island was part of Guangdong Province before it achieved provincial status in its own right in 1988. Simultaneously, Hainan became a Special Economic Zone (SEZ) alongside Shenzhen and the other three SEZ in South China. The developmental goal (implemented from the top down and led to a large extent by intellectuals from Beijing sent to Hainan for the purpose (Brodsgaard, 1998; Feng and Goodman, 1998) was to build on Hainan's position as a tropical island in the South China Sea, and open the island wide to foreign economic influences. Fairly rapidly, the result was significant foreign investment, loans and trade activity. Hainan gained a reputation as an almost completely uncontrolled society: the PRC's equivalent of the Wild West where 'anything goes', particularly socially. Economic growth was rapid until the early 1990s when overinvestment in real estate created a bubble that broke dramatically leading to considerably more restrained development.

Hainan Province is a highly compartmentalised society, with five different communities, each of whom has a competing vision of the island's identity and autonomy. A strong sense of history (especially around the experiences of the immediate post 1949 period), ethnic identity, linguistic difference, as well as clearly defined positions in Hainan's economic geography and political economy have combined to create largely self-identifying and self-contained communities. Of Hainan's seven million people, around two million are native born speakers of Hainanese, the descendants of fairly constant mainland migration to Hainan over several centuries to 1949. There are a million Li, the island's aborigines, and smaller groups of Zhuang, Miao and Cantonese speakers from the mainland immediately to the north who had also been in Hainan for several centuries.

The majority of the island's population belongs to three roughly equal-sized communities who have migrated here since 1949 (Weng, 2000)[20]. The first are the 'Old Mainlanders' who came here immediately after the formation of the PRC essentially to ensure the mainland's political control. The second are the Overseas Chinese resttled here to a place of safety after withdrawal from Southeast Asia during the difficult years for Chinese in the region during the 1950s and 1960s. The third community are the 'New Mainlanders' those who have come to Hainan during the late 1980s and early 1990s or their families. Many of those who migrated at that time were attracted by the economic opportunities, but there were also a substantial number from northern China concerned at the possible consequences in Beijing and the surrounding areas after the events of May–June 1989. Political and economic power lies very much with the two mainland communities (Feng and Goodman, 1997). The more Hainanese remain excluded from serving in senior positions on grounds that they speak inadequate Modern Standard Chinese, and through the introduction of a particularly draconian law of 'locality avoidance' that prohibited senior cadres from the same locality serving together in any administrative unit (Chen 1989; Ch'u 1962)[21].

The two mainlander communities live almost exclusively in the provincial capital, Haikou, which has more than doubled in size with the incorporation of neighbouring Qiongshan in 2002 into a Greater Haikou. Qiongshan was originally considerably more important than Haikou. From the Tang Dynasty on, Qiongshan was the main city on Hainan Island. Haikou was the port. This relationship lasted even under the CCP, until the mid 1950s. The change in Hainan's political centre of gravity probably came with the dismissal of Feng Baiju who had been based in Qiongshan. Feng was the long-time leader of the CCP in Hainan, a history which included the longest established CCP

Base Area, in the centre of the island (and with native Li support) from 1927 to 1949. As the CCP sought to centralise political authority there was a series of clashes between Beijing and local political leaders – of which this was one – all of which led the latter into difficulties even where they avoided yet more serious penalties (Teiwes, 1966).

The creation of a Greater Haikou follows decades of administrative chaos between the two neighbouring cities. There was, for example, environmental degradation as the two cities were unable to share sewerage provision and simply dumped waste on the other. Postal services broke down completely and in 2001 the Haikou City Government impounded more than a 100 Qiongshan taxis, on the grounds that they were an interference to the Haikou taxi system. The Qiongshan City Government appealed to the Provincial Government, and requested compensation from Haikou (Zhong, 2002).

Even allowing for the relative novelty of changed administrative arrangements, interviews conducted in Qiongshan a couple of years after the establishment of a Greater Haikou have confirmed the uneasy history of the past[22]. There was considerable pride expressed in the Qiongshan identity. Roughly 40 per cent of those interviewed saw Qiongshan's 'glorious history' as an economic advantage, not least because they saw its historical sites as being more likely to attract tourism. About 30 per cent thought that Qiongshan was now financially better off since its incorporation into the provincial capital. At the same time, about 30 per cent still saw Qiongshan as a separate entity and talked about 'its location close to the provincial capital'. On the other hand, about two-thirds thought that the development of Greater Haikou had been generally disadvantageous to the development of Qiongshan. Local industry had in their view, taken a hit on its performance, not least because Haikou's planning procedures worked to the disadvantage of Qiongshan as well as creating (necessary) discontinuities. Before 2002 there had been a plan for Qiongshan's industrial development and a scheme to develop a new industrial district. These had all now been shelved. Generally there was a feeling that the quality of Qiongshan's administrative services had declined and that the public security environment had worsened.

Migration is the key to understanding the development of contemporary Qiongshan. As already noted, while there are some pockets of native Hainanese in Qiongshan, particularly in its rural districts, the population is overwhelmingly comprised of either New or Old Mainlanders. With the relative economic slowdown of the last decade (to 2004 when fieldwork was undertaken in Hainan) a large proportion of the local population are also Old Mainlanders who have drifted to Qiongshan and Haikou in search of work from other towns and localities around the island (*Hainan sheng*). Of the women entrepreneurs interviewed in Hainan, two-thirds had migrated to Hainan since 1988, and the remainder had been Old Mainlanders divided almost equally between those from families who had initially settled in Qiongshan and those who had settled elsewhere but then more recently moved to Qiongshan. Six of the women entrepreneurs were not married. For those who were married, similar proportions of migrant background applied to their husbands. Only three of the women married Hainanese men. Migration from all over the PRC is indicated by the distribution of source provinces for the women and their husbands, though there were large numbers from Hubei and Jiangxi in the sample.

When questioned about their migration to Qiongshan, it is clear that family ties play a significant role. About a quarter moved before marriage and in each case they had a brother or sister already living on the island. Six of the women came to Qiongshan to seek economic opportunities along with their husbands, and two later followed their husbands once the latter had settled.

It is also clear that social networks from home towns and villages were important in determining migration and the development of new businesses. Three of the migrant couples, where the wife was interviewed, all came form the same village in Jiangxi, and all ran clothes shops on the same street in Qiongshan. In interviews the wives revealed that most people in their original home village in Jiangxi are engaged in clothes manufacturer and it is an established tradition for them to come to Qiongshan. [23] To take another example: a woman from Zhejiang Province who ran a glasses shop in Qiongshan said '80 per cent of the optical shops in Haikou are run by people from our township. Most Zhejiang migrants here are engaged in glasses retail sales or wholesale business.' [24]

Most of the New Mainlander women entrepreneurs interviewed became engaged in the service sector after migration to Hainan. Their businesses included beauty salons, art and design businesses, clothes manufacturing, clothes shops, insurance sales, restaurants, and opticians, as well as inevitably in Hainan, real estate. This is clearly no great surprise given that the service sector, as the planners had foretold in 1988, has now become the most productive part of the Hainan economy (38 per cent of GDP)[25] even if the enterprises of the women entrepreneurs interviewed were generally small scale.

It is clear that people are no longer streaming across the straits from the mainland as was the case during the late 1980s and early 1990s. Nonetheless, the interview sample suggests that for one social group Hainan still represents a safe haven and a chance to seek a new life: a role that it has not only played during the post-1949 era, but was also fairly constant even before the establishment of the PRC. Though the evidence may prove to be ecologically unsound, the interview sample contained a high number of women who came to Hainan after divorce on the mainland seeking a new start to life.

Ms Fang, one of those interviewed, had come to Qiongshan from Beijing. 51 years old when interviewed, Ms Fang had divorced her ex-husband in the early 1980s. In the early 1990s she was invited to come to Haikou to manage a restaurant. During the low tide of Hainan's economy, the owner withdrew his money and left Hainan. Fang and a partner took over the business. In 1998 the business partner also withdrew his money, and Fang invested 40,000 *yuan* to become the sole owner of the business. Since then, the restaurant has not developed beyond the dreams of avarice. Compared to its more splendid neighbours, it remains quite small and shabby. All the same Fang still managed to pay the wages of her eight employees, as well as her son's expensive tuition fees at university in Canada. In her own words, a single woman's life is not easy. 'If possible, I would choose to be a man in my next life'. Customers refused to pay bills and employees resisted her leadership, 'just because I'm a woman'. Fang had a low opinion of the Hainanese, though she had lived on the island for almost 15 years. In spite of all these difficulties, Fang would still rather take the opportunities presented locally: 'As I'd already made a mistake, I'd rather keep the mistake to myself'[26].

Another divorced interviewee, Ms Ma, came from Guizhou Province after being divorced. In her 40s when interviewed, before migrating to Hainan, she had been a middle-level leader in an enterprise in Guiyang. Her first job in Hainan was as manager of a four-star hotel. In 2000, she became a senior insurance agent. Within four years, she had established good relationships with both her supervisors and clients, and her business had been so successful that she had won many sales awards. Ma's family was no great burden: she had a casual worker to help with housework and her daughter was working in Guangzhou as an assistant lawyer. Ma chose to deliberately forget her former marriage. 'It was too long ago. I don't remember it anymore'.[27]

For the purpose of this examination of the impact of local culture in Qiongshan, gender has not been a necessary focus even though the source material has been drawn from a survey of women entrepreneurs. Nonetheless, it is interesting that most of the best-known figures in Hainan's history are women. These include The Red Detachment of Women made famous after 1949 and by Jiang Qing's Modern Revolutionary Ballet by that name for their role in the CCP's conquest of power; as well as the Song sisters – Song Ailing, Song Qingling, and Song Meiling. It is often claimed that capable women have provided the island with a 'maternal civilisation' [母性文明 *muxing wenming*] and an emphasis on 'soft, peaceful and natural beauty' according to the writer and scholar Yu Qiuyu (Feng, 1999).

Visitors are often surprised at the extent to which women are involved in the work force in Hainan. Jobs usually seen elsewhere in the PRC as being exclusively 'male', such as butchers or pedal rickshaw drivers are often carried out by women[28]. One usual local explanation of this is that 'traditionally' men used to support families by fishing. When they were away at sea, their wives were forced to shoulder all the tasks that came their way back on dry land, as well as taking care of the family. The tradition became so well embedded that even when men did not go fishing anymore, their wives still retained their role in labour outside the home. There is certainly evidence of a relaxed and easy going attitude to life among Hainan men. The tradition of 老爸茶 (*Laobacha* [Old Father Tea]) male tea houses is peculiar to Hainan. Here men can sit all day very cheaply shooting the breeze with each other. The custom even led one representative to the Hainan People's Congress in 2005 to suggest that Hainan men should 'treat women better and take a more significant role in production and at home'[29].

Among the women entrepreneurs interviewed in Qiongshan, there were some fairly acerbic comments made about Hainan men and their attitudes to both work and their families. A large proportion commented that 'Hainan men don't work' or 'Hainan men are lazy' and that 'Hainan men don't know how to look after their wives.' One woman entrepreneur from Hubei Province said (more than somewhat ruefully) that her husband (also from Hubei) had already adopted the 'regretful habits of Hainan men'[30].

7.1.4   Narratives of change

Three examples of the relationship between local culture on the one hand, and economic change and business development on the other cannot but be representative of themselves though they may sustain the argument that PRC culture needs to be disaggregated. Even so defining the term 'culture' in terms of local narratives of change, as has been attempted here, is clearly not without its dangers. While the distinctive may be more local than not, other cultural influences certainly exist both in terms of economic endeavour (social class and business practices for example) and even in terms of the Confucian Tradition and the practices of either the Chinese state or high culture. The extent to which those additional cultural influences may in the longer term be regarded as parts of Chinese culture though is not only a project in progress but depends necessarily on who is telling the story.

NOTES

1. Yadong Luo writes 'Guanxi (interpersonal relationship) is one of the major dynamics of Chinese society. It has been a pervasive part of the Chinese business world for the last few centuries. It binds literally millions of Chinese firms into a social and business web. It is widely recognised to be a key determinant of business performance, because the life-blood of the macro economy and micro business conduct in the society is the guanxi network. Any business in this society, including local firms as well as foreign investors and marketers, inevitably faces guanxi dynamics. No company can go far unless it has extensive guanxi in this setting. In China's new, fast-paced business environment, guanxi has been more entrenched than ever, heavily influencing Chinese social behavior and business practice.'

2. Even that appellation is a 20th Century invention as well as a misunderstanding. The character for 'middle' (zhong) in the Chinese character version of 'China' (zhongguo – Middle Kingdom) also means 'central' and the adoption of the term actually refers to the location of central authority within the imperial system on the 'Central Plains' a mythical and political rather than a physical location.

3. Research was undertaken in Taiyuan, 1998–1999; Xunhua, 2001–2003; and in Qiongshan, Hainan during 2004–2005, as part of various projects generously supported by the Australian Research Council. In each location, research could not have been undertaken without the cooperation and support of many local people. Research on Hainan was undertaken jointly with Chen Minglu. None of these people, nor any of those interviewed in connection with this project is responsible for any of the views or comments expressed here.

4. 1949–1999 Shanxi wushi nian [Fifty Years of Shanxi 1949–1999] Zhongguo tongji chubanshe, Beijing, 1999, p.700 (Taiyuan data) and p.155 (provincial data.) The currency of the People's Republic of China [PRC] is the Renminbi (RMB) or *yuan*: approximately RMB8 = US$1.

5. 143 interviews were conducted with 33 rural entrepreneurs; 35 private entrepreneurs; ten managers of joint venture enterprises; 23 managers of private enterprises; and 42 owner-operators.

6. Interview with Ma Jiajun, Deputy Director of Shanxi Provincial Economic and Trade Commission, Taiyuan, 12 July 1996.

7. Zhongguo tongji nianjian 1998 [1998 China Statistical Yearbook] Zhongguo tongji chubanshe, Beijing, 1998, p.419; Shanxi tongji nianjian 1998 [1998 Shanxi Statistical Yearbook] Zhongguo tongji chubanshe,

Beijing, 1998, p.26, and p.211; 1949–1999 Shanxi wushi nian [Fifty Years of Shanxi 1949–1999] Zhongguo tongji chubanshe, Beijing, 1999, p.465 ff, p.482 ff.

8. For example: Li Anmin, Antai International Enterprise Group Company, Jiexiu; Liang Wenhai, Shanxi Huanhai Group Company, Yuci; and Han Changan, Lubao Coking Group Company, Lucheng, all of whom have been national model entrepreneurs of various kinds. Li and Liang have been delegates to the Provincial People's Congress, Han was elected to the National People's Congress in 1998. 'Li Anmin' in Liu Liping et al. (ed.) Zhongguo dangdai qiyejia mingdian – Shanxi tao [Contemporary Entrepreneurs in China – Shanxi volume] Beijing, Gongren chubanshe, 1989, p.302; and Wang Yonghai, Liu Yaoming, Wang Jikang, Zhang Guilong 'Shanxi Huanhai jituan yougongsi zhongshizhang Liang Wenhai yu tade Huanhai shiye he huanbao zhanlüe' ['General manager of the Shanxi Huanhai Group Company, Liang Wenhai, his Huanhai business and environmental strategy'] in Shanxi Ribao [The Shanxi Daily] 22 September 1996, p.4. Additional information derived in discussions with Li Anmin, interviewed in Yi'an Township, Jiexiu City, 1 June 1996; Liang Wenhai, interviewed in Yuci, 29 October 1996; and Han Changan, interviewed in Dianshang, Lucheng, 14 October 1998.
9. Approximately 80,000 out of the total 10,000 Salar live in Xunhua.
10. Information on Xunhua County from interview with Ma Fengsheng, County Head, 5 August 2002, Jishizhen, Xunhua.
11. Interviewed in Jishizhen, 6 August 2002. Ma and Han are the most common Salar surnames. Ma is usually equated with Muhammed, of which it is the first syllable. The names of those interviewed have been changed to preserve anonymity, except where identification is obvious, germane and explicitly approved by the interviewee.
12. Interviewed, Wajiangzhuang Village, Qingshui Township 6 August 2002.
13. Interviewed, Dasigu Village, Qingshui Township, 6 August 2002.
14. Interviewed, Gaizi, 4 August 2002.
15. Interviewed, in Gaizi, 4 August 2002.
16. Unfortunately he somewhat marred this worldliness later over lunch by remarking that he had 'greatly enjoyed the thick chocolate cake and the Alps last time he visited Australia'. A clear reference to the other 'Australia' lying next to Switzerland that produced W.A. Mozart.
17. Interviewd in Gaizi, 5 August 2002.
18. Interviewed, 6 August 2002.
19. Interviewed in Gaizi, 7 August 2002.

20. 'Hainan de Yimin' ('Migrants in Hainan') at http://www.hn.
chinanews.com.cn/html/hainanxt/103.html; 'Chuanghai qiang: chuanghai
ren de guangrong yu mengxiang' ('The Go-to-Hainan Wall: Dreams of
glory') at www.hntqb.com/news/read.php?news_id=14596&news_class_
code=12

21. In imperial times a 'law of avoidance' restricted officials from serving in
their native place or where they might otherwise have some particular
connection, such as a relative in office.

22. 63 interviews were conducted under the auspices of the local branch of
the Women's Federation with women entrepreneurs and ten interviews
with local officials.

23. Interview, Qiongshan, 30 April 2005.

24. Interview, Qiongshan, 10 May 2005.

25. Hainan Province Statistical bureau Hainan tongji nianjian 2004 (Hainan
Statistical Yearbook 2004) Beijing, Tongji Chubanshe, 2004, p.40.

26. Interview, Qiongshan, 13 May 2005.

27. Interview, Qiongshan, 27 November 2004.

28. Yifang shuitu yang yifang ren, Hainan nüren mianmian guan at
http://hq.xinhuanet.com/news/2004-07/20/content_2522835.htm

29. 'Renda Daibiao Liu Hairong Guiquan Hainan Nanren: Yao Shandai
Nüren' ('Liu Hairong, Representative of the People's Congress
admonishes Hainan men to treat women better') at
http://www.hinews.cn/pages_xw.php?xuh+33945. For the record Liu
Hairong is a man.

30. Interview, Qiongshan, 3 December 2004.

REFERENCES

Breslin, Shaun (1989), 'Shanxi: China's Powerhouse', in David S.G.
Goodman (ed.), *China's Regional Development*, London: Routledge, pp.
135–152.

Brodsgaard, Kjeld E. (1998), 'State and Society in Hainan: Liao Xun's Ideas
on "Little Government, Big Society"', in Kjeld E. Brodsgaard and D.
Strand (eds), *Reconstructing Twentieth Century China: State Control,
Civil Society and National Identity*, Oxford: Clarendon Press, pp. 189–125.

Ch'u, T'ung-tsu (1962), *Local Government in China under the Ch'ing*,
Standford, CA: Stanford University Press.

Chen, X. and C.C. Chen (2004), 'On the Intricacies of the Chinese *Guanxi*: A
Process Model of *Guanxi* Development', *Asia Pacific Journal of
Management*, **21** (3), 305–324.

Chen, J. (1989), 'New move in Hainan: avoidance system for cadres', *Ban Yue Tan* [Bi-Monthly Issue], **15**, 71–75.

Clissold, Tim (2006), *Mister China*, New York, NY: Collins.

Dikotter, Frank (1997), *The Construction of Racial Identities in China and Japan*, London: C Hurst and Co.

Fei, Xiaotong (1981), *Towards a People's Anthropology*, Beijing: Foreign Languages Press.

Feng, C. (1999), 'Seeking Lost Codes in the Wilderness: The Search for a Hainanese Culture', *The China Quarterly*, **160**, 1036–1056.

Feng, Chongyi and David S.G. Goodman (1997), 'Hainan: Communal Politics and the Struggle for Identity', in David S.G. Goodman (ed.), *China's Provinces in Reform: Class, Community and Political Culture*, London: Routledge, pp. 53–80.

Feng, Chongyi and David S.G. Goodman (1998), 'Hainan in Reform: Political Dependence and Economic Interdependence', in Peter T.Y. Cheung, J.H. Chung and Z. Li (eds), *Provincial Strategies of Economic Reform in Post-Mao China: Leadership, Politics, and Implementation*, New York: M.E. Sharpe, pp. 342–371.

Fitzgerald, John (1994), '"Reports of my Death have been greatly exaggerated": The History of the Death of China', in David S.G. Goodman and Gerald Segal (eds), *China Deconstructs*, London: Routledge, pp. 21–58.

Gillin, Donald G. (1967), *Warlord Yen Hsi-shan in Shansi Province, 1911–1949*, Princton, NJ: Princeton University Press.

Gold, Thomas, Douglas Guthrie and David Wank (eds) (2001), *Social Networks in China: Institutions, Culture, and the Changing Nature of Guanxi*, Cambridge: Cambridge University Press.

Goodman, D.S.G. (1995), 'Collectives and Connectives, Capitalism and Corporatism: Structural Change in China', *The Journal of Communist Studies and Transition Politics*, **11** (1), 12–32.

Goodman, David S.G. (1997), 'China in reform: the view from the provinces', in David S.G. Goodman (ed.), *China's Provinces in Reform: Class, community and political culture,* London: Routledge, pp. 1–15.

Goodman, David S.G. (1999), 'King Coal and Secretary Hu: Shanxi's Third Modernisation', in Hans Hendrischke and Feng Chongyi (eds), *The Political Economy of China's Provinces: comparative and competitive advantage*, London: Routledge, pp. 323–356.

Goodman, David S.G. (2000), *Social and Political Change in Revolutionary China*, New York, NY: Rowman & Littlefield.

Goodman, D.S.G. (2002), 'Structuring local identity: nation, province and county', *The China Quarterly,* **172**, 837–862.

Goodman, D.S.G. (2004), 'Qinghai and the Emergence of the West:

Nationalities, communal interaction, and national integration', *The China Quarterly*, **178**, 379–399.

Goodman, David S.G. (2004) 'Localism and Entrepreneurship: History, Identity and Solidarity as Factors of Production', in Barbara Krug (ed.), *China's Rational Entrepreneurs: The Development of the New Private Business Sector*, London: Routledge, pp. 139–165.

Goodman, D.S.G. (2005), 'Exiled by Definition: The Salar in Northwest China', *Asian Studies Review,* **29** (4), 325–343.

Goodman, David S.G. (2006), 'Regional Interactions and Chinese Culture: Openness, Value Change and Homogenisation', in James Goodman (ed.), *Regionalization, Marketization and Political Change in the Pacific Rim*, Universidad de Guadalajara Press, pp. 123–143.

Guo, Yingjie (2003), *Cultural Nationalism in Contemporary China*, London: Routledge.

'Hainan de Yimin' ['Migrants in Hainan'] (2006), http://www.hn.chinanews.com.cn/html/hainanxt/103.html, 1 June.

Hainan Sheng [Hainan Province] (2006), http://www.cpirc.org.cn/rdzt/rd_gs_detail.asp?id=685, 1 June.

Hainan Te Qu Bao [Hainan Special Zone News] (2004), *'Chuang hai qiang: chuang hai ren de guangrong yu mengxiang'* ['The Go-to-Hainan Wall: Dreams of glory'], www.hntqb.com/news/read.php?news_id=14596&news_class_code=12, 28 April.

Hainan Te Qu Bao [Hainan Special Zone News] (2004), *'Yifang shuitu yang yifang ren, Hainan nüren mianmian guan'* [Natural, cultural, and social environment for life: Women in Hainan province], http://hq.xinhuanet.com/news/2004-07/20/content_2522835.htm, 20 July.

Harrell, Stevan (1994) 'Civilizing Projects and the Reaction to Them', in Stevan Harrell (ed.), *Cultural Encounters on China's Ethnic Frontiers,* Seattle, WA: University of Washington Press, pp. 3–36.

Hayes, R.W. (2005), 'China's Modern Power House', http://news.bbc.co.uk/2/hi/programmes/from_our_own_correspondent/4298284.stm, 1 October.

Hu, Fuguo (1996a), *'Renminde shengchang yao dui renmin fuze'* ['The people's governor must be responsible to the people'], in Hu Fuguo *Jiang zhenhua, ban shishi, zuo biaoshuai: zaichuang Sanjin huihuang* [Tell the truth, make things happen and set an example: Reconstructing Shanxi's Glory], Beijing: Zhonggong zhongyang dangxiao chubanshe, pp. 11–21.

Hu, F. (1996b), *'Quanmian guanche dang de jiben lilun he jiben luxian wei shixian xingJin fumin de kuashijie mubiao er fendou'* ['Fight to ensure the global goal of *A Prosperous Shanxi and a Wealthy People* through thoroughly implementing the CCP's basic theories and policies'], *Qianjin*

[Forward], **2**, p. 10.

Jacobs, J. Bruce (1980), *Local Politics in a Rural Chinese Cultural Setting: A Field Study of Mazu Township, Taiwan*, Canberra: Contemporary China Centre, Australian National University.

Jia, Lijun (1998), *'"Hongmaozi" zhende ganzhaima?'* ['Has the "Red Cap" really been removed?'], *Shanxi fazhan dabao* [Shanxi Development Herald], 19 May, p. 2.

Keng, C.W.K. (2001), 'China's future economic regionalization', *Journal of Contemporary China*, **10** (29), 587–611.

Keng, C.W.K. (2006), 'China's Unbalanced Economic Growth', *Journal of Contemporary China*, **15** (46), 183–214.

Liu, Liping et al. (ed.) (1989), *Zhongguo dangdai qiyejia mingdian – Shanxi tao* [Contemporary Entrepreneurs in China – Shanxi volume], Beijing: Gongren chubanshe.

Luo, Yadong (2000), *Guanxi and Business*, World Scientific Publishing Company.

Ma Wei, Jianzhong Ma and Kevin Stuart (eds) (2001), *Folklore of China's Islamic Salar Nationality*, Lewiston, Edwin Mellen, p.33.

Nee, V. (1992), 'Organisational Dynamics of Market Transition: Hybrid Forms, Property Rights, and Mixed Economy in China', *Administrative Science Quarterly,* **37** (1), 1–27.

Provincial China, (1998), 'The 1997 Statistical Yearbook in Provincial Perspective', **5**, 85–86.

Pye, Lucien (1982), *The Dynamics of Chinese Politics*, Cambridge, MA: Oelgeschlager Gunn & Hain.

Renda Daibiao Liu Hairong Guiquan Hainan Nanren: Yao Shandai Nüren' ['Liu Hairong, Representative of the People's Congress admonishes Hainan men to treat women better'] (2006), http://www.hinews.cn/pages_xw.php?xuh+33945, 1 June.

Salazu jianshi bianxiezu [Salazu History Editor Group] (eds) (1982), *Salazu jianshi* [Concise History of the Salar Nationality], Xining: Qinghai renmin chubanshe.

Shih, Chih-yu (2002), *Negotiating Ethnicity in China,* London: Routledge.

Teiwes, F.C. (1966), 'The Purge of Provincial Leaders, 1957–1958', *The China Quarterly,* **27**, 14–32.

Tilly, Charles (2001), 'Welcome to the Seventeenth Century', in Paul DiMaggio (ed.), *The Twenty-First-Century Firm: Changing Economic Organization in International Perspective*, Princton: Princeton University Press, 200–207.

Touzi daokan [Investment Guide] (1996), 'Shanxi Jianhang xindai zhanlue he zhizhu chanye xuanze ['The Shanxi Construction Bank's credit strategy and selection of industries for support'], 1 February, 9.

Wang, Yonghai, Yaoming Liu, Jikang Wang and Guilong Zhang (1996), *'Shanxi Huanhai jituan yougongsi zhongshizhang Liang Wenhai yu tade Huanhai shiye he huanbao zhanlüe'* ['General manager of the Shanxi Huanhai Group Company, Liang Wenhai, his Huanhai business and environmental strategy'], *Shanxi Ribao* [The Shanxi Daily], 22 September.

Weng, Bao (2000), *'1985–1988: jiqing niandai'* [1985–1988: Years of passion'], *Nanfeng Chuang* [South Wind Window], 4.

White, Lynn T. III (1998), *Unstately Power Vol. 1: Local Causes of China's Economic Reforms*, New York, NY: M.E. Sharpe.

Wong, Y.H. and T.K.P. Leung (2001), *Guanxi: Relationship Marketing in a Chinese Context*, Bingham, NY: Haworth Press.

Young, S. (1989), 'Policy, Practice and the Private Sector in China', *Australian Journal of Chinese Affairs*, **21**, 57–80.

Young, S. (1991), 'Wealth but not Security: Attitudes Towards Private Business in China in the 1980s', *Australian Journal of Chinese Affairs*, **25**, 115–137.

Zhongguo tongji chubanshe [China Statistical Press] (1998), *Shanxi tongji nianjian* [Shanxi Statistical Yearbook], Beijing: Zhongguo tongji chubanshe.

Zhongguo tongji chubanshe [China Statistical Press] (1998), *Zhongguo tongji nianjian 1998* [1998 China Statistical Yearbook], Beijing.

Zhongguo tongji chubanshe [China Statistical Press], *Zhongguo tongji nianjian 1999* [1999 China Statistical Yearbook], Beijing.

Zhongguo tongji chubanshe [China Statistical Press], *1949–1999 Shanxi wushi nian* [Fifty Years of Shanxi 1949–1999], Beijing.

Zhong, Weizhi (2002), *'Da Haikou Zhengjiu Hainan'* ['Would a Greater Haikou save Hainan?'], *The Economic Observer*, http://www.eobserver.com.cn/ReadNews.asp?NewsID=1940, 22 October.

Zhongguo tongji chubanshe [Hainan Province Statistical bureau] (2004), *Hainan tongji nianjian 2004* (Hainan Statistical Yearbook 2004), Beijing: Beijing Tongji Chubanshe, 2004, p. 40.

8. Networks as Business Networks

Hans Hendrischke

8.1 INTRODUCTION

Hardly any company is set up or business deal made in China without the help of personal connections – *guanxi* – and the ubiquitous business networks. Yet, in China and among China experts, the notion of business networks and of personal connections, which are the building blocks of business networks, remain influenced by the concept of traditional family networks in Taiwan, Hong Kong and the Overseas Chinese Diaspora (Weidenbaum and Samuel, 1996). The cultural explanation views trust, reciprocity and long-term commitment, which hold these networks together (Redding, 1990; Tong and Yong, 1998; Peng, 2004; Luo, 1997), as family commitments, much in the same way as for centuries religious and customary ties were underlying the trading networks of Maghribi traders in the Mediterranean (Greif, 1993). The paradigm of traditional Overseas Chinese business networks still dominates the description and analysis of business networks in the PRC, even though it is unlikely that the private sector in the PRC could have achieved its size, complexity and level of international integration on the basis of family based structures. Annual field interviews with local entrepreneurs in Jiangsu and Zhejiang from 2000 to 2006 suggest that it might be time to take a fresh look at Chinese business networks and attempt an economic explanation for their role and operation in China's newly privatised economy. Three initial findings prompt this attempt.

First, business networks extend far beyond family structures and include seemingly unrelated businesses as well as local administrations. This raises the questions of how networks are established and expanded in China's new corporate environment. Have traditional family structures been replaced by business networks able to expand beyond traditional loyalties and to create mutual commitments without a previous history of personal connections? Can the governance of these networks be better explained by current network theories than by reference to Chinese traditions?

Second, business networks seem to operate as economic actors in their own right and to have the ability to create and control assets. This raises the issue of corporate ownership and of the dividing line between firms and networks. This in turn raises the question of the role of entrepreneurs versus firms as the primary drivers of corporate activity. If entrepreneurs have a choice between a commitment to networks and a commitment to firms, the role of networks is much stronger than generally assumed, which has important business implications.

Third, local business networks, beyond facilitating business transactions, also play a role in the privatisation process by linking local administrative and corporate interests and contributing to the coevolution of new business procedures and institutions at local level. This has implications for privatisation trajectories, local state support for enterprises, taxation and, more generally, the future development and formation of a unified national business system.

The following attempt to explore these issues is first of all an exercise in rethinking habitual concepts and moving from a cultural towards an economic explanation. There is a practical dimension as well. If Chinese business networks are based on cultural and family values, one has to be Chinese to be part of them; if they operate based on economic rationale, one needs to know the rules to participate.

The following account describes enterprise-level business networks in their local administrative environment from an institutional perspective and perceives individual entrepreneurs as embedded in their surrounding economic, social and political institutions. This local perspective departs from the grand unified narratives of 'Confucianist China' or the 'Authoritarian State' as well as from China's central administration's view in Beijing that economic policies are being implemented in a controlled top-down process (e.g. Garnaut et al., 2001). The author's field research on the emergence of private enterprise over the last five years produced a wealth of detailed observations which were not available to earlier studies (Qian, 2003; Peng and Zhou, 2005) and which point to the crucial role of business networks in enabling nascent local businesses to operate in largely unregulated local business environments. The challenge facing this study is to sketch an overarching institutional architecture that links national policies and local diversity.

The following chapter is based on interviews with approximately 200 entrepreneurs in the rapidly expanding private sector in the Eastern Chinese provinces around Shanghai [1]. Section 2 starts off with a conceptual description of Chinese business networks that covers formation, membership, borders and cultural embedding. Section 3 shifts the focus to the corporate role of networks, including their role as economic actors, their control over assets and their interaction with markets. Networks here are seen to operate at a deeper level than just in facilitating business transactions. Two case studies will be presented to better illustrate the functioning of networks. Section 4 extends this analysis to the coevolution between business networks and local governments and the institution-building capacity of networks in China's transition to a market economy. Section 5 proposes some general conclusions.

8.2   NETWORK GOVERNANCE

There is general agreement on what constitutes the core elements of network structures. The main ones are entry and exit, the typology of ties, e.g. weak, strong, dyadic ties, density of the network, including structural holes, and boundaries of networks (Powell, 1990; Granovetter, 1993; Uzzi, 1996; Nooteboom et al., 1997; Borgatti and Foster, 2003). For China, the description of networks is dominated by the cultural account which is based either narrowly on family structures and extensions thereof, such as the group loyalties found in the Overseas Chinese Diaspora, or more broadly on Confucianism (Tsang, 1998; Lovett et al., 1999; Bian, 1997). An alternative, more politically oriented paradigm for describing and analysing networks originates from field studies in the PRC (Gold, Guthrie and Wank, 2002). Both approaches find external reasons for the formation of business networks. In this sense, both accounts are not satisfactory in explaining the dynamic business development in contemporary China and even less able to make any predictions. Family values and Confucianism are a-historical concepts that bear little relation to China's dynamic environment. The political account catches some of the dynamism in the PRC, but there is general agreement that political change happens much more slowly than economic change and is therefore not helpful in analysing or predicting economic changes. One way to overcome these limitations is to use an institutional account that views networks as originating from an economic rationale. Such an account will have to incorporate elements of the cultural as well as of the political account, but put them on their economic feet, so to speak.

The institutional account presented below is conceptually derived from the generalisation of case studies. The ideal type presentation of findings seems reasonable for this section, as the many observations concern informal structures which cannot easily be caught in formal interview processes or in anonymous questionnaires. On the other hand, they are open to any participant observer familiar with local institutions, culture and language. An institutional explanation will be proposed for each of the major elements of networks structures listed above.

8.2.1 Entry and Commitment

In the cultural account, entry into Chinese business networks is based on family links or other forms of attachments, such as membership of the same cohort of students or the same dialect group or similar. Implied in the conditions of entry is the type of commitment that sustains the network. Commitment is hardly questioned in this account, as entry in a family network implies acceptance of family values, much the same way as being part of a network of a school cohort implies acceptance of the culturally defined norms related to this role.

While in the cultural account, membership of a group comes first and participation in the control of resources second, an economic account has to begin with control over resources and then add the social dimension. In other words, entry into business networks is governed by two conditions. One is acceptance of a social code of conduct; the other is control over resources of interest to the network. In family networks, these two conditions are met through family socialisation and inheritance rights to family assets.

In the institutional account, entry and form of commitment have to be separated and their order of importance reversed. This means that networks are constituted around assets and resources which are contributed by their members. It is control over assets rather than familiarity among people that makes an economic network and members only join the network if they are able to contribute to its resource base. Resources have to be understood in a wide sense, ranging from physical assets to intellectual resources as well as access to power structures, non-tradable information and social capital, in brief, everything that is required to constitute exploitable assets. Only when a resource base is established and assets can potentially be put into operation, can the people who control these resources form networks which then need to rely on a set of social rules to assign members their share of control and benefits. We will now turn to these rules and return to assets in the following section. First, we propose a simple institutional model to explain the role of social rules and commitments of networks.

Acceptance of the social code of conduct commits entrants to some basic, unwritten rules intended to create trust that gives both stability and flexibility to the network. The first rule is that members have to be personally acquainted with other members of the network. This produces the one to one (dyadic) structure that is crucial for interpersonal trust among members (Chen and Chen, 2004). The second rule is that members agree to establish personal acquaintance with potential new members. This way they avoid what is know in network literature as structural holes (Burt, 1992). The third requirement for constant communication is often overlooked as a rule, because it is seen as part of natural social interaction rather than as a specific rule. This refers to the density of networks, i.e. frequency of contact (Boisot and Child, 1988).

As a result, these networks are characterised by dyadic ties, strong interpersonal trust, few structural holes and high density. This concurs with the cultural account, according to which Chinese networks are characterised by high density, interconnectedness, stability and durability (Batjargal, 2005). In contrast to the cultural account, however, the institutional account does not have to rely on vague notions such as 'Confucian emphasis on social harmony[which] facilitates trust building among members of a *guanxi* cluster over time' or 'the doctrine of the middle that avoids extremes, and the balance between the *yin* and the *yang*' (Batjargal, 2005: 20; see also Luo, 1997).

The weakness of the cultural account is that the density and Confucianist ideology are automatically interpreted as exclusionary devices. This is based on a limited understanding of how the creation of *guanxi* under business aspects actually works and the fact that traditionally in Chinese representation family analogies and personal affective terms (old friendship) are used which in fact hide an underlying economic rationale. The best example of the economic rationality of an affective term is 'old friend' (*lao pengyou*) which is in popular usage often presented as a relationship akin to family membership.

8.2.2   Old Friend as an Informal Agreement

At first sight it appears as if the social commitment within a network substitutes the emotional closeness of traditional family ties by a specific notion of friendship, thus confirming the cultural account that business ties grow out of personal links. However, this friendship with its fluid borderline between utilitarian and emotional aspects can be created nearly at will by activating cultural and social conventions. 'Old friend' which reflects an ambivalent closeness that can be economically or personally motivated or preferably both, is an informal status between two or more people that is usually established after several personal meetings, often banquets and other forms of social entertainment which encourage a relaxed personal atmosphere. The procedure can be shortened in the case of urgent business demands. Usually it culminates in the mutual affirmation of now being 'old friends', with the implication of now being open to future business proposals on the basis of the newly formed trust (for a description of the process, see Yang, 1994).

In institutional terms, 'old friends' have established sufficient trust to make their personal affinity strong enough to withstand surrounding formal institutions or to make up for the lack of formal structures in a weak institutional environment. 'Old friends' have established sufficient trust to jointly face the risks involved in overcoming or disregarding external institutional constraints. In the flexible institutional environment of China's transitional economy, 'old friends' are able to create their own procedures and institutions. Conversely, in areas of stronger institutional environments, these personal links can be used to circumvent formal institutional constraints, including laws and administrative regulations, and may become the source of illegal or corrupt conduct (see also Xin and Peace, 1996).

This brings us back to our previous discussion. If 'old friend' status is comparable to an informal contractual agreement between parties to circumvent or disregard formal institutions and constraints should that be in their common interest, this has consequences for the density of the network and the strength of ties. The practical obligations under such an agreement include constant accessibility and responsiveness to demands for cooperation from other members (whether these demands are accepted or not), and a commitment to loyalty and confidentiality within the network. The requirement of confidentiality is a consequence of the institutional borders that networks draw around themselves. The strength of ties is to be measured less in proximity of personal or social ties than in the commitment to consensual institution building, either in order to overcome the absence of formal institutions or to resist or undermine formal institutions that are deemed disadvantageous to the economic interests of the network. The borders of networks are defined by the ability to overcome external constraints, rather than by closed membership.

8.2.3   Weak and Strong Ties

Commitment to the network is not uniform across its membership. Anthropology and management studies sometimes differentiate between strong and weak links (Granovetter, 1993; Bian, 1997). From an institutional perspective, networks are better divided into an active and a dormant sphere. The active sphere comprises those members who are linked to each other by joint economic activity, more specifically, by joint exploitation of a resource base. Active links constituted by joint exploitation of assets form the core of networks. Dormant links form a periphery of unrealised cooperation and represent the potential of a network. The dormant sphere encompasses members who are joined by mutual acquaintance to members of the active network and who when required might be called upon to contribute their resources, but who are not currently engaged in joint exploitation. This is not the same as the differentiation between weak and strong ties. Weak and strong ties are based on personal and social ties, whereas the differentiation between active and dormant links rests on economic criteria, specifically on the involvement in the exploitation of assets. From this perspective, the degree of overlap between different networks, or between different cores, depends on the endowment of individual members with control over assets.

8.2.4 Dormant and Active Networks

Entry can be made into the active or the dormant sphere of the network. The former occurs when an entrant controls resources or assets which are immediately required by other network members. Entry into dormant membership occurs when someone has control over resources or assets which at the time cannot be configured into an exploitable asset but are of potential interest to the members of the network. From this perspective, dormant membership serves to store social capital which can be activated for the mobilisation of resources. Membership in a network is therefore highly flexible and deliberately open to potential contributors, even allowing potential members to compete for access. Active membership, on the other hand, can revert to dormant status once resources are no longer required. This normally does not mean exit from the network.

8.2.5 Boundaries of Networks

In institutional terms, the border of a network is defined by the social commitment to cooperate with the network members and the actual or potential contribution of resources. The size of networks is hard to pin down as there is no clear borderline for dormant membership. The active part of membership is more clearly defined as comprising those members who have pooled resources and assets for specific business purposes. Also, active membership in one network does not preclude membership in other networks as long as there is no conflict in the use of assets. Active and dormant members can belong to different and overlapping networks as long as there are no personal or economic conflicts of interest. Networks can include dormant members who at the same time may be dormant or active members of other networks. However, such links across networks do not constitute links between the original networks.

8.2.6 Exit

Exit from the network is as flexible as entry and happens through transition to dormant status and further cooling off once a member's resources have lost their actual or potential usefulness for the network. Outgoing members move to the periphery of the network, which is defined by the distance from involvement in exploitation of assets. This fading out is more likely than explicit exit or expulsion. Expulsion would occur if trust is broken or if a member relied on formal institutions to exploit a network controlled asset in the form of individual profit-taking. The network would then employ formal or social sanctions.

Unlike families, business networks exist for economic purposes. This is not necessarily expressed in these terms when dormant networks are set up, because the social function tends to overshadow the economic purpose. The economic purpose becomes obvious when dormant networks become activated around a business concern and when assets and resources are accumulated and assembled to form assets. The core function of business networks is to provide an environment enabling the formation and exploitation of business assets when existing institutions are lacking or dysfunctional. We will now take a closer look at how networks assemble and utilise assets.

8.3   NETWORK CONTENTS

There is a vast and detailed literature on what Peng and Zhou (2005) call the contents of Chinese business networks, such as their business to business economic role (Hamilton, 1996; Schlevogt, 2002) or their business to government social and political role (Boisot and Child, 1998; Wank, 1995; Gold, Guthrie and Wank, 2002). The underlying general assumption is that networks operate between firms. This assumption is questionable on the ground that in a transition economy like the Chinese in the last decade, assets are seldom given or static. Ownership and control rights may be contested and legal titles unenforceable (Krug and Polos, 2004). To function in this dynamic environment, assets frequently require additional input or reconfiguration to bring them in line with the constantly changing regulatory and market environment (Stark, 1996). The same is true for the ownership of assets. In China's gradual transition process, assets can have a stronger continuity than the property rights attached to them; put differently, informal ownership through networks can survive changing formal ownership. The reason for this is that assets are not privatised in a straightforward fashion, but instead come under the control of local governments in the wake of China's devolution policies (Qian, 2000, 2003). At the local level, further privatisation happens in a step-wise process that is negotiated through networks between local governments and entrepreneurs (Krug and Hendrischke 2003). Correspondingly, assets change their formal status in this process, but not necessarily their informal status. This dynamism can be expressed by differentiating forms of network control.

Below, the terms 'network concern', 'network asset' and 'private asset' will be used to distinguish assets according to the way in which they are controlled by networks and private interests. Network concern will be used for a potential asset, i.e. a collection of resources under consideration by a network of people who are intent and able to convert them into a functioning business asset. Network asset will be used for an asset that has been put together and is being exploited by a network of people who are controlling the exploitation. Network asset denotes a functioning business asset that has been constituted from the contributions of the network members and is being commercially exploited without being defined in legal terms and without assignment of formal property rights. Private asset will be used for assets that are incorporated and have clear legal property rights attached. Before taking these considerations any further, a short case study might help explain the background for these considerations (Hendrischke, 2004).

> **Case study 1: Setting up a firm through social capital**
> Street Lighting Factory Ltd. emerged from a business opportunity conceived by the managers of a Shanghai based state-owned enterprise (SOE) and a local Bureau of Industry and Commerce in a near-by city in Zhejiang Province. The Shanghai SOE wanted to supply technically advanced components of street lighting to a Sino-foreign joint venture. They could have expanded their own existing operations but instead chose to privatise. For this purpose, they activated a network of contacts in order to locate resources, including management skills and finance. The choice fell on the respondent, Mr. Li, because he was known to the Shanghai enterprise and recommended by leaders and colleagues of his local Bureau of Industry and Commerce. As a physics graduate of Fudan University, he had embarked upon a technical career in the 1960s, managed a glass factory in the 1980s and had ended up heading the local Bureau of Industry and Commerce. His decision to accept the offer and to set up the new enterprise involved considerable risks, as he was not offered a binding supplier's contract, but simply the reasonable chance to enter a lucrative market, provided that he was successful in setting up a new production facility and able to meet the challenges of new technologies, quality control and reliability.
> Finance was also organised by the network. The project required an initial RMB500,000 of which RMB400,000 were for equipment and RMB100,000 for running costs. Mr. Li and his deputy, his former chief engineer from his time as a factory director, contributed RMB60,000 each in return for informal shares of 13 per cent of the registered capital. Five smaller investors who were

interested in employment with the company acquired total of 14 per cent. The bulk of 60 per cent came from a local private entrepreneur who owned an electrical goods company. This ownership structure was set up informally in 1993 and remained unchanged. Only in 2000, the company formalised the property rights by registering as a Limited Liability Company.

Interestingly, the Shanghai SOE managers and the local Bureau of Industry and Commerce, who had initiated the project, held no formal shares or positions and were excluded from the formal distribution of profits. After incorporation, the company operated according to the Company Law, with the majority investor holding the position of Chairman of the Board of Directors and the operational side of the business remaining the sole responsibility of Mr. Li, the general manager. However, the profit distribution was unusual and reflected the history of privatisation. Sixty per cent of profits were re-invested and of the remaining 40 per cent, Mr. Li received half as his dividend. This exceeds by far his entitlement on the basis of his 13 per cent share of registered capital. This additional benefit is an indication of the remaining network influence, even under formal corporate structures. No information was given about any informal entitlements that other members of the founding network might have received.

The network, however, did not guarantee the operation or support it commercially. During the start-up period the company did not receive any orders from the Sino-foreign Joint Venture for which it was originally set up. Initially, the new company only managed to sell to smaller domestic clients in South China and to one Middle Eastern country. By 1995, the quality of their products had reached a level where the Sino-foreign Joint Venture finally accepted them as a supplier. From then on, their production expanded rapidly. By 2000, 60 per cent of their production was sold to the Joint Venture.

In this case, we have an example of a network concern in the conceptualisation of a future asset (the street lighting factory) by a network of people which includes local government, a state-owned enterprise, and private entrepreneurs and investors. The active sphere of this network can be seen in those members who conceived the business idea and had control over the initial assets and resources. They needed to activate their dormant contacts in order to complete a functioning asset (for example, by finding a general manager to run the plant). The network concern was the basis from which the availability of required assets and resources, such as technology, finance, land and personnel, could be explored. Once a network of active contributors had been formed around this business concern, the asset was assembled and put in operation. This is when the network concern became a network asset. At this stage, it is appropriate to differentiate between the network concern and network asset, because this change marks the dividing line between exploration and exploitation (see Graph 1). Also, at this stage, coordination between the network members becomes a necessity in order to distribute risks and profits. The final step towards privatisation through the formalisation of property rights under the Company Law remains a separate transition. In legal terms, this step establishes private property rights. Yet, the interesting point in this final step is that it does not fully extinguish the underlying informal rights of the original network. In the case above, this is outwardly reflected in the larger profit share of the general manager. This case describes a relatively simple transition from hybrid to formal property rights and the role that a network can play.

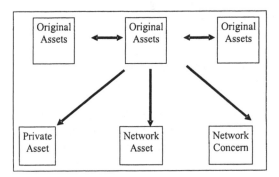

Figure 8.1   Networks and the allocation of assets

A more complex transition is shown in the next case of the privatisation of an existing state-owned asset, in this case a hotel.

Case study 2: From manager to co-owner
In Suzhou, an internal Party document specified privatisation procedures through 2002 and until April 2003, when public auctions were made mandatory. Up to that date, local authorities had the option to proceed by 'internal transformation (neibu gaizhi)' or 'Internal agreement (neibu xieyi)', which allowed them to negotiate individual settlements with preferred clients. Since April 2003, in this local instance, a reserve price for assets has to be established on the basis of an asset evaluation, and investors are invited to submit their bids. The ensuing auction has to be repeated

at least once if the reserve price is not reached. Only in exceptional cases are local authorities allowed to deviate from this procedure.

The management buy-out (MBO) in which Mr. Niu was involved happened just before a public auction became mandatory, but included already competitive bidding between different interested parties. Mr. Niu's bid for the hotel he was managing was also no longer the traditional take-over of an asset, but a more sophisticated operation in a highly dynamic environment. Mr. Niu is a self-made man who had made his way up from the bottom of the hierarchy before becoming general manager of a state-owned three star hotel in the Suzhou New Development Zone in 1997. By 2003, he had acquired a university education in night classes and was on the way to getting an MBA degree. The owner of the hotel, the local government-owned Suzhou New Development Zone Management Group also owned a four star hotel and three commercial companies. Mr. Niu had achieved occupancy rates of 95 per cent and was without serious competition.

Before his hotel came up for privatisation in 2002, Mr. Niu had witnessed one of the last cases of first generation MBO in his group. The general manager of the group-owned four star hotel was able to negotiate for himself a share of 35 per cent in a deal that was worth over RMB100m. He borrowed the required capital from a local bank which accepted the hotel, i.e. his future share in the hotel, as a security for the loan. These kinds of deals were banned by the time Mr.Niu prepared his bid.

For the privatisation of Mr. Niu's hotel, the management corporation as the owner used 'internal agreement' procedures to find investors and finally came up with a list of five interested parties. All competing parties approached Mr. Niu and made him various offers, seeing that Mr. Niu was crucial to manage the asset profitably. Mr. Niu eventually decided to throw in his lot with the only group of investors that offered him a share in the deal. Once Mr. Niu had reached agreement with the three investors, the deal with the management corporation was finalised within a week, as his group offered the best price. The three investors acquired shares of 38 per cent, 32 per cent and 25 per cent respectively and financed Mr. Niu's share of 5 per cent of the deal worth 21.5 million yuan.

Unlike many of the first generation MBOs, this deal did not secure Mr. Niu control over the asset, or tie him to his position indefinitely. On his insistence, the contract he signed with his co-shareholders was limited to three years. Mr. Niu had calculated his

options very carefully. The period of three years was the medium
term for which he could foresee that he would be able to maintain
his competitive position in the local market. More importantly, he
had decided not to push for a larger share, although he knew that
his investors had granted a ten per cent share to another general
manager in a similar project elsewhere. What counted more for him
was that the share he held jointly with them served as an entry into
their business network and would turn him from a manger into a
shareholder. The three business partners, keen to keep Mr. Niu
committed to their hotel enterprise, offered him shares in other
investment projects and gradually expanded his role to become a
fourth shareholder in their real estate and agricultural businesses.
What appeared like a management incentive share turned out to
become a substantial form of co-ownership. It would allow Mr. Niu
to withdraw from the hotel and concentrate on other activities once
the land on which the hotel was situated would be re-zoned for
residential usage. The resulting profit would be a windfall for the
investors, now including Mr. Niu.

The case shows that the transition from network concern to network asset can
also be reversed. Here the cooperation between network members starts with
a given asset through which a new member gains entry into the network. The
manager in his original function can be regarded as a dormant member for the
original network of the three investors. He becomes an active member of
their new network that disassembles the asset and converts it to a network
concern. The existing asset is disestablished on an informal basis and
superseded by a network concern controlled by the now four members.

Underlying these movements are two different paths of business operation.
An exploitation path leads from the conceptual level through steps of
implementation to the establishment of an asset where commercial
exploitation becomes possible. In the reverse direction, an exploratory path
leads from an existing asset to its disestablishment and reassembling in a
different configuration of assets and network members with a view to realise
a higher commercial potential.

Networks enable these seemingly complex transactions by providing a
relatively secure form of informal ownership, as network members can rely
on the inherent trust within the networks to guard them against the risk of
losing control over the assets. They trade off their active involvement in and
the concomitant immediate benefits from a network asset (which might be
linked to formal property rights) against their involvement in a network
concern. However, as the cases show, this change in the forms of control
over assets does not preclude the institution of private property rights in the

form of legal titles to play a role. We will argue that there is a hierarchy in control over assets, in the sense that informal control of network concerns and network assets takes precedence and overrides formal control established by legal property rights.

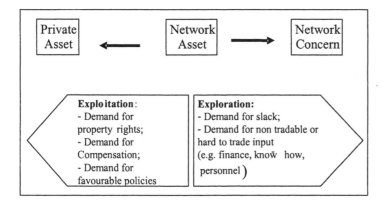

Figure 8.2   Exploitation and exploration at the network level

8.3.1   Network Assets and Private Assets

Both cases show that in the transition process network assets can be transformed into private assets by attaching legal titles and that this process is also reversible. This reduces the importance of formal property rights as legally defined property rights become subordinate to informal property rights. In fact, as ownership becomes obscured to those outside of the network, the role and relevance of legal property rights needs to be reconsidered.

The two case studies highlight two particular features. First, private property rights can be assigned by a network on an agreed basis to network members who can be regarded as agents of the network. This assignment does not need to reflect the actual contribution by members to the asset nor include all network members who are stakeholders. Second, once a network asset is disestablished, the attached formal property rights lapse and are substituted by the informal rights the owners hold in the network. In practical terms, these informal rights are manifest as informal claims to participation in future network assets. This transition between formal and informal property rights parallels the transition between private assets and network assets (see Figure 8.3).

First, the transition from informal to formal ownership turns the asset from a network asset into a private asset. This does not mean that network ownership is extinguished. Ownership remains predominant in substantial terms, but becomes overlaid by a formal property rights structure. This transition corresponds to the exploitatory path from network asset to private asset. As formal usage rights are assigned to network members, the economic benefits from the network activity become legalised, taxable and freely transferable and can be enjoyed by the members to whom the assets were assigned. In this way, the network formalises (at least part of) the benefits which the members derive from their assets in order to comply with surrounding formal institutions such as tax laws. Such a move reduces transaction costs related to the governance of the network and avoids the semblance of corruption when, for example, officials are involved in the network. However, the network does not relinquish its informal rights which remain in the background and can give the network access to cash-flow and other form of interference to the degree that these interventions are compatible with the formal status of the asset. If informal interventions in the formal structure come into obvious conflict with the latter, the network will have to change the formal structure, as follows.

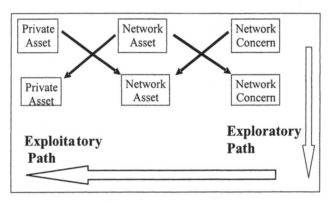

Figure 8.3   The dynamics between exploitation and exploration at the network level

Second, the reverse transition from formal to informal ownership corresponds to the exploratory transition path from private asset to network asset. The networks needs to remove the formal property rights attached to an asset in order to be able to exercise control over the asset. While network members might forego their formal rights to the asset, they will not loose their informal rights embedded in the network. This informal residual power is stronger than and can override the formal rights linked to the asset.

Such a dynamic process points to a predominance of informal over formal structures that has important consequences for the general transition process as well as for business transactions in the future, transformed environment, as it creates a path dependency. The ability to switch an asset flexibly from exploitatory to exploratory mode explains the robustness of private enterprise and the ability to deal with incomplete property rights, weak formal institutions as well as the dynamic mix of formal and informal institutions that can be observed in China. Several consequences are worth exploring, in particular with regard to corporate identity, asset specificity and, more broadly, links between the corporate and the government sector. The next section will turn to the role of networks as intermediaries between local entrepreneurs and local governments.

8.4   NETWORKS AND LOCAL GOVERNMENT

Networks also straddle the divide between the local corporate and government sectors, where 'local' in terms of scale is understood as the locality where enterprises are registered and taxed. This section will attempt to define the economic interests that place them in his position. The network links between local government and the local corporate sector have been well documented by political scientists and sociologists and explained in concepts such a clientelist networks (Wank, 1995) and local state corporatism (Oi, 1999). These are useful concepts to capture the degree to which local governments have tolerated and supported a fledgling private sector to emerge in their jurisdictions. These concepts are less helpful when it comes to explaining the mutual dependence between corporate and local government sectors that lies at the root of public-private networks.

Public-private networks are a product of China's transition strategy and by most accounts have only a transitory role and limited life expectancy. While it is quite likely that these local networks will disappear once legal property rights and legal procedures are ubiquitously implemented, this process might take a long time and create path dependencies which will give these networks a more lasting influence than is predicted.

The overall co-evolution between local firms and government becomes quite complex when one considers factors such as local taxation and public governance in local jurisdictions which compete for firms and where firms depend on government support and cooperation in form of subsidies, tax reductions and procedures (see Chapters 5 and 6). Proceeding from the preceding line of argumentation, this section will concentrate on the aspect of the role of public private networks in the transition process.

The initial reason for the emergence of public-private networks was that authority over local state-owned and collective enterprise was allocated to township and county governments who had the right to decide, within the limits of policies issued at the higher prefectural or provincial levels, how to implement privatisation policies at their local level. Public-private networks emerged when previously government appointed leaders of collective enterprises or public servants had to sever their links with the government to take over managerial functions in new enterprises (Rozelle, 1998; Rozelle et al., 2000). The need for this arose out of the slow process of privatisation during which local governments, for example in the provinces of Zhejiang and Jiangsu, could hold shares in 'transforming' enterprises for a period of over ten years. With local governments thus integrated in local businesses, newly emerging private enterprises likewise had to seek their support in view of the lack of support from central government legislation and central administration. This is the origin of the so-called 'red hat' enterprises which as private enterprises changed their status to collectives in order not to attract unwanted political attention. The outcome in either case was the formation of networks with local governments. The distinction between types of networks assets also works for these public-private networks, albeit in a dynamic sense, as state intervention is gradually being reduced.

In the initial stages of reform, i.e. the 1980s and 1990s, local government authorities were still directly involved in assets, frequently as shareholders. Their participation in private assets served directly to fund local government tasks. As reforms progressed, in particular since 2000, local governments came increasingly under pressure to withdraw their direct shares from enterprises and consequently lost access to the revenue streams from private assets.

However, local government still had a hold on network assets through their control over public assets such as land and their authority over local taxation. To this day, these remain areas of coordination between local government and enterprises (see Chapter 5). The benefits that local governments can derive from their involvement in networks assets are less tangible than those from private assets. They might simply consist in higher tax revenue or in non-budgetary benefits such as enterprise participation in social welfare tasks. The expanding regulatory environment is gradually reducing arbitrariness in the use of resources.

At the level of network concerns, local governments would coordinate their activities with enterprises in order to attract investment or in structuring broader industrial policies. In graphic form, the gradual withdrawal of the local state from networks would follow the following trend.

Such a representation has only limited validity, as it does not consider the regional variances in privatisation policies. For other provinces, the time line would be quite different to the effect that some stages in the graph above would fall together. The argument of this section is that the withdrawal of the local state is not a political issue that can be resolved by local political decision-making or by central legislation, but only in an extended process of establishing local procedures and public governance.

Table 8.1   The withdrawal of the (local) state at the network level

Reform Stages in Zhejiang/Jiangsu	Initial privatisation mid 90s	Privatisation late 90s	Deepened reform 2002/3	Post reform
Network concern	Public private	Public private	Public private	Private
Network asset	Public private	Public private	Private	Private
Private asset	Public private	Private	Private	Private

8.5   CONCLUSION

To conclude, the term business network is understood differently from the traditional usage in Chinese business networks mentioned above. 'Entrepreneurial networks' or 'resource mobilising networks' (Hendrischke, 2004) are more appropriate terms to denote that the networks discussed here are not agents of a family or a circumscribed group of people and do not operate in the sense of a club. They are understood as collective economic actors who have the ability to adapt their membership and structure to changing institutional and commercial opportunities. These new entrepreneurial networks are therefore not culturally specific; they are found in other economies in different forms (Ghewamat and Khana, 1998). In China, they bridge the institutional gaps left by the end of state planning and have become part of a path dependency that will structure China's emerging business environment and inform the behaviour of Chinese entrepreneurs in domestic and global markets. An understanding of these networks is of interest beyond China, as they display characteristics and behaviours similar to the networks that are transforming Western business environments.

NOTES

1.   The Data set is described in Chapter 5.

REFERENCES

Batjargal, B. (2005), 'Comparative social capital: Networks of entrepreneurs and investors in China and Russia', Ann Arbor, MC: William Davidson Institute, Working Paper No. 783, p. 29.

Bian, Y. (1997), 'Bringing Strong Ties Back In: Indirect Connection, Bridges, and Job Search in China', *American Sociological Review*, **62**, 266–285.

Boisot, M.H. and J. Child (1988), 'The iron law of fiefs: bureaucratic failure and the problem of governance in the Chinese economic reforms', *Administrative Science Quarterly*, **78**, 237–273.

Borgatti, S. and P. Foster (2003), 'The Network Paradigm in Organizational Research: A Review and Typology', *Journal of Management*, **29**, 991–1013.

Burt, R. (1992), *Structural Holes: The Social Structure of Competition*, Cambridge, MA: Harvard University Press.

Chen, X. and C.C. Chen (2004), 'On the Intricacies of the Chinese Guanxi: A Process Model of Guanxi Development', *Asia Pacific Journal of Management*, **21**, 305–324.

Garnaut, Ross, Ligang Song, Yang Yao and Xiaolu Wang (2001), *Private Enterprise in China*, Canberra: Asia Pacific Press.

Ghemawat, P. and T. Khana (1998), 'The Nature of Diversified Business Groups: A Research Design and Two Case Studies', *Journal of Industrial Economics*, **XLVI**, 35–61.

Gold, Thomas, Doug Guthrie and David Wank (eds) (2002), *Social Connections in China: Institutions, Culture, and the Changing Nature of Guanxi*, Cambridge: Cambridge University Press.

Granovetter, M. (1993), 'The Strength of Weak ties: A Network Theory Revisited', *Sociological Theory*, **1**, 201–233.

Greif, A. (1993), 'Contract Enforceability and Economic Institutions in Early Trade: The Maghribi Traders' Coalition', *The American Economic Review*, **83** (3), 525–548.

Guthrie, D. (1998), 'The Declining Importance of Guanxi in China's Economic Transition', *The China Quarterly*, **154**, 254–82.

Hamilton, Gary G. (1996), 'The theoretical significance of Asian business networks', in Gary G. Hamilton (ed.), *Asian Business Networks*, pp. 283–298.

Hamilton, Gary G (ed.) (1996), *Asian Business Networks*, Berlin and New York: Walter de Gruyter.

Hendrischke, Hans (2004), 'The Role of Social Capital, Networks and Property Rights in Chinas Privatization Process' in Barbara Krug (ed.), *China's Rational Entrepreneurs: The Development of the New Private Business Sector*, New York and London: Routledge, pp. 97–118.

Krug, B. and H. Hendrischke (2003), 'China Incorporated: Property Rights, Privatisation, and the Emergence of a Private Business Sector in China', *Managerial Finance*, **29**, 32–45.

Krug, Barbara and L. Polos (2004), 'Emerging Markets, Entrepreneurship and Uncertainty: The Emergence of a Private Sector in China', in Barbara Krug (ed.), *China's Rational Entrepreneurs: The Development of the New Private Business Sector*, New York and London: Routledge, pp. 72–96.

Lechner, C. and M. Dowling (2003), 'Firm networks: external relationships as sources for the growth and competitiveness of entrepreneurial firms', *Entrepreneurship & Regional Development*, **15**, 1–26.

Lovett, S., L.C. Simmons and R. Kali (1999), 'Guanxi versus the Market: Ethics and Efficiency', *Journal of International Business Studies*, **30**, 231–247.

Luo, Y. (1997), 'Guanxi: principles, philosophies, and implications', *Human Systems Management*, **16**, 43–51.

Nooteboom, B., H. Berger and N.G. Noorderhaven (1997), 'Effects of Trust and Governance on Relational Risk', *Academy of Management Journal*, **40**, 308–332.

Omta, S.W.F., J.H. Trienekens and G. Beers (2001), 'Chain and network science: A research framework', *Journal on Chain and Network Science*, **1** (1), 1–6.

Oi, J. (1999) *Rural China takes off institutional foundations of economic reform*, Berkley, California: University of California Press.

Park, S.H. and Y. Luo (2001), 'Guanxi and Organizational Dynamics: Organizational Networking in Chinese Firms', *Strategic Management Journal*, **22**, 455–477.

Peng, M. and J. Qi Zhou (2005), 'How Network Strategies and Institutional Transitions Evolve in Asia', *Asia Pacific Journal of Management*, **22**, 321–336.

Peng, Y. (2004), 'Kinship Networks and Entrepreneurs in China's Transitional Economy', *American Journal of Sociology*, **109**, 1045–1074.

Powell, W.W. (1990), 'Neither Market nor Hierarchy: Network Forms of Organizations', *Research in Organizational Behaviour*, **12**, 295–313.

Qian, Y. (2000), 'The Process of China's Market Transition 1978–98: The Evolutionary, Historical, and Comparative Perspectives', *Journal of Institutional and Theoretical Economics*, **156** (1), 151–171.

Qian, Yingyi (2003), 'How Reform Worked in China', in Dani Rodrik (ed.), *In Search of Prosperity: Analytic Narratives on Economic Growth*, Princeton, NJ: Princeton University Press, pp. 297–333.

Redding, S. Gordon (1990), *The Spirit of Chinese Capitalism*, Berlin and New York: Walter de Gruyter.

Redding, Gordon S. (1996), 'Weak organizations and strong linkages: managerial ideology and Chinese family business firms', in Gary G. Hamilton (ed.), *Asian Business Networks*, pp. 27–42.

Rozelle, S. and G. Li (1998), 'Village leaders and land-right formation in China', *American Economic Review*, **82** (2), 433–438.

Rozelle, S., A. Park, J. Huang and H.H. Xin (2000), 'Bureaucrat to entrepreneur: The changing role of the state in China's Grain Economy', *Economic Development and Cultural Change*, **48** (2), 227–252.

Schlevogt, Kai-Alexander (2002), *The Art of Chinese Management: Theory, Evidence and Applications*, Oxford: Oxford University Press.

Stark, D. (1996), 'Recombinant Property in East European Capitalism', *American Journal of Sociology*, **101**, 993–1027.

Tong, C.K. and P. Kee Yong (1998), 'Guanxi bases, Xinyong and Chinese business networks', *British Journal of Sociology*, **49**, 75–96.

Tsang, E.W.K. (1998), 'Can guanxi be a source of sustained competitive advantage for doing business in China', *The Academy of Management Executive*, **12**, 64–73

Uzzi, B. (1996), 'The sources and consequences of embeddedness for the economic performance of organizations: the network effect', *American Sociological Review*, **61**, 674–698.

Wank, D.L. (1995), 'Private Business, Bureaucracy, and Political Alliance in a Chinese City', *Australian Journal of Chinese Affairs*, **33**, 55–71.

Wank, David L. (2000), 'Cigarettes and Domination in Chinese Business Networks: Institutional Change during the Market Transition', in Deborah S. Davis (ed.), *The Consumer Revolution in Urban China*, Berkeley: University of California Press, pp. 268–286.

Weidenbaum, Murray and Hughes, Samuel (1996), *The Bamboo Network: How Expatriate Chinese Entrepreneurs are Creating a New Economic Superpower in Asia*, New York, NY: The Free Press.

Yang, Mayfair M. (1994), *Gifts, Favors, and Banquets: The Art of Social Relationships in China*, Ithaca, NY: Cornell University Press.

Yang, M.M. (2002), 'The Resilience of Guanxi and its New Developments: A Critique of some New Guanxi Scholarship', *The China Quarterly*, **170**, 459–476.

Xin, K.R. and J.L. Pearce (1996) 'Guanxi: Connections as Substitutes for Formal Institutional Support', *Academy of Management Journal*, **39**, 1641–1658.

9. Whom are We Dealing With? Shifting Organisational Forms in China's Business Sector

Barbara Krug and Jeroen Kuilman

9.1 INTRODUCTION

China's economic transformation has led to firms taking a multitude of different forms, some of them quite bewildering to Western observers:

- listed companies need not indicate that they have private shareholders (Opper, Chapter 1)
- foreign–domestic joint ventures need not always involve a partner from outside the PRC; sometimes the 'foreign' partner is actually a domestic firm's Hong Kong-registered subsidiary (Zhang and Reinmoeller, Chapter 3).
- incorporating a firm can be seen as a way of setting up a partnership (Greeven, Chapter 4)
- private firms are usually those whose assets are predominantly in private hands, but they can also be parts of collective firms contracted out to a private manager (Goodman, Chapter 7)
- the term 'collective' as found in official statistics might suggest that a local community operates a firm, but it is sometimes used to describe a multi-market company or a holding company managing an asset portfolio (Hendrischke, Chapter 8)

In short, nothing is what it seems in Chinese business. Any attempt to analyse the existing and future business sector must first collect firm-level data, then understand the many new organisational forms for which the rest of the world has no easy description. That China's economic transformation has led to new business forms should not be surprising. They evolved as the Chinese government haltingly dismantled its socialist planned economy which had previously known only one type of firm – the bureaucratic organisation operating as part of a larger and superior bureaucracy. Even today, such state firms (SOEs and collective enterprises) still contribute 36.3 per cent of GDP, while the private sector (i.e. firms whose assets are held by domestic or foreign private owners) amounts to 61.5 per cent (2003 data from OECD 2005, Table 2.1). What is surprising, however, is the multitude of ill-defined organisational forms that fall somewhere between conventional socialist firms and what Williamson terms 'market-conforming firms'[1] – between hierarchy and the market, to use the Williamson (1985) terminology. Until recently, these types of firms have been badly treated in economics or organisation theory, and often ignored in studies of economic transformation. They have been regarded as 'anomalies' which reflect corruption (Li, 2005) and local state intervention (Oi 1995; Walder 1995), or as 'hybrids' which will disappear once the market functions more effectively (Powell, 1990). Transaction cost economics explains these hybrids by showing that firms dealing simultaneously with contracts, incentives and governance structures need to take on different forms if transaction costs are to be minimised (Aoki, 2001; Williamson, 1985). Organisational ecology (Carroll and Hannan, 2000), on the other hand, draws attention to changes in the resource environment and the availability of market niches to explain the formation of new organisational populations and their subsequent survival.

It is time to take a step forward in terms of defining organisational forms in China, and in understanding the changes in these forms over time. Both transaction cost economics and organisational ecology can be helpful in this regard. Recently, researchers have regained interest in defining forms (e.g. Hannan, Pólos, and Carroll, 2007), but the situation in transition economies has received scant attention and is less clear-cut. From a theoretical point of view, studying transition economies such as China's is of great importance because such economies are characterised by weak selection mechanisms (Krug and Pólos, 2004) where one can isolate specific kind of transaction costs, namely those specific to the economic transformation process – 'transformation costs' in the terminology of Grabher and Stark (1997). For ecologists, transition economies such as China's offer ample opportunity to study the process of identity and boundary formation with respect to organisational forms which might not be viable in any other context.

In the case of China, the study of organisational forms is of more than academic interest. Managers and entrepreneurs badly need to know what form China's future business system will take. Will a few large companies, perhaps even Chinese multinationals, dominate the business sector? Or will the market be driven by a multitude of small and middle scale firms as is the case in Taiwan? Moreover, will organisational diversity continue to characterise the Chinese economy, or will market selection start to reduce the diversity of organisations? And finally, does the economy need different kinds of firms because of the different culturally determined ways Chinese economic actors organise production?

This chapter will apply transaction cost economics and organisational ecology to categorising organisational forms in China. Transaction cost economics, which is firmly rooted in conventional economics, and organisational ecology with its roots in sociology offer different perspectives on organisational forms. Between them, they can perhaps account for the many new organisational forms that have emerged in China. A resource space will be defined which can then be applied to develop a dynamic analysis of organisational change in China based on the principles of organisational ecology. The chapter ends by examining whether the two approaches can be combined, and whether such a combination might allow empirical tests of their utility.

9.2   IDENTIFYING ORGANISATIONAL FORMS IN CHINA

Why should we try to single out different types of organisations (organisational forms) in the first place? The simple observation that in essence every organisation is unique ignores the fact that some organisations are clearly more similar than others. Further, social (aggregate) entities can be distinguished within the world of organisations, and these social forms are useful because the organisations they comprise respond similarly to environmental variations and share a common fate (Hannan and Freeman, 1977). That makes these organisational forms appropriate units of analysis. By delineating such organisational forms, we can learn more about general patterns of economic and social change, as these patterns correspond closely with the diversity of forms. According to Grabher and Stark (1997), transition economies with greater diversity adapt more easily to environmental change because their variety of organisational forms can be seen as a repository of available solutions for coping with the uncertainty inherent in environmental change.

Delineating organisational forms is by no means an easy task. Of course one can always distinguish between organisational forms in hindsight. For example, one could *ex post facto* apply statistical techniques such as cluster analysis to group organisations on the basis of any underlying dimension. Such an approach, however, provides little guidance in recognising new forms as they evolve. For this, we need a sharp definition or some guiding principles of categorisation. First-generation theories in organisational ecology mainly focused on organisations' structural features. Hannan and Freeman (1984), for instance, proposed categorising an organisation in terms of 1) its stated goals, 2) the forms of authority within the organisation (its governance structure in the language of transaction cost economics), 3) the core technology used to transform inputs into outputs (its production function), and 4) its marketing strategy. These four features stand in a rough hierarchy, where goals are regarded as the most highly constrained element of an organisational form, while marketing is much less subject to constraints. Similarly, transaction cost economics (Williamson, 1985) distinguishes between different types of organisation on the basis of two behavioural assumptions (opportunism and bounded rationality) and three context-specific variables (uncertainty, asset-specificity and frequency of contracts). Transaction cost economics subsequently argues that the most efficient form is the one that minimises the transaction costs generated by context-specific variables — the costs incurred in making economic exchanges.

In contrast with these approaches to delineating forms, recent advances in organisational ecology have increasingly recognised that structural elements are not the key to defining forms, but that instead the social perceptions of outside audiences such as industry regulators, critics, consumers, or activists matter more. This social constructionist approach is based on the assumption that the social support for an organisational form has a strong impact on the survival chances of organisations adopting that form. Hannan et al. (2007) define an organisational form as a category that is taken-for-granted by relevant audiences. Audiences in such cases have default expectations about what it takes for an organisation to be part of a form. Organisations that aspire to be part of a form but fail to meet these default expectations generally do not fare well (Zuckerman, 1999; Pólos, Hannan and Carroll, 2002). Thus, an organisational form is an externally enforced identity that is subject to social norms (Pólos et al., 2002).

There are certain well-established organisational categories, such as the old SOEs and foreign-owned enterprises, which certainly can be considered as distinct and legitimate organisational forms in China. From an identity perspective, it is clear that SOEs, as remnants of the socialist past, are distinct from the many new organisational forms which have emerged as a result of China's business policy reforms. Similarly, foreign firms have an identity distinct from their local counterparts. For instance, Kuilman and Li (2006) in their study of banking in Shanghai note that histories of banking in Shanghai as well as modern media reports invariably categorise banks as either 'foreign' or 'local'. This difference in social identity reflects structural differences, as these different forms of ownership convey much information about differences in structure, size, corporate governance and employment practices. How, then, to define identities for the multitude of organisational forms which have emerged during the transformation process?

Both approaches to defining organisational forms display limitations when it comes to 'hybrids'. Structural approaches (Williamson, 1985; Hannan and Freeman, 1984) are in this context of limited explanatory value, taking into account the results of empirical research in which most of the firms studied changed their ownership and their products more than twice during the course of the study (Krug and Hendrischke, 2006; Li, 2005). But defining forms in terms of their social identity also has its limitations. It has been argued (Krug, Chapter 5) that firms are the outcome of ongoing institutional change in the political arena, and of organisational/institutional innovation in nascent markets. With the exception of the old SOEs and conventional foreign-owned enterprises, all other firms in China would therefore have a weak social identity, operating in an environment where violations of default expectations are rarely sanctioned effectively (Krug and Pólos, 2004). Moreover, Chinese official data are of limited use in applying either a structure-based or identity-based perspective, as they still link firms to administrative levels and frequently change their classifications. The original commune enterprises, for example, were re-labelled township and village enterprises (TVEs) in 1984, but today's TVEs are private companies, no longer managed by a township (see also Goodman, Chapter 7).

Given these considerations, only close institutional analysis can help in identifying and singling out (potential) organisational forms in China's collective and private domains. Such an analysis should be sensitive to structural factors determining organisational form – the core features of Hannan and Freeman (1984) or the cost structure emphasised by Williamson (1985) – and identity differences between forms (Hannan et al., 2007). The assertions in this chapter will therefore be based on the fieldwork described by Krug (Chapter 5) and on the analyses of the other chapters. It should be read as a cautious first attempt to model the process of organisational change that accompanies economic transformation.

9.3 EMERGENT ORGANISATIONAL FORMS

Seen from the transaction cost perspective, different organisational forms reflect the organisational choices of entrepreneurs or owners seeking the governance structure which will minimise transaction costs. In order to show that transaction cost considerations dominate organisational choice, empirical evidence is needed to show that Chinese firms do react systematically to changes in the institutional environment. Another test is to see whether foreign firms in China react similarly once they are exposed to a similar set of transaction costs, or whether similar forms have evolved in other cultural settings. In fact, the database is too small for a comprehensive study, but

Krug's fieldwork (Chapter 5) offers enough illustrative evidence to give some confidence that the forms chosen reflect transaction cost considerations of a particular kind — namely, those which are generated by the transformation process itself. It thus appears that it is not so much the Williamson type of transactional alignment which matters most to organisations (Silverman, Nickerson and Freeman 1997; Argyres and Bigelow, 2006), but instead the minimisation of transformation costs (Grabher and Stark, 1997). Managers and entrepreneurs of the new firms appear to choose the organisational form which they feel best fits the external environment, in the sense that they opt for what they determine to be the most effective governance structure

- to cope with the political architecture when they seek to align the interests of political actors and other stakeholders with the interests of managers or entrepreneurs. Such alignment promises access to prior information about further reform steps, protection of property rights and business agreements, if not participation in political decision making at the local level.
- to respond to market shifts when they search for organisational solutions that mitigate the effects of market fragmentation, lack of market information, and local embeddedness. Effective governance structures allow appropriating arbitrage, jurisdictional arbitrage, as well as generating enough leverage to limit local government intervention.
- to align the interests of the firm with the interests of potential investors by designing incentives which secure (ongoing) private investment; exclusive access to shared or jointly produced knowledge, information or business routines; and ultimately, a commitment by investors and mangers that limits moral hazard..

Table 9.1 links some organisational forms common in China with these three features of the external environment. Not all firms are dealing with the same political architecture, and competitive markets develop earlier in one sector than in another, so not all firms have the same ability to form or enter equally effective networks. A diversity of organisational forms is only a natural consequence. Thus, for example, as long as some banks are still controlled by local regulators, access to bank loans in one location may best be secured through political deals with local government agencies, while in other jurisdictions where the local state no longer interferes with lending practices, access to bank loans may depend on conventional economic calculations. In the first case, firms have an incentive to invest in alliances with local government agencies; in the second case they have an incentive to invest in collateral and competent cost control. In a local environment characterised by 'interventionist' government agencies, protecting property rights may involve offering 'shares' to local politicians[2].

Table 9.1 New organisational forms, alignment to the environment, and incentive effects

Organisational form (hybrids)	Alignment with political architecture	Alignment with emerging markets	Incentives for resource mobilisation
Township or village enterprise (early in the reform process)	Village-owned	Low transaction cost in the local economy	Incentive contracts for managers
Privatised TVE	Management buy-outs (MBOs) creating private owners and a local non-state tax base	Expansion to other sectors and locations	Access to bank loans and private capital; Mitigating spatial risk
Multi-market firm	Increasing autonomy via subsidiaries in different sectors or markets	Spreading market risk	Exploiting scale economies in tangible assets i.e. influence on political government agencies
Public/private partnership	Informally allocated ownership shares within or across jurisdictions	• Access to local information • Securing contracts with SOEs as suppliers or customers	• Preferential treatment in taxation and regulation • Investment in complementary infrastructure
Incorporated firm	• Codification of ownership shares • Enlarging the non-state tax base	• Defining of corporate assets • Limiting government access to cash flow • Jurisdiction arbitrage	• Converting intangible social capital into corporate assets • Hardening property rights • Experimentation
Networked firm	Leveraging market power and political power	• Internal competition as a surrogate for missing external competition	• Competition for network resources • Scale built on non-tradable assets (reputation, influence with the bureaucracy)

All in all, organisational choice in China reflects a search for the best match with the external environment (cf. Hannan, 1986) or, more precisely, a search for the most effective way to minimise transaction costs that are specific to the political control and procedural uncertainty that characterise this nascent market. The diversity of the resulting organisational forms reflects the unequal distribution of risks, business chances and incentives connected with missing property rights and opportunistic behaviour.

These different organisational forms are not, however, completely independent. In particular, networking generates what Milgrom and Roberts (1990) have termed 'complementarity: synergy effects' arising when concentrating more on one activity increases the return on other activities (or assets). Investing in networks, for example, helps to expand inter-firm business, while at the same time increasing the value of business agreements and offering a platform for sharing hard-to-exchange knowledge. This can, in turn, enhance the value of intangible assets such as political influence or reputation. In this way, offering crop sharing (incentive) contracts to managers of TVEs was originally seen as a device to secure and motivate scarce managerial talent, but at the same time increased the 'returns' from privatising formerly collective assets. There are cases in which a single firm has embraced all different organisational forms of Table 9.1, being at once:

- incorporated (a limited liability firm)
- a multi-market firm (with operations spread across industries)
- a geographically dispersed firm
- a firm whose expansion leads to subsidiaries with discrete ownership structures, each of which acknowledge local government agencies as shareholders
- a networked firm whose activities are co-ordinated by long-term agreements which are governed via informal institutions

Such a 'generalist' approach should help to maximise an organisation's survival chances. In contrast to SOEs and foreign firms (which predate the transformation process and often stand outside the transition economy), in Reform China's modern firms, all these new organisational forms can in principal be combined. For instance, to mitigate risk by spreading operations across several jurisdictions is compatible with all kinds of ownership structures, so long as ways can be found to solve the principal-agent problem (Stark 1996) between the parent company and its local representatives, offices, or subsidiaries.

The organisational ecology perspective involves a similar line of reasoning. Hannan et al. (2007) develop the notion of grades-of-membership, in which social actors can fall partially into one organisational form while also partially displaying the features of other forms. In China, such multiple low grade memberships can be a way of ensuring at least some degree of legitimacy when dealing with a rapidly changing environment. Stark (1996) notes that in post-socialist societies, savvy strategists adopt robust identities that potentially correspond to many different organisational forms. In short, having a weak organisational identity may sometimes actually be strength in a transitional economy. As has been argued by Krug (Chapter 5), entrepreneurship in China does indeed involve finding ways of identifying and coping with 'volatilities' in the environment as much as converting a new product idea or a new technology into a tradable product or process. Entrepreneurship in China involves the ability to configure an organisation so that it can identify and monitor volatile key resources and search for governance structures and routines which can efficiently cope with external shocks or variance in the behaviour of potential business partners or government agencies (see also Casson, 2005).

Such organisational or corporate governance arrangements provide an explanation for the lack of distinct and sharply defined organisational forms in China's new business sector. According to organisational ecology, new organisational forms are most likely to come into existence when the organisations requiring that form do not already derive part of their identity from other, already existing forms[3]. To turn the argument around, as most firms reflect transformation of an inherited socialist form, hybrid forms of organisation would be expected to evolve, rather than completely distinct forms, a finding that is compatible with the transaction cost argument introduced earlier.

9.4 RESOURCE SPACE IMAGERY AND ORGANISATIONAL CHOICE

In order to understand the dynamics of organisational forms in China, it might be helpful to envision a resource space in which (potential) organisational forms can be mapped[4]. Organisational ecology has used this approach extensively, starting with Carroll (1985) who studied shifts in the resource space for newspapers. In a transition economy, any resource space would usually encompass the central bureaucracy, local government agencies, networks, employees, suppliers, consumers, and other actors and institutions that are potential providers of resources. A resource space can in principle be characterised by several dimensions (see Péli and Nooteboom, 1999), but in the interest of simplicity this discussion will be confined to one dimensions only: the state socialist vs. market orientation of the resource providers (Figure 9.1). The abscissa in the figure represents a state socialist vs. market continuum. At one extreme, resource access is controlled by political-bureaucratic allocation, at the other by market allocation, while the market centre is dominated by network allocation which might involve a mix of market and bureaucratic mechanisms. The resource space in transition economies is further assumed to be characterised by a normal distribution[5] of physical assets, finances, and human resources along the state socialist vs. market continuum.

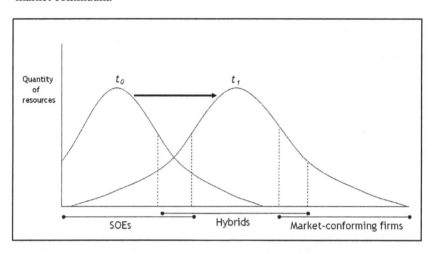

Figure 9.1   Hypothetical organisational landscape in China

At any given time, an organisation occupies one position along the state socialist vs. market continuum. Empirical studies have shown that, depending on the organisation's position, there is an appeal to a particular set of political and economic actors. On the right-hand side we find organisations that operate under pure market conditions. Only a few companies in China can claim to work in such an environment, most probably found in foreign trade where WTO regulations encourage price competition and lower entry barriers. For convenience, the organisational form of such companies can be called 'market-conforming'. At the other extreme are (unreformed) SOEs still subject to plan quotas and controlled by government ministries. In between these two extremes, a multitude of hybrid organisational forms has emerged after regulatory reforms acknowledged the legitimacy of such organisations. As argued earlier, their weak organisational identity and 'messy' boundaries do not indicate market failure, let alone lack of innovation or competence. The hybrid forms evolved because they promised to better cope with the political and economic diversity confronted during the transition period.

Figure 9.1 portrays two hypothetical resource distributions along the chosen dimension, focussing on three separate forms only: the SOEs; the market-conforming firms (at the beginning of the reform period exclusively foreign firms, but later including some private firms); and the broad category of hybrids, which combine all or some of the features described earlier. The left bell-shaped curve described the resource distribution in the early 1980s (at time t_0). Most resources were then assigned to firms with a state socialist ideology, i.e. the SOEs. The SOEs were in this period clearly positioned in the market centre, defined as the place with the peak in the resource distribution. Figure 9.1 also displays a second bell-shaped curve in which the centre of the market has shifted on the state-socialist vs. market continuum, reflecting the more contemporary period (at time t_1). Hybrids and market-conforming firms have started to attract a larger proportion of the available resources. As a result, SOEs now operate on the periphery of the economy, while market-conforming firms have shifted from the periphery toward the centre. That hybrids attract most of the resources is not only predicted by transaction cost and organisational ecology analysis, but supported by the many empirical studies which have gone beyond the official statistics.

From the transaction cost perspective, the positions of firms in the resource space reflect their organisational choices in response to the different resource allocation mechanisms they face. State allocation via quota or other bureaucratic means defines one extreme; the price mechanism defines the other extreme namely the point from which firms act within the Williamson scenario of organisational choice. On the left, political capital is essential, and SOEs (almost by definition) represent the best fitting form. On the right, the business environment is characterised by effective capital markets, functioning liability and tort laws, open entry for firms and functioning market mechanisms. The middle is characterised by co-existing and overlapping allocation rules when ad hoc bargaining can offset 'official' regulation but also limit the functioning of markets. A firm must normally ensure access to resources via all three allocation mechanisms. As the use of markets, bureaucratic hierarchies and networking is not costless, firms will search for an organisational form which minimises their transaction costs. Firms of different size, ownership, or sector will face different transaction costs, so, for example, small firms in the consumer goods sector where political agencies do not interfere will come to depend more on competition in product and factor markets than do large firms operating in state controlled sectors, depending on state controlled inputs, or with SOEs as their main customers. Subsequently firms have an incentive to search for a corporate governance structure, i.e. an organisational form that allows best use of all three kinds of allocation mechanism.

It is the need to flexibly exploit different mixes of the allocation mechanisms which explains the diversity of the hybrid forms, as well as the fact that firms choose to keep their organisational boundaries flexible. Transaction cost considerations also explain why firms migrate toward the hybrid, which makes best use of networking to bridge between bureaucratic control and market competition.

9.5   A DYNAMIC PERSPECTIVE

From a dynamic perspective, two types of changes should, over time, affect which organisational forms are successful and which are not. These shifts are not mutually exclusive, but will for analytical reasons be treated separately:

1.   *A shift in the resource distribution.* Ongoing reforms in the form of further liberalisation and less state intervention liberate resources as they become no longer politically or bureaucratically co-ordinated. Such moves lift an income constraint or shift the opportunity set, leaving more resources for network or market co-ordination. Subsequently, the value of political capital declines leaving fewer resources at the disposal of SOEs (Nee, 2005). This does not necessarily mean that the SOEs will disappear. As long as the state protects them and nurtures them with cash, bureaucratically distributed input and personnel, they will remain and claim a part of the total resources available. The shift in the resource distribution does not, however, depend on further reforms alone. Increasing the share of income and investment outside state control increases the stock of resources open for network or market co-ordination. The boundary of network organisations and market-conforming firms is fluid, so when, for example, networks find it advantageous to make use of the market by establishing and then contracting out to quasi-independent competitive firms (Hendrischke, Chapter 8), the move to the right will not lead to a skewed distribution around an unchanged mean. Such a move can be expected once liberalisation of the financial sector has started. The number of organisational forms relying on state allocated financing will decline, while 'private equity' firms on the right of Figure 9.1 will increase, leading to more resources being allocated according to the economic rationale of the capital markets (rate of return, creditworthiness, availability of collateral). The majority of firms will, however, still depend on bank loans, access to which might still depend on who control the banks, a process on the left side of the continuum. Another substantial and increasing body of firms depends

on capital accumulated within networks or brokered by networks, for which they have to compete. They too, therefore, need to behave as if they were market-conforming firms.

2.   *A change in the position of the organisational form* as firms search for new resources and change their location on the state socialist vs. market continuum. For instance, firms seeking to exploit economies of scale will try to serve the market centre where there is an abundance of resources (Carroll, 1985). A result might be a gradual, incremental change in the position or even identity of the organisational form. TVEs, for example, being collective firms, started well on the left side of the state socialist vs. market continuum. In the late nineties, when increasing competition for customers, suppliers and capital threatened their resource base, they used management buy-outs to mitigate commercial risk and as a means of gaining legitimacy. This helped them to mobilise additional investment and secure bank loans. In other words, they moved from the left of the continuum more toward the right. Foreign multinationals investing in China provide another example. In the 1980s it was expected that the multinationals could use their well-tested blueprints and enter the Chinese market via joint ventures. Yet, once having invested in China and thus become vulnerable, they quickly learned that they needed to localise their operations and invest in alliances with local government agencies and in local networks. As a result, they came to look more and more like Chinese companies, investing in unrelated lines of production, going for a wide geographical spread, becoming involved in local politics, and joining Chinese-foreign networks. In other words, they moved from the extreme right of the continuum toward the middle[6]. It is worth stressing that this phenomenon of foreign firms imitating or blending with domestic organisational forms contradicts the claim that the Chinese form of business networking is China-specific[7]. It rather supports the claim that in China too, organisational choice follows transaction cost considerations, in particular transformation cost considerations (Grabher and Stark, 1997).

What determines whether an organisational form will ultimately be successful in the resource space and perhaps comes to develop a more distinct identity? One of the characteristics of the hybrid organisational forms is that they operate under weak survival constraints, insulated to some extent from market competition and political persecution. As a result, these hybrid forms survive longer than they would in an environment with strong selection pressures. Only SOEs, which can rely on ongoing state control formulated at the central level, and market-conforming firms working in generally accepted markets are exposed to one constraint only. In contrast, the hybrids aim at a position where they can leverage their economic power (over investment and job creation) and their tax payments to wield political influence. Their political power can then feed back into economic power. It is this effect that limits the explanatory power of transaction cost or public choice approaches that rely on exogenously determined market or political constraints. Fieldwork has demonstrated that such selection mechanisms can be weakened via negotiation, so other analytical tools then need to be employed. Institutional game theory (Bates, 1998; Greif, 1998; and also the contribution by Zhu and Krug, Chapter 6) confirms that changes in organisational form should reflect only partly a systematic response to changes in the relative prices of exploiting different political or social institutions. Changes also occur as the result of interactions among firms and political agents.

While economics focuses on the marginal firm, organisational ecology reminds us that success in the market is mainly a function of positioning in the resource space. Competitive overlap in this space is among the main determents of which organisational forms survive. The empirical results discussed in chapter five have shown that it is less competition for customers that characterises the business sector, but rather competition for capital in all its forms. In the transformation context, this refers to tangible and intangible assets, and a set of resources which can be labelled as political capital, social capital, or market capital. The more overlap an organisational form has with other organisational forms in terms of these assets and resources, the lower its survival chances ought to be (Hannan et al., 2007). In this connection, Hannan and Freeman (1977) have invoked the principle of 'competitive exclusion'. This principle states that when two similar organisational forms occupy an identical position in the resource space, one of the forms will prevail and the other will disappear. Recently, Ruef (2006) confirmed this principle in his study of the demise of organisational forms, a study which also considered other possible explanations, including declining material resources and lack of political support. Crowding has also been noted by Grabher and Stark (1997) as a factor that limits organisational diversity, and they discussed 'compartmentalisation' as a way to maintain diversity, that is to organise the resource space such that forms are buffered from each other.

It seems, then, that the most successful forms should be those that can insulate themselves from competition from other forms, but also those that include organisations that can minimise transformation costs by positioning themselves such that they can best exploit their particular combination of political, social and market capital. An optimal position would thus be a differentiated niche close to the market centre, which is assumed to be characterised by a combination of accumulated political, social, and some market capital. As we have argued, hybrids can best exploit such resource niches. In the end, the greater flexibility of hybrid forms, in particular the network form, but also increasingly the market-conforming form, will lead to their occupying the market centre, and best coping with the demands of the market (Krug and Pólos, 2004).

9.6   CONCLUSIONS

The objective of this chapter has been to move a step forward in defining organisational forms in China and in understanding changes in the organisational landscape over time. To this end, we have applied insights both from transaction cost economics and from organisational ecology. While acknowledging the role of market competition in explaining the prevalence of particular organisational forms, transaction cost economics tends to focus on efficiency considerations and traditionally has a cross-sectional focus. Organisational ecology, on the other hand, stresses social processes such as legitimacy and social identity in the evolution of organisational forms and has a longitudinal orientation. This does not mean, however, that transaction cost economics and organisational ecology are at odds. According to Carroll, Spiller, and Teece (1999: 69), 'there is nothing inherent in the two theories that precludes a synthesis'. The findings of Silverman et al. (1997) indeed suggest that organisational ecology and transaction cost economics are highly complementary. They have shown that incorporating both transaction cost considerations and ecological variables in market models can lead to significantly sharper predictions of organisational mortality. (See Geroski (2001) for other ideas that combine ecology and economics.)

Transactional alignment improves a firm's survival chances (Silverman et al., 1997), and this seems to be especially so when markets are characterised by strong selection pressures (Argyres and Bigelow, 2006). Grabher and Stark (1997) have argued that transactional alignment is also relevant in transition economies with weaker selection pressures, but in these countries it concerns transaction cost considerations of a different kind, namely transaction costs specifically generated by the country's ongoing economic transformation process. A logical extension would thus be to test the relationship between 'transformational alignment' and organisational failure in China. An empirical study would test the assertion that hybrid and market-conforming firms should have improved survival chances. It would also stimulate a further synthesis between organisational ecology and transaction cost economics.

In attempting to apply these insights more widely, some may argue that the Chinese context is too specific in terms of its culture and the predominance of networks. As a counterargument, the primacy of transaction cost considerations even in China seems to be confirmed by the quick response of Chinese firms to changing institutions and policies. The relatively smooth transition toward market-conforming behaviour by firms in the Pearl River delta (greater Hong Kong) and in the Yangtze River delta (greater Shanghai) testifies to this. Other examples are the disappearance of the traditional TVEs, and the organisational changes which have been made to accommodate foreign direct investment. Moreover, the claim that networking is the essence of Chinese business behaviour can no longer be justified. Networking in China is an adaptation to weak institutional architecture, and as such is not linked to the Chinese case only. There is an increasing literature on networks and business groups which, following Greif (2006), shows that networking is not just a historical carry-over from the time when there was no modern judiciary, which necessitated relation-based trade. Rather, this organisational form can be found today in countries as different as India, Mexico, Russia and France (for a more complete list and a comprehensive analysis, see Ghemawat and Khanna, 1998).

Both ongoing reforms and private investment remove constraints and encourage firms built around private capital. At the same time, increasing competition is forcing firms to build clearer boundaries, in particular when it comes to political interference. Does this mean that firms with a clearer identity will emerge? At the beginning we found only two kinds of firms with a strong identity, those at the opposite ends of the state socialist vs. market continuum, namely the foreign firms and traditional state firms. After almost 30 years of transformation, we can point to state owned firms organised as stock-listed companies on the left, and limited liability companies with a clear product profile (and increasingly with a brand name) on the right. When the incorporation of firms is seen as a requirement for getting bank loans, or when the increasing use of written contracts asks for a legal person as the contracting partner, firms have an incentive to better delineate their identity. Thus, well-defined firms can come to help solve some asymmetric information problems, leading to lower transaction costs. Similarly, private firms have also profited from their increasing social legitimacy. Even in official government documents, their existence is not only acknowledged but regarded as beneficial for overall economic development. Thus, more firms with a clear identity can be expected to emerge at the extremes of the continuum.

NOTES

1. Market-conforming firms in what follows is a label used for the kind of firms one finds in functioning market economies and whose organisational form is assumed to reflect transaction cost minimisation of the kind Willliamson (1985) analysed.
2. Offering shares free of charge to local decision makers informally is a powerful means to harden property rights compatible with operating across jurisdictions, or even internationally, yet still subject to considerable Communist Party control (Opper, Chapter 1).
3. McKendrick and Carroll (2001), for instance, in a study of disk drive array producers, concluded that in this case no new organisational form came into existence because many of the organisations involved in producing disk drive arrays were also involved in other activities ranging from the manufacture of computers and motherboards to distribution and retail activities. From a social identity perspective, such a lack of perceptual focus impeded the development of a sharply defined and coherent organisational form for disk drive array manufacturers (McKendrick and Carroll, 2001).
4. On the product level, such an approach resembles that of Hotelling (1929), which was later to be extended to account for a potentially infinite number of dimensions by Lancaster (1971), where each dimension represented a product characteristic.
5. We assume a unimodal resource distribution in the interest of simplicity. Of course it is also likely that in a transition process a second peak emerges. This possibility of a bimodal resource distribution is considered by Dobrev (2000). Dobrev (2000) studied the dynamics of Bulgarian newspapers after the fall of Communism and noted that two market centres had emerged: one centre represented the pro-Communist readers and the other centre represented their political opponents.
6. It has been widely documented that for state–owned enterprises such changes are much less likely. Large state-owned enterprises are known to exhibit a high degree of inertia in their structures and strategies, which prevents these organisations from making adaptive moves. Nee (2005) provides an extensive analysis of factors that create and reinforce structural inertia in Chinese state-owned enterprises. According to Nee (2005: 59), the old organisational rules and routines employed by SOEs are no longer effective means of organising in China's contemporary transitional economy; and, 'because the old organisational rules and routines are enmeshed with the interests and identity of individuals in

powerful networks entrenched inside the state-owned firms, organisational inertia is reinforced, resulting in structural rigidities that lock these firms into inefficient economic performance.'
7. The most influential articles are Xin and Pearce (1996), Luo (1997), Guthrie (1998), Tong and Yong (1998), Tsang (1998), Park and Luo (2001), Peng (2001), Fan (2002), Lechner and Dowling (2003), Zhou et al. (2003) and Peng (2004).

REFERENCES

Aoki, Masahiko (2001), *Toward a Comparative Institutional Analysis*, Cambridge, MA: The MIT Press.
Argyres, N. and L. Bigelow (2006), 'Do Transaction Costs Matter for Firm Survival at all Stages of the Industry Lifecycle?', Working Paper, Boston, MA: Boston University.
Bates, Robert H., Avner Greif, Margaret Levi and Jean-Laurent Rosenthal (eds) (1998), *Analytical Narratives*, Princeton, NJ: Princeton University Press.
Carroll, G.R. (1985), 'Concentration and specialization: Dynamics of niche width in populations of organizations', *American Journal of Sociology*, **90**, 1262–83.
Carroll, Glenn R. and Michael T. Hannan (2000), *The Demography of Corporations and Industries*, Princeton, NJ: Princeton University Press.
Carroll, Glenn R., Pablo T. Spiller and David J. Teece (1999), 'Transaction Cost Economics: Its Influence on Organization Theory, Strategic Management, and Political Economy', in G.R. Carroll and D.J. Teece (eds), *Firms, Markets, and Hierarchies: The Transaction Cost Economics Perspective*, New York, NY: Oxford University Press, pp. 60–88.
Casson, M. (2005), 'Entrepreneurship and the theory of the firm', *Journal of Economic Behavior & Organization*, **58**, 327–48.
Dobrev, S. (2000), 'Decreasing concentration and reversibility of the resource partitioning process: Supply shortages and deregulation in the Bulgarian newspaper industry', *Organization Studies*, **21**, 383–404.
Fan, Y. (2002), 'Questioning *guanxi*: Definition, classification and implications', *International Business Review*, **11**, 543–61.
Geroski, P.A. (2001), 'Exploring the niche overlaps between organizational ecology and industrial economics', *Industrial and Corporate Change*, **10** (2), 507–40.

Ghemawat, P.J. and T. Khanna (1998), 'The nature of diversified business groups: A research design and two case studies', *Journal of Industrial Economics*, **46**, 35–61.

Grabher, Gernot and David Stark (1997), 'Organizing Diversity: Evolutionary Theory, Network Analysis, and Post-Socialism', in Gernot Grabher and D. Stark (eds), *Restructuring Networks in Post-Socialism*, New York, NY: Oxford University Press, pp. 1–32.

Greif, A. (1993), 'Contract enforceability and economic institutions in early trade: The Maghribi traders coalition', *American Economic Review*, **83**, 525–48.

Greif, A. (1998), 'Self-enforcing Political Systems and Economic Growth: Late Medieval Genoa', in R.E.A. Bates (ed.), *Analytical Narratives*, Princeton, NJ: Princeton University Press, pp. 23–63.

Greif, A. (2006), *Institutions and the Path to the Modern Economy.* Cambridge: Cambridge University Press.

Guthrie, Douglas (1998), 'The declining significance of *guanxi* in China's economic transition', *The China Quarterly*, **154**, 254–82.

Hannan, Michael T. (1986), 'Uncertainty, Diversity, and Organizational Change' in Neil Smelser and D. Gerstein (eds), *Social and Behavioral Sciences: Discoveries over Fifty Years*, Washington, DC: National Academy Press, pp. 73–94.

Hannan, M.T. and J.H. Freeman (1977), 'The population ecology of organizations', *American Journal of Sociology*, **82**, 929–64.

Hannan, M.T. and J.H. Freeman (1984), 'Structural inertia and organizational change', *American Sociological Review*, **49**, 149–64.

Hannan, Michael T., László Pólos and Glenn R. Carroll (2007), *The Logics of Organization Theory: Social Codes and Ecologies*, Princeton, NJ: Princeton University Press (in press).

Hotelling, Harold (1929), 'Stability in competition', *Economic Journal*, **39** (153), 41–57.

Krug, B. and László Pólos (2004), 'Emerging Markets, Entrepreneurship, and Uncertainty: The Emergence of a Private Sector in China', in Barbara Krug (ed.), *China's Rational Entrepreneurs: The Development of the New Private Business Sector*, New York and London: Routledge, pp. 72–96.

Krug, B. and H. Hendrischke (2006), 'Framing China: Transformation and institutional change', *Management and Organization Review,* **2** (forthcoming).

Kuilman, J.G. and J. Li (2006), 'The organizers' ecology: An empirical study of foreign banks in Shanghai', *Organization Science*, **17** (3), 385–401.

Lancaster, Kelvin (1971), *Consumer Demand: A New Approach*, New York, NY: Columbia University Press.

Lechner, C. and M. Dowling (2003), 'Firm networks: External relationships as sources for the growth and competitiveness of entrepreneurial firms', *Entrepreneurship & Regional Development*, **15**, 1–26.

Li, P.P. (2005), 'The puzzle of China's township-village enterprises: The paradox of local corporatism in a dual track economic transition', *Management and Organization Review*, **1**, 197–224.

Luo, Y. (1997), '*Guanxi*: Principles, philosophies, and implications', *Human Systems Management*, **16**, 43–51.

McKendrick, D.G. and G.R. Carroll (2001), 'On the genesis of organizational forms: Evidence from the market for disk drive arrays', *Organization Science*, **12**, 661–83

Milgrom, P. and J. Roberts (1990), 'The economics of modern manufacturing: Technology, strategy, and organization', *American Economic Review*, **80**, 511–28.

Nee, Victor (2005), 'Organizational Dynamics of Institutional Change: China's Market Economy', in Victor Nee and R. Swedberg (eds), *The Economic Sociology of Capitalism*, Princeton, NJ: Princeton University Press, pp. 53–74.

OECD (2005), *Economic Surveys: China*, **13**.

Oi, J.C. (1995), 'The role of the local state in China's transitional economy', *The China Quarterly*, **144**, 1132–49.

Park, S.H. and Y. Luo (2001), '*Guanxi* and organizational dynamics: Organizational networking in Chinese firms', *Strategic Management Journal*, **22**, 455–77.

Péli, G.L. and B. Nooteboom (1999), 'Market partitioning and the geometry of the resource space', *American Journal of Sociology*, **104**, 1132–53.

Peng, M.W. (2001), 'How entrepreneurs create wealth in transition economies', *The Academy of Management Executive*, **15**, 95–108.

Peng, Y. (2004), 'Kinship networks and entrepreneurs in China's transitional economy', *American Journal of Sociology*, **109** (5), 1045–74.

Pólos, L., M.T. Hannan and G.R. Carroll (2002), 'Foundations of a theory of social forms', *Industrial and Corporate Change*, **11**, 85–115.

Powell, W.W. (1990), 'Neither market nor hierarchy: Network forms of organizations', *Research in Organizational Behaviour*, **12**, 295–313.

Ruef, M. (2006), 'The demise of an organizational form: Emancipation and plantation agriculture in the American South, 1860-1880', *American Journal of Sociology*, **109**, 1365–410.

Silverman, B., J.A. Nickerson and J.H. Freeman (1997), 'Profitability, transactional alignment, and organizational mortality in the U.S. trucking industry', *Strategic Management Journal*, **18**, 31–52.

Stark, D. (1996), 'Recombinant property in East European capitalism', *American Journal of Sociology*, **101**, 993–1027.

Tong, C.K. and P.K. Yong (1998), 'Guanxi bases, xinyong and Chinese business networks', *British Journal of Sociology*, **49**, 75–96.

Tsang, Eric W.K. (1998), 'Can *guanxi* be a source of sustained competitive advantage for doing business in China?', *The Academy of Management Executive*, **12**, 64–73.

Walder, A.G. (1995), 'Local governments as industrial firms: An organizational analysis of China's transitional economy', *American Journal of Sociology*, **101**, 263–301.

Williamson, Oliver E. (1985), *The Economic Institutions of Capitalism,* New York and London: Macmillan.

Xin, K.R. and J.L. Pearce (1996), '*Guanxi*: Connections as substitutes for formal institutional support', *Academy of Management Journal*, **39**, 1641–1658.

Zhou, Xue Guang, Wei Zhao, Qiang Li and He Cai (2003), 'Embeddedness and contractual relationships in China's transitional economy', *American Sociological Review*, **68** (1), 75–102.

Zuckerman, E.W. (1999), 'The categorical imperative: Securities analysts and the illegitimacy discount', *American Journal of Sociology*, **104**, 1398–438.

Index